No Contact

No Contact

How a Seductive Ideology Broke Families and Friendships and How We Can Repair Them

NOELLE MERING

FORUM BOOKS

Forum Books
An imprint of the Penguin Random House Christian Publishing Group,
a division of Penguin Random House LLC
1745 Broadway, New York, NY 10019
forumconservativebooks.com
penguinrandomhouse.com

Hardcover ISBN 979-8-217-15200-1
Ebook ISBN 979-8-217-15201-8

The Cataloging-in-Publication Data is on file with the Library of Congress.

Printed in the United States of America

1st Printing

First Edition

The authorized representative in the EU for product safety and compliance is Penguin Random House Ireland, Morrison Chambers, 32 Nassau Street, Dublin D02 YH68, Ireland. https://eu-contact.penguin.ie

BOOK TEAM: Editor: Matthew Burdette • Production editor: Jessica Choi • Managing editor: Julia Wallace • Copy editor: Kayla Fenstermaker • Proofreaders: Jean Bloom, Megan Koch

Book design by Diane Hobbing

For details on special quantity discounts for bulk purchases, contact specialmarketscms@penguinrandomhouse.com.

To my late father Phillip, who taught me to think with great curiosity, and to my mom Irene, who showed me how to love with great affection.

Contents

Introduction

The most revealing sign of civic unrest is not the slogans shouted in public but the relationships abandoned in private. Since 2020, I've traveled around the country giving talks on a destabilizing ideology that seemed, almost overnight, to be everywhere. The Q&A sessions quickly became my favorite part of the evening—offering a glimpse into people's on-the-ground experiences and perspectives. Within the first year and with striking consistency ever since, one question emerged again and again: "What do I do about my grown children who not only have abandoned the faith and values they were raised with but have also estranged themselves from us?"

Late 2024 polling by the American Psychiatric Association reveals just how polarized American families are politically and ideologically. One in five Americans reported having become estranged from a family member (21 percent), blocked a relative on social media (22 percent), or skipped a family event (19 percent) because of political or ideological disagreements. These statistics underscore a cultural moment in which even our most intimate relationships are increasingly vulnerable to public polarization.[1] The divide in civic society now cuts through the heart of millions of homes.

This isn't an easy issue to untangle. Most of those who have shared their stories with me are strangers, and I can't presume to fully understand the complexities of their family histories—the layers of hurt, misunderstanding, and missteps that shape every intimate relationship. I imagine that if I heard from their adult children, an even more complicated picture might emerge.

In the case of the parents interviewed for this book, I was able to engage in much more personal and in-depth conversations than I could do at a public event. I would have welcomed the opportunity to speak with their children as well, but that was most often not an option. Their relationships were fragile if not entirely fragmented, and the parents were universally desperate not to jeopardize any possibility of reconciliation. For that reason, names and telling circumstances have been altered to protect anonymity. I also interviewed adult kids from other families who have struggled with staying in contact with parents.

Even when initially hearing only the parents' side, I could sense the complex spectrum of culpability within this phenomenon. Some parents were candid about the ways they had contributed to their children's pain—divorce, for instance, was often named as a likely root wound beneath the more explicit ideological reasons given for estrangement. A couple of parents seemed to recoil at taking any ownership at all. But by far most of the parents I spoke with seemed genuinely caught in a larger cultural moment shaped by shifting norms, fraying social bonds, and a rising intolerance for dissent. The majority of these parents have worked to examine their failures and taken ownership readily where it was warranted. While they had made missteps as parents, theirs were the ordinary parental failings that, in previous generations, would have been absorbed or forgiven rather than collected, catalogued, and marshaled retroactively to support a narrative of childhood harm.

One objection to a book examining the ideological underpinnings of the no-contact movement is this: No one would choose to cut off intimate family members without just cause (an objection that I will explore more deeply in chapter 1). It's true that many people have had to cut contact after trying to make a relationship work by every other avenue first. When someone makes this painful decision to avoid serious harm like abuse, it's understandable that they might feel defensive when someone suggests that some choose estrangement unnecessarily. It isn't my goal to exhume anyone's personal situation. Were I in conversation with someone and it came up that they had cut contact with a family member, my reaction would be to express compassion, assume this situation was tragic but unavoidable, and respect their privacy. If you are in the situation of having had to cut contact over an abusive relationship, this phenomenon and this book aren't about you.

Critiquing the ideological misuse of no contact isn't a condemnation of the legitimate practice itself any more than warning about antibiotic overuse is an attack on antibiotics. Antibiotics are lifesaving when used properly, but when they're prescribed too casually or for the wrong reasons, they breed resistance and undermine their own effectiveness. In the same way, when the prescription to go no contact is overapplied—when ordinary conflict or ideological disagreement is mislabeled as "abuse"—it dilutes the meaning of real trauma and harms those who truly need protection.

This book draws a sharp distinction between the legitimate use of no contact and its overuse. The no-contact movement, however, tends to effectively erase such distinctions. Some of that is due to an ideological precept that the victim is always right (to be discussed in chapter 1). Some of it might just be the sloppiness of discussions. Regardless, the overall effect of such conflation is the same: a collapse of the moral distinctions that once supported family obligation and social repair.

This conflation of examples is a tactic of cultural revolution that I call "trauma hijacking": using egregious forms of abuse to justify responses to much less severe experiences. Most examples of trauma hijacking follow a predictable pattern. First, identify a genuine phenomenon in which a personal trauma necessitates an alternative to an established social norm, particularly when those seeking the alternative are highly sympathetic, like victims of abuse who need to break free of obligations to their abusive families. Then amplify these stories relentlessly, creating the impression that the issue is widespread and demands urgent social intervention. Once that sense of urgency takes hold, people become hyper-attuned to similar violations, increasingly willing to accept that these range across a broad spectrum—from minor to major infractions. Subtly shift the narrative so that the norm itself—not the individual perpetrators of the trauma—becomes the perceived source of suffering. Reframe anyone who upholds the norm as, at best, outdated and, at worst, oppressive. Simultaneously portray those who benefit from the norm as privileged and incapable of recognizing the full scope of reality. Finally, leverage this manufactured moral imperative to demand the deconstruction of the supposedly artificial norm in the name of justice.

There is also the risk of manipulative or narcissistic parents using this thesis of ideologically driven estrangement to further claim a victim narrative for themselves. But this is the case with most any complex social phenomenon. For example, it's generally true that hyper-individualism and loosening sexual mores have contributed to the rise in divorce rates in the past. That reality doesn't negate the fact that there are clearly cases in which one spouse must leave and is entirely justified in doing so. Will a toxic spouse try to blame hyper-individualism and the sexual revolution to shield themselves from culpability after their marriage fails? Yes. But the misuse of something shouldn't deter us from its proper use, in this instance the importance of examining sociological factors that drive a broader trend.

Private sorrow and public trends aren't the same thing. Whatever the legitimacy of certain individual cases, there remains the broader reality: We are living through a sharp uptick in family estrangement, and such estrangements are increasingly colored by ideology.

For years now, loneliness has been a growing problem in the West, becoming a public health crisis marked by isolation, declining community life, and thinning personal commitments. Ideological estrangement is exacerbating and accelerating this crisis. When relationships are severed over politics, the loss is felt on both sides, leaving people more vulnerable to despair, bitterness, and the echo chambers that further divide us. My purpose here is not to paint a cartoon of heroes and villains, as if one side holds a monopoly on virtue and the other on cruelty, but to reveal how we are being influenced by social currents toward estrangement and how this dynamic is harming us all.

While this phenomenon is largely happening among parents and Gen Z, it certainly transcends age and relationship categories. In 2021 and 2025, writer Kate Mulvey published two essays. The first was titled "Why I'm Disinviting My Unvaccinated Friends from My Dinner Parties."[2] A few years later came the second: "I'm a Single Woman of 63, and I Feel Friendless and Lonely."[3] In the first, Mulvey makes a public case for social exclusion in the name of principle, saying, "If you won't have the vaccine, you're no friend of mine." In the second, she laments the deep ache of isolation in later life, wondering where all the meaningful connections have gone and why her phone has stopped ringing. She recounts one friend cutting her off after taking offense at something she wrote (perhaps her earlier piece about cutting off the unvaccinated, though it doesn't say). It would be easy to read this juxtaposition as poetic justice, but it's better understood as a sobering reminder of how desperately we all need more grace—to be extended and received. Read together, the two essays trace a cultural arc. They are a microcosm of a broader societal trend in which ideological purity and fear of contamination, moral or otherwise, have left many standing alone.

This same pattern is now playing out, often with even higher stakes, within families. The decisions once made about who to invite to a dinner party are now made about who will be welcomed to a wedding or who should be shunned on their deathbed.[4] The stakes are both deeply personal and broadly civilizational.

At the center of this phenomenon is the terminal choice to go no contact, to cut off ties entirely. Yet this book addresses the full spectrum of polarized relationships—from families and friends who remain in contact but live with tension, to those striving to regain contact or find peace despite the divide, and everyone in between.

The most common ideological reasons for going no contact fall into roughly three categories: disagreement over Covid policy, voting for Donald Trump, and gender ideology. In each category those on "the wrong side of History" are considered threats to society and, more often than not, threats to the lives of others. While the deconstruction of gender ideology isn't the point of this book, it occupies many of the illustrations of this phenomenon. It makes sense that it does. The transgender movement is at its core a rejection of one's own flesh, and that inevitably extends to one's own flesh and blood.

It should also be noted that, with the number of those who identify as transgender remaining relatively small (though it has risen sharply in recent years), they don't make up the entirety of those who have gone no contact over gender. Alongside them is a large, though largely overlooked, population of self-described allies and activists. This group often remains hidden in discussions of gender ideology. Yet their advocacy, and their intolerance of those who express even the slightest hesitation, can be even more zealous. With the conviction of crusaders who believe they are fighting on behalf of the vulnerable, allies often become the most uncompromising enforcers, cutting off relationships with stunning speed and finality.

Finally, this book also examines how political forces have both fueled and been driven by these ruptures. Ideology and alienation are intimately entwined. As our bonds fray, ideological estrangement and political hostility feed off each other, each intensifying the other in a cycle that is terminal—both to relationships and at times to life itself, as we have seen in the rise of political violence. If we can't hold fast to one another in the face of disagreement, we risk losing not only our most intimate bonds but also the architecture that makes a free, humane, and just society possible.

Part 1

A HOUSE DIVIDED

1

THE NEW SHAPE OF ESTRANGEMENT

Jack and Genevieve, empty nesters living in a leafy suburban neighborhood outside Chicago, had always shared a close and affectionate relationship with each of their five children, but their bond with their eldest, Liam, grew more distant after he finished college. Liam began expressing a newfound skepticism about the Christian faith in which he was raised. What began as doubt only grew, and eventually Liam, now a physicist, concluded he was an atheist. Jack was deeply saddened. Genevieve was more sanguine about it. Regardless, Liam and the family maintained their warmth and an easy, regular connection.

Things changed in 2020. Between Covid and the unrest following the death of George Floyd, much of the world felt on edge and, like in so many other families, what had once been easily overlooked differences suddenly seemed urgent and unavoidable. That same year Liam fell in love with a colleague, Krista, a slight and ethereal beauty with an intelligence that matched Liam's. The two bonded over social issues they cared about deeply and their common frustration with what they saw as the provincial intolerance of half the country.

Jack and Genevieve and Liam's siblings embraced Krista,

including her at all family events from baby showers to barbecues. Krista was more skeptical and perhaps unsure of their sincerity, seemingly testing them at times by making a point of wedging political comments into apolitical conversations. Some of the siblings felt this was off-putting and condescending, but Jack and Genevieve assured them that, while challenging, these were the natural growing pains of merging lives with very different outlooks. Upon Liam and Krista's request, they even agreed to keep one room in the house for Krista to retreat to when she needed to take a mental health break from them because of her discomfort with their differences.

The following year Liam and Krista announced their engagement. Liam's sisters offered to throw a bridal shower, and the parents had them over for a champagne toast. After the toast Krista announced she needed to make sure they all understood that, despite the engagement, their marriage might be open. For Krista, this felt like an important moment to be transparent with her future family. For Jack and Genevieve, this felt like an unnecessarily aggressive confrontation; they didn't want to know the inner workings of the couple's sexual life. They didn't argue, but the rest of the evening was chilled, and the conversation strained.

Liam emailed the family shortly after to let them know that a Covid vaccination would be a requirement for all guests attending their spring wedding. For Liam and Krista, the shot was a necessary step toward ending a scary chapter in the country and a duty of a responsible citizen. For the rest of the family, the coercion and censorship surrounding the discussion of the vaccine didn't engender trust in either its efficacy or its safety. They had quietly made the decision to avoid it and communicated this to Liam.

For the young couple, this decision was intolerable. Jack

and Genevieve offered to self-isolate the family prior to the wedding and take multiple Covid tests to ensure they weren't carriers of the virus, but Liam insisted that the vaccine was nonnegotiable. If they loved him, he insisted, they would do the right thing.

Liam and Krista felt the family was recalcitrant. Liam's parents and siblings felt the same about him. Both the family and the engaged couple believed the others had drawn a line in the sand that effectively elevated ideology over family. In an email to his parents and siblings, Liam expressed his bewilderment at their choice to not attend his wedding by refusing the vaccine. Jack, Genevieve, and Liam's siblings replied that it was Liam who had forced this situation by not accepting their offers of compromise.

With neither side willing to budge further, Liam and Krista made the decision to end contact with the family. They haven't spoken in more than three years.

—

The true story of Jack and Genevieve's family is sadly not an outlier. Family estrangement—or going no contact—isn't a new phenomenon. But in recent years it has gained significant visibility. Unlike previous decades when estrangement was often shrouded in shame and secrecy, today it's more openly discussed and sometimes celebrated as an act of courage and self-care, calling into question long-held social norms and beliefs about the importance of family. Digital platforms like TikTok, Reddit, and YouTube play a significant role in normalizing and amplifying stories of estrangement. Popular hashtags such as #ToxicFamily, #NarcissisticParent, and #ChildhoodTrauma offer a wealth of advice on going no contact. These platforms provide validation and community for individuals grappling with the decision to sever family ties, making estrangement more palatable.

Estrangement is less stigmatized today; it's also on the rise. A Cornell study found that approximately 27 percent of Americans are estranged from a close relative. That is roughly sixty-eight million people.[1] The reasons for this growing phenomenon are contested. Some suggest that destigmatization acts as a necessary corrective, giving permission to people who need to cut ties but fear social stigma. Others, including clinical psychologist Joshua Coleman, author of *Rules of Estrangement,* propose that the proliferation of discussion on estrangement on social media can also create a kind of social contagion: "Cutting out your toxic family member is becoming sort of an act of personal expression and identity, rather than what it often is, which is an expression more of avoidance."[2] The two explanations are not mutually exclusive: destigmatization can increase willingness in a good way, while normalization increases frequency by lowering the bar for severance in a way that can be damaging.

That our culture has destigmatized estrangement suggests that we have changed our minds about some of our most serious guiding principles. Many young adults perceive family relationships as chosen and conditional, hinging on shared values and mutual respect. Political and cultural divides within families can quickly take on a more intense and dire tone, with ideological differences increasingly cited as key reasons for estrangement (rather than abuse, for example). As a point of comparison, while approximately one in four Americans experience family estrangement, one in five experience estrangement over a political or ideological divide.[3] This phenomenon of politically driven estrangement isn't particular to people of faith, but I have found that they are disproportionately represented among those who have lost contact with family because of schisms over political or religious views.

This escalation of politically driven estrangement can unmoor society for generations to come. For centuries, close family bonds have been considered central to personal and communal well-being, yet for many today, family relationships are increasingly perceived as obstacles to mental health and personal growth. The generational divide underscores this change: A recent YouGov poll found that 70 percent of individuals aged sixty-five and older prioritize family relationships as most important, compared with only 50 percent of adults under thirty.[4] Younger generations often prioritize friendships or chosen communities over traditional family ties.

In 2024 *The New Yorker* examined this rising phenomenon in a long essay, "Why So Many People Are Going 'No Contact' with Their Parents."[5] The author profiles a young woman, Amy, whose story mirrors Liam's. Like Liam, Amy didn't experience any of the historically common reasons for estrangement such as abuse, addiction, divorce, or mental illness. Amy also had a religious upbringing that she began to question in college and eventually jettisoned.

Most strikingly, both Liam and Amy took the terminal step to go no contact over the issue of their parents' refusal of the vaccine for their weddings. Amy's mother also sought some sort of compromise that would allow them to attend while distancing. "I beg of you, do not respond to this imperfect email with anger," her mother pleaded. "Please see the love behind it."[6]

In reply, Amy sent a short email offering two choices: get the vaccination and attend or don't attend at all.[7]

A few months after the wedding, Amy asked for all contact to end. She struggled with the sadness of it but explained that, to reestablish connection, she would need not merely an apology or a smoothing over but a real commitment from her family to do a lot of work. She believed it was unlikely, so rather than holding on to false hope, she pressed on with her decision as the best way to move forward. She blocked family members' phone numbers and marked cards they sent "Return to Sender."

Despite the similarities between the stories of Amy and Liam, ideological estrangement didn't originate in 2020. While research remains relatively new, many experts agree that the phenomenon had been quietly building for at least a decade prior. The year 2020 did mark a pivotal turning point, though. The Covid-19 lockdown led to a steep decline in mental health and a dramatic rise in anxiety and isolation, with many flocking to online forums and communities in search of connection and meaning. The nation was simultaneously embroiled in racial tensions that spilled into the streets, and political divisions calcified among neighbors, friends, and families. In some ways 2020 can be defined as the year we all became strangers and threats to one another.

An angry and isolated populace is one that inevitably searches for a scapegoat, projecting collective frustration and fear onto visible targets. In such a climate, going no contact is increasingly reframed not as a failure of familial bonds but as a necessary purge, doing one's part to expunge from personal life those whose views make them toxic to public life. Estrangement of this sort is both a symptom and a reinforcement of broader civic division—both echoing and amplifying the polarization.

Research on adult child–parent estrangement shows that younger generations largely drive this dynamic and that the two parties interpret the breakdown in their relationship in divergent ways. Adult children often attribute the breakdown to generalized and intractable problems in their parents, such as narcissism or toxicity. Parents, on the other hand, tend to explain estrangement through external factors, such as the child's spouse, a therapist, or broader societal influences.[8] This divergence in perspectives complicates reconciliation efforts, as each party operates from a fundamentally different understanding of the cause of estrangement.

While the reasons for this growing phenomenon might be ideological, the consequences are profoundly and painfully human. Adult children who go no contact are left without a safety net when met with a crisis like a job loss, a health scare, or a difficult breakup. In such times, it's typically family that provides a unique source of support, stepping into places a friend or colleague might not. On the other side, estranged parents and grandparents experience a perpetual heartache they never anticipated, which some have described to me as living with a missing limb as they mourn the loss of relationship with their children and grandchildren.

This book seeks to understand what is driving the accelerated phenomenon of estrangement, with the goal of equipping families and friends to avoid ideologically driven estrangement or to repair their relationships if they have already fractured. The first step to overcoming ideological estrangement is to expose and analyze the factors that have made it a normal part of the culture today.

Through my conversations with families experiencing ideological estrangement and by sifting through hundreds of posts, videos, testimonials, and articles, I have identified five core conditions driving this phenomenon: (1) demythologizing the family, (2) social hygiene, (3) broadening the definition of trauma, (4) the infallibility narrative, and (5) cultural narcissism. What we are facing in the politics of estrangement is less like a steady current pulling us downstream and more like a wildfire. As a native Californian, I am very aware that such fires rarely have a single cause. Was it the unlucky convergence of weather events? Was it aided by human neglect, mismanagement of the land and the reservoirs? Was there arson involved that initiated or accelerated the destruction?

In the same way, the phenomenon of political estrangement has emerged like a cultural wildfire, where multiple forces (each powerful on its own) have converged at once. The dry tinder of spiritual and familial decline, the fuel of identity politics, the wind of therapeutic culture, the heat of political polarization, and the oxygen of social media all feed the flames. Estrangement is often a tangle of forces—some beyond our control, others very much within it.

At the root of these conditions lies a radical revision of what it means to be human, recasting the person around two opposing principles: the exaltation of autonomy and the incentivization of victimhood. I call this "the Empowerment Delusion," as it promises power but leaves people profoundly powerless. On one hand, individuals are told they possess near-absolute power to redefine core aspects of reality—such as sex, the body, and the meaning of life—according to personal preference. On the other hand, they are told that the locus of control over their lives is almost entirely external—and that their identity and capacity for success are under continual threat.

Both sides of the Empowerment Delusion lead to frustration and despair. The first, radical autonomy, claims power over what is fixed and unchanging. The second, incentivized victimhood, claims powerlessness over what can be changed by relocating responsibility for our successes and failures almost entirely onto systemic forces of society or by ascribing far too much power to those who have hurt us, thus freezing us in narratives of despair. Together these distortions breed nihilism: a sense of meaninglessness to our lives, our efforts, our flesh and blood. Across these pages, I will trace how these five conditions and this revision of anthropology through the Empowerment Delusion are reshaping both the individual and society and driving the politics of no contact.

Demythologizing the Family

The first condition at the heart of family estrangement today is the debunking of what some call "the family myth." This "myth" is the belief that familial relationships are worthy of special regard in a way that entails obligations. While the effort to demythologize the family has an older philosophical lineage, it has received renewed attention in our viral age. Influencers and online no-contact communities regularly challenge the belief that family merits unique loyalty, framing it as a social construct imposed on us rather than an authentic moral or natural imperative. For many, the universal mandate captured in the Bible to "honor thy father and mother" is now an antiquated notion that serves as a fig leaf to hide oppression, abuse, and other toxic behavior. A popular counterpoint to the old adage "blood is thicker than water" in these discussions is that such attachments are neither natural nor necessary and that we can simply deprogram ourselves out of them.

Therapist Patrick Teahan, a prominent online educator about childhood trauma and going no contact, welcomes this shift as a sign of cultural progress: "The movement right now is that we can break a cultural norm. The structure is becoming undone around 'family is everything.' I think it's a good thing."[9]

In a way, Teahan is correct. Family is *not* everything. In the case of someone enduring abuse, the idea that they can flourish and live a happy, connected life after estrangement can be important. One woman I spoke with, Cameron, a mother in her early forties, endured an abusive marriage to a mentally unwell husband. The court granted her full custody of her children after recognizing the emotional toll on the children. She told me how she found the strength and clarity to remove her ex-husband from her children's lives: "I thought about how when the kids were little, I tried to cultivate in them their natural instincts to recoil from things that might hurt them—to not play chase around an open bonfire as toddlers, to avoid a burner on the stove unless they could tell it was off and cooled. And I thought about what I was desensitizing them to by letting them bury their instinct toward self-protection from a harmful father." But for Cameron, cutting off contact was a necessary evil that she wishes could have been otherwise, not a good thing. She doesn't view the desire for a whole, intact family as a social construct. Rather, she understands that her children have lost something deeply human. "They were meant to have a father. There is no getting around that. They can heal and thrive, but the deprivation is real."

While one might be required to cut family ties in certain

contexts, a broader claim has emerged—that the institution of family itself is arbitrary, that it tends to serve harmful power interests, and that society can evolve beyond it. This view will be examined further in chapter 4, as it raises crucial and consequential questions, not only about what family means, but also about what it means to be human and what ramifications such a shift might have on civic life.

Social Hygiene

As family life is attenuated, our sense of belonging and safety becomes destabilized and displaced. We can see this most clearly in the rise of identity politics and the fragile sense of self that emerges from these weaker and yet more antagonistic self-conceptions. The slogan "The personal is political" emerged in the 1960s and was initially intended as a radical reframing of personal experiences through a lens of power and societal structures. With time, however, this focus on supra-personal forces has eclipsed older social attitudes that differentiated people more clearly from their politics.

While no person's identity can be fully understood in isolation from politics, identity did not used to be reduced to political positions. Historically, what made up a person's identity was a combination of character, familial relationships, cultural heritage, and religion.[10] As the latter three sources of personal identity have weakened, so the first, character, has undergone a transformation. A traditional society holds that a person's character is determined by their virtues or vices—lived habits that define personal morality. A virtuous person might hold political beliefs that diverge from your own, but you could still highly regard their moral stature.

With the rise of the politics of identity that emerged after the civil rights era and intensified in the 2010s, it has become more common to evaluate a person's character, and therefore their social acceptability, based on political tribe. Once your identity is subsumed by your political opinions, who you are is judged no longer by how you behave but rather by what you endorse, making virtue and vice abstract categories and leaving little daylight between political tribe and moral stature.

This fusion of politics and identity turns disagreements into existential threats. Where communities once worried that a person's vices endangered the common good, now it's a person's political beliefs and tribe that are a threat. This is somewhat understandable. In the past, political disputes were usually arguments about how best to achieve a shared goal: Do we reduce poverty more effectively by encouraging the proliferation of private enterprise or by a more robust social safety net? Today, political disputes are not merely about means but about *ends*—dealing with questions that go directly to the heart of what it means to be human.

In recent memory, for example, a number of mainstream publications featured commentary arguing that growing concern about population decline was in fact a matter of misogyny and white supremacy, evincing clearly that the political debate had shifted away from how best to make family life possible and had become a question of whether encouraging reproduction was even moral. When politics moves from debating how to achieve shared goals to disputing the goals themselves, it makes us not merely divided but mutually unintelligible, and it reinforces the suspicion that a person's politics determines their character and identity.

Increasingly, younger people project this concept of political alignment as the determinant of moral stature onto an older generation that generally doesn't view disagreements in the same way. A recurring sentiment expressed by estranged adult children is "My parents reject something fundamental about who I am." They understand their political convictions as core parts of their identities, so disagreement is indistinguishable from rejection or even enmity. For Liam and Krista, the decision to go no contact with Liam's parents was deeply rooted in this dynamic. Liam and Krista believed Jack and Genevieve were being immoral by not getting vaccinated and were ready to reject the relationship because of it. But they also believed that Liam's parents' traditional views on sexual ethics were a fundamental threat and an implicit rejection of Krista as a person. They considered his parents unacceptable and assumed that they were unacceptable to his parents. If family members with opposing views are not just wrong but harmful to one's identity and sense of self, the concept of personal acceptance despite deep disagreement isn't possible.

A further psychological dimension is at play here as well, in that progressive ideology leads to a dynamic of low differentiation, a concept that arises out of Bowen family systems theory. Developed by psychiatrist Murray Bowen in the mid-twentieth century, the theory describes differentiation as the ability to maintain one's own convictions and emotional stability while staying connected to others, even in the presence of disagreement or tension. Families and societies, Bowen observed, exist on a spectrum of tolerance for differences, from low to high.[11]

People with low differentiation can't tolerate much difference at all. They tend to experience it as a personal threat, respond with emotional reactivity, and easily turn disagreement into relational conflict. Their concept of unity is collapsed into uniformity.

In contrast, those with high differentiation can engage

with others who think or act differently without feeling destabilized or pressured to conform. They can stand firm in their own beliefs while allowing space for others to hold their own, avoiding both defensiveness and the loss of self that comes with placating others.

This sense of political identity as personal identity combined with low differentiation results in "social hygiene"—scrubbing our social circles clean of toxic ideas by cutting contact with those who hold them.

In cultural commentary, few social rituals have come to represent this tension as starkly as Thanksgiving dinner. In 2022 the Biden White House released a list of talking points to help progressives navigate political discussions over their holiday dinner. Talking points ranged from celebrating the specific successes of the Biden administration to warning family members that extremists will try to institute a national abortion ban.[12] Pass the potatoes.

Nearly a decade earlier during the Obama administration, a similar message was projected with the infamous Pajama Boy campaign featuring a hipster in plaid onesie pj's, encouraging young adults to advocate for health insurance at family gatherings over the holidays. Pajama Boy (who was a grown man) offered young adults a to-do list for their holiday time with family: "Wear pajamas. Drink hot chocolate. Talk about getting health insurance."[13] While the campaign was widely mocked, it signaled the growing intrusion of political ideology into the intimate spaces of family life. Earlier administrations hadn't leveraged disagreements within families to promote policies nor appealed to the young to correct the old, setting up and hardening generational conflict. What seemed at the time a one-off moment of political advocacy foreshadowed a deeper societal shift.

The election of Donald Trump intensified the dynamic, shifting Thanksgiving talking points toward avoiding the meal altogether with Trump-supporting relatives. Countless pundits talked about or published think pieces on how to navigate, or simply skip, holiday gatherings in the wake of the election. The question was no longer about persuasion but about disgust and the dawning belief that half the country was simply beyond repair.

This approach to politics creates an environment where estrangement is a looming, implicit threat. One young woman I spoke with, Kaitlyn, has an aunt who goes in and out of no contact with Kaitlyn's family. At their most recent Thanksgiving dinner, the aunt showed up tense, though she relaxed as the evening progressed and conversation remained devoid of anything controversial. After dinner, however, she grew agitated and stepped outside. When Kaitlyn checked on her, her aunt reassured her that she was having a lovely time, that the conversations were pleasant, and that everyone was being kind. Then she sighed and said, "I just can't be at peace knowing that I'm in a room full of people who probably voted for *him*."

Despite her experience enjoying all of them, the aunt felt cognitive dissonance akin to how someone might feel morally sullied if the hosts had stolen the turkey from another family's home. With moral stature relocated to political identity, a person can become complicit through proximity not to an act but to a person. Kaitlyn's aunt felt her personal relationships with them were deceptive, obscuring the reality that they were likely carriers of toxic political views that could contaminate others through exposure and poor social hygiene. She offered a terse thank-you to Kaitlyn, asked her to grab her purse, and excused herself from the rest of the evening. She needed distance and clean air.

When every personal relationship becomes a stage for political performance, loyalty and affection are subordinated to ideological alignment. The family, once a sphere protected from the demands of public life, becomes yet another battleground. This blurring of boundaries is central to the rise in ideological estrangement: Convictions that might once have been debated around the table are now treated as grounds for exile from it.

Broadening the Definition of Trauma

Another condition contributing to ideological estrangement is the expanding notion of trauma. Over the past four decades, the formal definition of trauma in the *Diagnostic and Statistical Manual of Mental Disorders* (DSM) has gradually broadened. What was once limited to extraordinary, catastrophic events like combat or surviving a train crash, now includes a wider range of experiences, such as witnessing harm to others, being exposed to the details of a traumatic event, or being bullied. While these changes have improved recognition of genuine psychological injury, they have also blurred the lines between trauma and hardship.

In the popular lexicon, especially on social media, the concept of trauma has expanded further into the "big *T*" / "little *t*" distinction, in which chronic stressors, personal slights, and ordinary conflicts are framed as traumas. Additionally, participants in no-contact forums commonly speak of the experience of having a relationship with someone with different values as a source of trauma. These shifts lower the threshold for seeing relationships as unsafe and make permanent estrangement appear necessary for self-preservation.

Psychologist Nick Haslam has documented what he calls concept creep: the steady expansion of ideas like abuse, trauma, and harm to encompass increasingly ordinary human experiences. As a result, behaviors once considered normal, like strict parenting, some emotional stoicism, or high expectations, are now more easily labeled as profoundly harmful.[14] While a case can be made for each behavior becoming pathologically injurious in particular instances, these broader definitions risk catastrophizing normal familial conflicts and foster the unreasonable expectation that life can be lived without adversity or emotional injury—things that are inherent to the human condition.

Furthering the conflation of "big *T*" / "little *t*" trauma, victims of physical or sexual abuse often share online platforms with individuals estranged from their families over political disagreements or unmet emotional needs. Users describe extreme cases of abuse alongside stories of more common familial hurts and challenges. These forums, such as the Estranged Adult Child forum on Reddit (with thirty-nine thousand members), frequently put such profoundly different experiences on the same continuum of *degree* rather than acknowledging radical differences in *kind*, making it difficult to assess the validity of individual cases of estrangement.

The new definition of trauma has become culturally normative. Universities, for example, often provide counseling services, "safe spaces," and other resources in response to political events, framing them as traumatic. Following Donald Trump's 2024 victory, Chico State offered painting, coloring, and journaling to help students cope.[15] While well-intentioned, these measures inadvertently train young people to view political differences as emotionally harmful and existentially threatening to their psyches and well-being. In *The Coddling of the American Mind*, authors Greg Lukianoff and Jonathan Haidt argue this kind of framework creates cognitive distortions in young people—patterns of thought that cognitive-behavioral therapy (CBT) aims to correct. As CBT helps individuals challenge and reframe distorted thinking, practices like trigger warnings, the overemphasis on emotional safety, and the belief that disagreement is a threat reinforce these distortions rather than countering them.[16]

This emotional training has left kids fragile and relationships brittle, with a massive influx of therapists and therapeutic approaches rushing into the void. In her bestselling book *Bad Therapy*, Abigail Shrier writes of iatrogenesis, the phenomenon of harm caused by attempts at healing.[17] She describes what she calls the treatment-prevalence paradox: The more we intervene to prevent psychological distress, the more distress we can seem to produce. Shrier argues that the hyperfocus on the emotional state of adolescents and young adults can contribute to, and even cause, the very mental instability that mental health interventions intend to cure. Training them to place undue importance on their feelings—which are by nature unreliable—tends to induce an increase in negative feelings and make them feel more anxious, not less, leading to an ongoing cycle of further interventions.[18] In the same way, a broadened and ever more elastic understanding of trauma trains young people to search for it in their own lives, and perhaps even retroactively project it onto their past. Recognizing that we experienced hardships or hurts in childhood is different from telling ourselves that we endured trauma, that we are *traumatized*.

People like Liam and Amy, who might have endured emotional adversity and family disagreements, shouldn't be lumped together with victims of physical, sexual, or emotional abuse.

The Infallibility Narrative

Many who advocate going no contact believe that no one makes this decision unless it's the only remaining reasonable option. The adult child's choice is therefore always presented as self-justifying, creating an atmosphere where questioning the act of severing ties is seen as dehumanizing or condoning abuse. Like the expansion of the concept of trauma, this sort of unfalsifiable claim of the righteousness of those who go no contact risks conflating extreme cases of abuse with more ordinary familial disagreements by covering all with a hedge of inscrutability.

With more than two hundred thousand followers on TikTok and more than eight hundred thousand subscribers on YouTube, Patrick Teahan is highly sought after for his insights on childhood trauma and going no contact. In one pinned TikTok video, he explains how toxic families tend to see their children as cardboard cutouts and, when the adult child starts to go no contact, the parents will push back—which he implies is always unjustified. "It'll sound like this: 'We used to have amazing conversations. We used to be so close. I don't know what happened to us. Now you're all moody,'" Teahan says. "The real mind F of all that is we start to see [from] the way that they double down . . . that the family never really knew you to begin with."[19]

In a video on his YouTube page, Teahan explains not only that parents are wrong to question their adult child's decision regarding estrangement but also that their questioning demonstrates the family's toxicity: "When estranged parents reactively believe that their child has been wrongfully influenced by a therapist or whatever, by TikTok or whatever, it kinda implies that the child has no . . . thoughts of their own and that . . . the parents [see] them as an object and not as an individual. It's kind of like a clue."[20]

And what if other family members question the adult child's narrative? They are subject to the same judgment as the estranged parents. A slide from one of Teahan's presentations asks, "Are there any safe members who get the abuse and fully support you?" If the answer is no, then he doesn't suggest reevaluating the decision but rather suggests considering cutting off those family members as well. The same slide tells readers that any of the following traits qualifies as abuse: if someone is unloving, toxic, exploitive, entitled, physically unsafe, abusive, self-consumed, or refuses ownership or reality.[21] Teahan never acknowledges the obvious: that while pushback from siblings, parents, or other relatives can be a toxic refusal to acknowledge abuse, it can also be a normal, inevitable response to an unnecessary estrangement.

Moreover, the claim that going no contact is always a last recourse isn't well supported. For example, participants in a study on the psychological effects of estrangement noted enjoying the reactions of shock and curiosity from others when discussing their choice, suggesting that, for some, having a story of childhood trauma and estrangement may serve a psychological or even social function.[22] Particularly in trans youth communities, sharing one's story of parental estrangement can be a sort of social ritual or induction into the tribe, mimicking the ritual of sharing one's testimony in evangelical circles to show how God worked in one's life. In the same way, trans-identifying youth often share how family trauma worked in their lives. The claim of last recourse ignores the very human and powerful allure of identifying ourselves as victims and the sort of social capital given to those who have endured oppression.

This is the one-way nature of moral credibility in estrangement narratives: The infallibility narrative flows only toward the adult child. Ana Yudin, who holds a doctorate in clinical psychology and has more than six hundred thousand YouTube subscribers, reinforces this asymmetry. While she believes that adult children who go no contact are self-justifying, she insists that the parents' perspectives deserve intense scrutiny. She cites a *Journal of Family Communication* article cautioning that "the causes of a person's behavior are rarely this simple or straightforward, and thus children's assessment of their parents' behavior may be incomplete or inaccurate."[23] However, Yudin dismisses this caution as gaslighting. To suggest that adult children might bear any responsibility in repairing the parent-child relationship, she warns, is a slippery slope—one that dangerously undermines and harms adult children of dysfunctional parents.[24]

This asymmetry plays out in the no-contact community. Parents who have been cut off and tell their stories online are regularly subjected to derision and armchair psychoanalysis, while adult children are almost unanimously affirmed in their decision in such forums. For these communities and the therapists that advise them, there can be powerful incentives to defend adult children against all scrutiny—not necessarily out of ill will but because doing so affirms their own interpretive framework and reinforces a model of care centered on continued therapeutic dependence.

In response to genuine past injustices, our society has a strong impulse to sacralize victims in a reactionary and indiscriminate way. Just as the slogan "Believe women" (in the sense of "Believe all women") was an excessive correction to the injustice reflected in the Me Too movement, so is a growing narrative of "Believe all adult children." This black-and-white sorting of good versus bad categories of people echoes other identitarian divides. When combined with prevailing narratives, such as "Disagreements are dangerous," "Family is expendable," and "Daily life is infused with trauma," it's almost more surprising when a young adult chooses *not* to go no contact in the face of any level of familial conflict.

Cultural Narcissism

The final underlying condition driving estrangement is the rise of narcissism on both sides of the generational divide. Christopher Lasch's 1979 book *The Culture of Narcissism* makes the case that modern American society fosters widespread narcissistic behavior because of cultural, political, and economic shifts—particularly the rise of consumerism and individualism and the erosion of traditional social structures like family and community.[25]

Lasch's argument has only become more relevant since his writing. Results of the Narcissistic Personality Inventory between 1979 and 2006 show a significant rise in narcissistic traits among college students in the United States.[26] Over several decades researchers tracked the values and attitudes of high school seniors and college freshmen. What their responses revealed is a clear generational shift: Young adults have become more focused on external rewards like money, fame, and image than previous generations were at the same age. Empathy scores, meanwhile, have declined. This research by psychologist Jean Twenge and her colleagues points to a broader cultural movement toward self-focus and away from psychological well-being. The cumulative effect is an erosion of the interpersonal resilience required for healthy disagreement and the repair of long-term relationship.[27]

More recently, John Burn-Murdoch analyzed striking data from USC for the *Financial Times* documenting a decline in conscientiousness among the younger generations. The study covered the period from 2014 to 2025 and showed a dramatic drop in traits like discipline, reliability, and follow-through, alongside a dramatic rise in neurotic traits like emotional fragility and self-preoccupation. Both extroversion and agreeableness declined steeply as well.[28]

Taken together, these shifts help explain why relationships and commitments have grown more brittle across generations, even as the pattern is most pronounced among the young.

Social media has only exacerbated the rise in narcissistic traits by exponentially increasing an addiction to appearance over substance, perpetuating a disembodied abstract sense of community over the intimacy of a familial one, and habituating us to using others to satisfy our desire for cheap affirmation. All these tendencies, if not curbed and corrected, are terminal to a thriving family life.

Developmentally, narcissism is appropriate in young children; there is a "healthy narcissism," and that is precisely what family life exists to form us beyond. In the intimacy of a healthy family life, each person is invited to learn, in a setting of safety and unconditional love, to work through the inevitable clashes of will and to grow in self-knowledge and forgiveness.

A true narcissist, by contrast, is in a state of arrested development. Today's prolonged adolescence produces adults who have never been coaxed beyond the early stage of childhood preoccupations with the fulfillment of their own needs and desires. Because of this arrest, the narcissist is almost constitutionally incapable of self-knowledge. Deflection, projection, and a preference for fantasy and grandiosity over reality characterize the thought patterns of the narcissist, erecting an almost-impenetrable fortress around the person's psyche, protecting what is actually a very fragile, undeveloped sense of self. As narcissism rises, relational stability predictably declines.

With the rise in narcissistic traits, there has been a simultaneous surge in accusations of narcissism. This overlap is not incidental: A culture increasingly shaped by self-focus naturally becomes more alert—sometimes hyper-alert—to narcissism in others. At the same time, because we are soaked in pop therapeutic language, we tend to use the word *narcissism* imprecisely and gratuitously. "I'd say before 2020, people were not using this word at all outside of therapy circles," Israa Nasir, MHC, stated in an interview on the ubiquity of the term. "Now, I hear people in my personal life use it while describing relationships, dates gone wrong, as well as in therapeutic environments while talking about their parents. The term has proved super sticky, and has quickly skyrocketed into our public consciousness."[29]

Younger people are more likely to interpret interpersonal conflict through a lens of narcissism.[30] It's very common for adult children on no-contact forums to claim that they were raised by narcissists. The real increase in narcissistic traits and the emotional charge of family conflict make such accusations feel justified, even as they far exceed any clinical basis. Complicating matters further, narcissistic traits themselves tend toward projection, making it easier to locate the problem exclusively in others. What is clear is that though traits of narcissism have risen sharply, our use of the term greatly outpaces actual clinical diagnoses of the disorder. This makes it inevitable that some adult children are taking difficult human behavior, pathologizing it, saying that it's incurable and that they aren't implicated in the demise of these relationships.

Reconsidering the Ties That Bind

We hear the five conditions driving the no-contact movement reflected in the slogans and sentiments we encounter online, in therapy rooms, and in everyday conversation: "The family is a social construct." "The personal is political." "Protect your peace." "Believe victims." "#ToxicParents." Embedded in each phrase and each condition is the Empowerment Delusion of radical autonomy and victimhood. Together they dry out the cultural underbrush, making every relationship more flammable. And these ideas can spread quickly—from a single household to entire communities, from one rupture to a culture of rupture.

A young woman I spoke with who had recently gone no contact noted that people often tell her they are her family now, but it rarely ends up being true. "It feels like an easy, comforting thing to say, but there is a lack of action to back it up." For her, this gesture at connection feels like a repeated source of abandonment in her adult life.

Embedded within the promise of liberation through going no contact is the sad reality that this will leave many with no contacts. They often end up lonely and without a stable support system. There is good reason to think this is a sadness that doesn't get better with time. In fact, one of the most common regrets people have at the end of life is not having given sufficient time and priority to their closest relationships.[31]

Family dynamics are inherently complex, making it tempting to avoid deeply interrogating the phenomenon of estrangement, as it often feels too varied, emotionally charged, and subjective. Who would willingly choose such a painful path? It seems likely that very few make the decision to go no contact lightly. However, significant cultural, ideological, and psychological conditions are fueling this rising trend—forces that may operate beyond the conscious awareness of any individual. We see something similar in cases of marital estrangement. The likelihood that you will divorce increases significantly just when a friend has another friend who is getting a divorce, indicating how social contagion acts as a strong driver of our behavior.[32]

The line between the tragically necessary and the tragically unnecessary types of estrangement isn't always clear. Examining such a deeply personal phenomenon is undeniably fraught. On one hand, the complexity should serve to warn us against dismissing estrangement as a trivial or passing trend; on the other, it reminds us of how vulnerable any of us are to error when grappling with such complexity. The stakes, then, make deeper analysis both a challenging task and a responsibility too important to ignore.

For Jack and Genevieve, it has been a long and painful three years since Liam cut contact with them and his siblings. They kept thinking perhaps they'd run into one another on visits to the city, but they never did. One brother eventually saw a former colleague of Liam's and learned that the couple had moved out of state six months earlier.

Jack and Genevieve maintain hope that things might be repaired someday. Genevieve admits that sometimes it's hard not to blame Krista, but she's quick to correct that instinct and sees Liam as just as much an adult with agency and responsibility. Some of the siblings have said candidly that family gatherings feel easier now. But they all have a strong sense of sadness and loss. Several say Liam shows up here and there in their dreams. Holidays, celebrations, and family photos never feel complete. And the sense that it didn't have to be this way hovers over them all.

2

THE ROAD TO CULTURAL AMNESIA

Jeffrey Marsh is a bestselling author, coach, and queer advocate who identifies as non-binary. A caption to an article by Marsh on Oprah's website reads, "With their message of positivity and self-acceptance, red-lipsticked Jeffrey Marsh is a master of the six-second video on Vine, where they've amassed 260 million views—and counting."[1]

Marsh, with his signature five-o'clock shadow, colorful eyeshadow, and playful, childlike disposition, has only grown in prominence, though he's since moved from Vine to TikTok, where he regularly encourages his followers to go no contact: "It's that time of year again, when you start thinking about going no contact." Marsh tells them they're going to love it, despite the guilt they might be encountering at present: "Every time you think about going no contact, you just feel this thing in your chest and in your stomach and you don't want to be *that* person. And 'How could you?' 'But she's your mother.' And all this stuff that culture tells you."

Marsh then slows and quiets his voice as he pointedly reassures his viewers that with time it will all be worth it: "It'll make *you* content. Happy. Calm. And in love with life."[2]

Marsh isn't merely a TikTok influencer. His work has taken

him from the United Nations to partnerships with brands like Target. As a reporter, he has covered LGBTQ issues for a wide range of publications and networks, including *Good Morning America*, *The New York Times*, *Variety*, and the BBC. He also served as an advisor for Elizabeth Warren's 2020 presidential campaign and consulted for MTV, New York University, Condé Nast's *Them*, and *Teen Vogue*.

In another video Marsh describes having gone no contact with his entire family—parents, siblings, extended relatives alike—after working through a period of intense guilt. But, he realizes, he was giving priority to his family's feelings and potential hurt and not prioritizing his own feelings. He continues, shifting his language from his story to one shared with his audience. "Why is it that we never consider *our* mental health? *Our* feelings? Why do we want to go no contact in the cleanest way possible so that *they* will not be upset? What about the trillion times when *we* were upset?" He assures viewers that he loves them and that the pain of going no contact can't compare to the pain of remaining in relationship. His tone then shifts from tender concern to exuberance. "Have a good time going no contact!"[3]

The video's title, "How to Know If No Contact Is the Answer," suggests that viewers will receive guidance to discern whether estrangement is the right choice. The answer seems to be an unqualified yes. Marsh's role is not to help viewers weigh their decision but to encourage them to take the leap.

The hashtag #ToxicFamily has 267,000 posts on TikTok, and figures like Marsh hold influence that is hard for many to imagine—particularly those from older generations. If the word *TikTok* makes you think of the sound of a clock and not a social media platform, the no-contact movement likely feels bewildering. Even savvy journalists write about it with a puzzled tone, sensing that it signifies fundamental shifts in our understanding of family and our criteria for estrangement.

On the London-based social networking site for grandparents, Gransnet, user Eugenia's post speaks to the bewilderment: "My generation, boomers, born from the 50's to 60's, we literally NEVER heard of estrangement." Even in families that struggled, she recalls, people still maintained ties.

By contrast, she says, now estrangement is everywhere: "I did a search once, to look up Toxic adult children, and guess what?? Everything that popped up was about parents! Only one, lone website addressed adult children who mistreat or take advantage/demanding of their parents. It's pretty clear, there is a bias out there, and I don't know why." She questions why "toxic people" are so readily sorted by age or parental status and compares it to blaming infidelity on only one sex: "It's like saying all cheaters are men . . . that would be untrue and misleading."[sic][4]

Eugenia's bewilderment highlights just how dramatically and quickly the conversation around estrangement has shifted. While older generations experienced it as a rare, almost-unthinkable phenomenon, today it has become a much-talked-about topic framed around victimhood and liberation. Family estrangement isn't an entirely new phenomenon, but the modern, ideologically driven no-contact movement doesn't easily fit within the lineage of an older tradition that saw estrangement as an extreme measure, justified only to preserve social cohesion, maintain order, and reinforce communal stability. Today's estrangement, however, has a newer lineage—one that prioritizes not social preservation but social disruption and reinvention. Rather than reinforcing shared norms, this movement often functions as a tool of ideological purification, severing individuals from their past to reshape the future.

In the twentieth century, family estrangement underwent a multipronged transformation, paving the way for the modern no-contact movement. First, estrangement had functioned to uphold communal stability and reinforce cultural norms. In the last century, it was reframed as an act of liberation from inherited tradition and a means of destabilization. Second, familial divisions had often been unintended consequences of larger societal forces, like war or exile. In contrast, modern ideological movements have increasingly treated estrangement as *an end in itself*, a way to break generational continuity and subordinate relationships to a new, revolutionary future. And last, whereas in the past banishment was most often initiated by an elder, the ideological denunciations of the last century have generally come from the young.

Today's no-contact movement is the direct heir of this revolutionary approach to estrangement, carrying forward its logic of liberation, generational rupture, and reinvention.

—

Throughout history, familial ties have been a matter of life or death. Survival and cohesion depended on members providing support to one another from infancy to old age. In ancient agrarian societies, individuals could rarely sustain themselves (especially during times of scarcity) without the labor and benefits afforded by family and community. Being expelled from one's family or tribe was effectively a death sentence. Because of this, most societies have regarded severing ties with a relative as an extraordinary measure.

As foreign as it might seem to our modern sensibilities, family exile was a means of reinforcing communal memory and moral order. A banished person was often cast out to serve as a cautionary tale, a reminder of the importance of the values they had violated and the gravity of the community's commitment to protect civic stability. The exiled individual remained a part of cultural memory, either as a tragic lesson or as a figure of redemption. Biblical and medieval notions of exile, such as Cain's punishment or royal excommunications, reinforced the authority of religious or political institutions and kept the past alive in the collective memory.

In ancient Greece, familial banishment might occur if someone committed treason or another crime that shamed their family and threatened social stability. In ancient Rome, the paterfamilias (head of the family) had authority akin to a military commander's to disown members for disobedience or dishonor, particularly women for infidelity or men for cowardice. Ancient laws, such as the Code of Hammurabi, included provisions for banishing those guilty of crimes like incest or breaking religious laws.

In medieval Europe, noble families might disown or exile members who betrayed their country or faith through actions like treason or heresy. Banishment occurred in Puritan and other colonial settlements for offenses including adultery and heresy. In many indigenous and non-Western societies, it's still considered a form of purification or atonement to expel individuals from the family or tribe for violating sacred customs. To this day, the Catholic Church uses formal excommunication as a rare medicinal, rather than punitive, form of righting the unrepentant sinner. While remaining a member of the church, the excommunicant is no longer able to receive the sacraments nor hold any ecclesiastical position until they are reconciled. Throughout time, the stakes of belonging have been high and clearly defined.

The no-contact movement doesn't find its antecedents in

this lineage that wielded estrangement for the sake of social preservation and continuity. Instead, it echoes more recent efforts to narrate anew the past and redefine family in a way that liberates the individual from both. It fits more neatly into the lineage of Stalinist Russia or Maoist China's Cultural Revolution, where young people were encouraged to denounce their families in the name of ideological purity. In both cases, relational ties were recast as political battlegrounds.

Initially presaged by the French Revolution's Reign of Terror, where massive bloodshed, denunciations, and torture were justified to enforce ideological purity and social progress, totalitarian regimes in the twentieth century cemented this new paradigm, portraying enemies not simply as opposing forces but as threats to humanity and obstacles to progress. The enemy no longer was confined to battle lines or identifiable by a uniform but could be in your home, uncovered through whispers, suspicions of dissent, or the retention of traditional beliefs. This shift transformed religious and familial pieties into a religious-like loyalty to the state, making atrocities more prevalent and denunciations of family members more zealous.

The Russian Revolution of 1917 embodied this shift. Soviet leaders urged the youth to align with the Communist Party and denounce their parents as class enemies, often leading to arrests or executions. After Lenin's death, Stalin leveraged denunciations and loyalty to party over family into a central tool for maintaining control and promoting loyalty to the regime. Stalin's secret police encouraged reporting any anti-Soviet behavior among family and neighbors, fomenting widespread paranoia.

As the paranoia grew, the fearful sensed that they could

deflect suspicion from themselves and demonstrate state loyalty by accusing others. Soviet leadership became not only a surrogate family but also the center of a surrogate religion, with Stalin portrayed as both the "father of peoples"[5] and a godlike figure.

The party imposed a kind of examination of conscience, interrogating members to unearth their sins against the party. Chief among those was the sin of not having sufficiently purged oneself or one's family of the superstition of traditional religion.

One such documented examination from a party cell meeting went as follows:

> *Did you baptise your children?*
>
> The last one to be baptised in my family was my daughter in 1926.
>
> *At what date did you break with religion?*
>
> In 1923.
>
> *It seems that there are still icons in your house.*
>
> Yes, that's because my mother-in-law doesn't want me to take them down![6]

School curricula and youth propaganda celebrated stories of children denouncing their parents for anti-Soviet attitudes or actions. According to Soviet lore, a young Siberian boy, Pavlik Morozov, was murdered by his family in 1932 after informing authorities about his father's alleged disloyalty to the state. Pavlik, said to be a devoted member of the Communist Young Pioneers, knew that remaining silent about disloyalty would make him morally complicit. During Stalin's campaign of farm collectivization and the persecution of kulaks (wealthy peasants), Pavlik reportedly demonstrated his loyalty and courage by exposing his father for aiding exiled kulaks.

The story of Pavlik, the child hero and martyr who bravely denounced his father, was told and retold to schoolchildren. Children demanded vengeance for his murder, wrote poems and sang songs of his sacrifice, made pilgrimages to his statue, and wondered how they, too, might be brave enough to turn in their parents. There was just one problem: The story seems to be almost entirely untrue Soviet propaganda.[7] The regime needed a martyr to rally peasants to their cause against landowners and to silence dissent. Those who knew the truth of Pavlik were cowed into silence.[8]

Yet even the Soviet state eventually recognized the social danger of the message it had unleashed. By the late 1930s, Stalin grew concerned about the instability caused by such dissolution. Children denouncing their parents had been so effective that they were no longer useful, and so he reintroduced a sense of paternalism to Soviet families and refocused loyalty to the state as exemplified in self-sacrifice over denunciations.

Even so, the habits of suspicion and fear had carved deep and lasting divisions in social life. According to *The New York Times*, "One memoir of the time describes a woman who had denounced so many neighbors that she suffered a paralyzing stroke when she learned that labor camp inmates were being rehabilitated after Stalin's death in 1953 and would be coming home."[9]

The craze of denunciation wasn't limited to Soviets. During the Spanish Civil War, propaganda on both sides urged citizens to identify ideological enemies, deemed "enemies of the revolution" (by the Republican side) or "enemies of Spain" (by the Nationalist side). In some Republican-held areas, radicalized youth denounced their devoutly religious parents of political disloyalty. Conversely, in Nationalist-held territories, children of Republican sympathizers often faced public shaming or were sent to Francoist institutions for reeducation under the guise of inherited guilt.

In Germany under the Third Reich, children were taught that loyalty to the Führer superseded loyalty to family, leading many to accuse their parents of being backward for not supporting Nazi ideology. Such reporting could lead to arrests and executions, even as the children were encouraged to interpret their actions as moral service to the regime.[10]

In China, Mao Zedong's campaign to enforce Communist orthodoxy through cultural revolution led to brutal widespread persecution and ideological purges. Mao made clear that collective happiness would come by way of toppling what he called "the four olds": old ideas, old customs, old culture, old habits. As Mao knew, religion and familial bonds foster competing allegiances and serve as conduits for cultural continuity. His goal was not continuity but rupture. Memory itself is a problem for totalizing regimes, and no one has a longer memory than the old.

Practically, this liberation from the old translated into literal and figurative parricide as children were used as the vehicle of revolutionary rage against their parents, teachers, and religious authorities. Leaders urged children to denounce representatives of the four olds as counterrevolutionaries and harborers of bourgeois tendencies. The accused were publicly shamed, beaten, tortured, sent to labor camps, or executed by a single shot to the back of the head or by a firing squad.

Author Xi Van Fleet, who lived through Maoism in China, says of her experience under Chairman Mao, "It was indeed a world turned upside down full of insanity and violence. Things we had taken for granted were condemned as bourgeois and counterrevolutionary and needed to be canceled or destroyed. We were asked to question everything that was traditional. And we were told there were enemies of Mao (*oppressors*) in the midst of us which could even include friends, neighbors, family members, even our own parents and that we needed to expose and report them if discovered. Everyone was frantically trying to align themselves with the 'correct' side (*oppressed*) to avoid ending up as the target of the Red Guards."[11]

Ji-li Jiang, who was also a young girl during the Maoist Cultural Revolution, recounts the immense pressure she faced to denounce her father, who was labeled as a class enemy. Jiang initially saw Mao as a savior and felt a great loyalty to him and the future he promised. Everything shifted for her when the authorities learned that her grandfather had been a landowner, a revelation that had dire implications for the family. It didn't matter that her grandfather had passed away thirty years prior. Jiang and her siblings became outcasts at school. Her father, a theatrical performer, was detained by the authorities, and her grandmother was forced into manual labor. Eventually, the party came and ransacked their home, taking all their furniture, including their beds.

When she was fourteen, the authorities came to Jiang's school, demanding that she denounce her father at a "struggle meeting." Her father was to stand onstage hanging his head with a sign around his neck condemning him. She would be onstage, too, announcing his sins against the state to the crowd. They told her, though this might seem difficult, if she took the right attitude, this wouldn't be hard to do. They spoke with praise of another girl who, filled with righteous rage for her country, slapped and denounced her mom onstage. But Jiang was close with her family, and she had never heard or seen her father say or do anything that was against Chairman Mao and their country. She decided not to report to the authorities for the struggle meeting. Her father was recategorized as a landowner, though he was only the son of one, and they sent him to work in the countryside even without her denunciation. Jiang managed to evade complicity in her father's condemnation, but she doesn't blame those who succumbed to such pressure. "I don't think we should blame those kids, because they were so confused; they were brainwashed," Jiang says.[12]

In his dystopian novel *1984*, George Orwell captures how ideological loyalty can unravel and invert the most intimate human ties. One memorable example is Parsons, Winston Smith's neighbor in Victory Mansions. A bumbling but loyal Party man, Parsons feels great pride over his children's zeal for the Party. At one point, he boasts to Winston about how his daughter identified a man as an enemy and accused him just based on his appearance.[13]

Later in the novel, Winston encounters Parsons in the Ministry of Love—the regime's grim facility for torture and ideological reprogramming. Parsons has been arrested for thoughtcrime. When Winston asks who turned him in, Parsons replies, with a kind of pitiful pride, "It was my little daughter. . . . She listened at the keyhole." She had overheard her father saying in his sleep, "Down with Big Brother!" and reported this failure of loyalty the next day.[14]

The dynamics look different in our culture, but the principle remains eerily similar: Ideology, once internalized, can turn children into moral enforcers against their parents.

Today we see this pattern emerging, not through a formal,

state-imposed ideology, but through individuals and institutions influenced by ideology gone viral. This creed reframes family as an outmoded social construct and personal grievances and political disagreements as moral indictments. Unlike organic boundary-setting, modern ideological estrangement is shaped by online influencers, pervasive and often-imprecise therapeutic language, and a demand for ideological conformity. The shift from social protection to social engineering is stark: If past generations distanced themselves from harmful relationships to preserve personal well-being, today's no-contact movement often encourages estrangement as a signal of liberation—an act of moral progress unburdening ourselves from the past in service of an imagined future. The question is no longer "Should I distance myself from harmful people?" but "How could I remain among those who are on the wrong side of History?"

Cultural Subversion

Even as revolutionary regimes sought to remake society through political force, some Marxist theorists concluded that lasting change required a transformation of culture, one that would take root from within. This turn toward culture did not represent a single, centrally coordinated strategy, and the thinkers associated with it differed in method and emphasis. Yet across these varied strands of Western Marxism ran a shared conviction: Socia consciousness is formed through institutions such as family life, parental authority, sexuality, education, and civil society. Drawing in part on psychoanalytic theory, they examined how these domains shape and reproduce the status quo, making them pivotal arenas for lasting social change.

Within this broader effort, Wilhelm Reich emerged as a key figure. Reich moved to the United States in 1939 shortly after publishing his book *The Sexual Revolution*. Having seen the horrific rise of authoritarianism in Europe, he was convinced that cultural revolution was the necessary path forward. To that end, Reich wrote extensively about the need to educate the young toward total sexual liberation, empowering them to question and reject the moral and cultural authority of their parents. He believed that family and religion, as the main transmitters of sexual normativity, are central tools of authoritarianism, used to maintain power and suppress individuality. Like other Freudian Marxists of his era, Reich explicitly linked sexual liberation to broader revolutionary aims, arguing that true societal transformation required addressing both economic *and* sexual oppression.[15]

Throughout the mid-twentieth century, as these revolutionary ideas took hold and younger generations embraced sexual liberation, parents—especially those with traditional or religious values—often reacted with alarm and resistance. The speed of change produced sharp generational conflict. Some parents responded severely, rupturing relationships with children over promiscuity, cohabitation, homosexuality, among other disagreements. While conflicts over sexual morality weren't new, the pace and scope of the sexual revolution made such clashes more common and polarizing.

In the decades that followed, however, social acceptance of sexual liberation rose while parental rejection declined. I spoke with Fr. Philip Bochanski, formerly of Courage International, who spent years working pastorally with persons with same-sex attraction and their parents. He observes that, in the moment of their child coming out, parents are hit with multiple cognitive crises at once. They must confront the reality that who they understood their child to be wasn't altogether accurate. They also must confront the prospect of a very different future for their child than the one they imagined. While the child has often spent a good deal of time processing all this, the parents haven't. Most parents with whom he spoke feel some degree of regret about how they initially reacted to the news and feel they would have done it differently in hindsight, indicating that even if agitation is the initial reaction, it's often not the permanent one.

Over the years, Fr. Bochanski has seen countless examples of devoutly religious parents in such situations who remain happily engaged in their child's life and affirm their child's dignity and goodness without abandoning or compromising their religious convictions or devotion to God. In fact, it's often their religious devotion that *spurs* them to see the fundamental dignity of their child and to fight for grace and connection amid deep disagreement—belying the predominant narrative that religion leads people in a straight line toward bigotry or hatred. Such relationships require grace from each side. But what happens if only one side is willing to extend such grace? What happens if the son or daughter believes that anything short of total affirmation—including of activity and/or preferred pronouns—is a condition of love?

The Authoritarian Self

While the era of parents harshly rejecting their children is happily waning, the rise of the transgender movement has coincided with a sharp increase in adult children rejecting their parents. Although the no-contact movement reaches well beyond such identity issues, features specific to the trans movement tend to intensify family conflict and push divisions toward estrangement. I spoke with writer and researcher Sarah Mittermaier about how trans ideology maps onto the no-contact movement. "Unlike other ideological shifts, it requires active participation from loved ones," she explains. "Gender identity demands not just tolerance but enthusiastic buy-in. If parents have doubts, it creates an existential crisis for the child. This demand for affirmation is sweeping, asking everyone in a person's life to co-sign and celebrate self-rejection. Parents are tolerated only to the extent that they are willing to be reeducated."

Throughout history, the justifications for family estrangement have taken three primary forms: offenses against God, offenses against the state, and offenses against the self. Each kind of offense—whether religious, political, or personal—can justly warrant estrangement. For instance, if a relative were actively practicing Satanism, I wouldn't want them around my family. Similarly, those who commit treason or acts of terrorism against their country have long been subject to social and legal exile. And no one should feel compelled to endure personal abuse simply out of familial obligation.

However, each of these justifications can become corrupted and devolve into authoritarianism, leading to family estrangement. Cult leaders often assume godlike authority and demand that adherents sever ties with their families under the guise of religious purity. Totalitarian regimes under Stalin and Mao justified familial betrayals by invoking loyalty to the state, but—having displaced any notion of a higher authority—their true aim was the preservation of their own absolute power.

Like a cult leader or a totalitarian state leader, contemporary therapeutic culture can elevate the claims of the self into an unassailable moral absolute, dissolving any higher standard by which those claims might be judged. The modern ethos of expressive individualism, which is the pervasive belief that fulfillment is found chiefly through the expression of our authentic inner selves (to be discussed in the next chapter), redefines personal identity by severing it from external sources of meaning like family duties, faith, and civic belonging. Identity is relocated entirely within the self. Every person becomes the sole author of themselves, bound by nothing higher than the demand to be true to themselves. Yet this self-created identity is ironically fragile: a self that is made *by* itself and *for* itself must be endlessly affirmed by others in order to endure.

In an interview, LGBTQ advocate Jeffrey Marsh offers a revealing glimpse into how deeply the creed of self-authority has become embedded in contemporary thought. Discussing his second bestseller, *Take Your Own Advice,* the interviewer asks Marsh about his "journey into stepping into the authority of [his] authenticity," to which Marsh replies, "That is the only way we can do it. It is possible, obviously, to be an authority on a subject—to be a subject matter expert. That happens all the time. But there is no one else that is an authority on your experience, on your worldview, on the things that have shaped what you care about. So to me, one thing that's essential is accepting that you are an authority. You are an author of this human being's outlook, and you can make conscious choices to express that in ways that help bring people together."[16] And, by implication, ways that cut others out.

The culture of political estrangement can't be understood apart from this view of personal authenticity and authority. When the self is the chief authority, the choice to go no contact needs no justification. Of the five conditions driving the no-contact movement, this is the fourth (the infallibility narrative), which, when paired with the third (broadening the concept of trauma), transforms our wounds into moral mandates.

In this framework, severing relationships need not be an option of last resort; it can be a default response to the discomfort of disagreement. Instead of providing opportunities for reconciliation and growth, grace and resilience, the convergence of these conditions encourages rupture as a means of self-actualization, leaving in its wake not just broken families but a culture increasingly suspicious of the very bonds that once defined human belonging. Each of the five forces presupposes and reinforces the others.

Unlike the twentieth-century denunciations, no state authorities are formally orchestrating the no-contact movement, nor are parents facing show trials or labor camps for voting wrongly or not using preferred pronouns. But neither is coercion entirely absent today. Instead of state authorities coercing the youth to denounce mom and dad at a formal struggle meeting, public school systems are urging kids to use preferred pronouns, encouraging social transitioning, and keeping it a secret from parents. Pop therapists with large platforms and financial incentives are inducing young people to scrutinize their family members for signs of toxicity or political unacceptability. Rather than an unstable, paranoid totalitarian state that requires coercion to maintain control, an unstable, novel notion of personal identity requires language manipulation and endless external validation. Instead of the godlike state, we now have the godlike self—who inevitably demands a godlike state to enforce its coercion.

This reality is the combination of the five powerful conditions, sparking an inferno that leaves behind a barren social wasteland. Boundaries, once understood as a means of protecting healthy relationships and individuals *within* relationships, have become utterly subjective, sacrosanct, beyond scrutiny—and destructive to the very things they are meant to protect.

The Power of Forgetting

In *The Book of Laughter and Forgetting,* Milan Kundera, a Czech dissident author censored and exiled under Communist rule, wrote, "The struggle of man against power is the struggle of memory against forgetting."[17]

Any effort to remake what it means to be human must first *unmake* what has come before it. The violent attempts of the twentieth century to remake humanity and society brought with them an urgent need to forget. In their quest to forge a radically new future, social engineers required the erasure of the past. Estrangement within families, in this context, was not just a personal tragedy but a political necessity.

Memory is the currency of family life. Memory bonds us, wounds us, stirs a longing within us, and holds us accountable. It animates our relationships, for better or for worse, making estrangement a rupture, not only of affection and connection, but also of our personal history and identity. Because of this reality, memory stands in the way of both the authoritarian state and the authoritarian self as an obstacle—and antidote—to this authoritarianism.

Transgender ideology isn't the only expression of the authoritarian self, but it's the one that most urgently depends on forgetting. More importantly, it acutely reflects the broader social embrace of the Empowerment Delusion's belief in the individual's total autonomy over reality. It bears reiterating that this mindset extends far beyond the relatively small number of people who identify as transgender. It encompasses the millions who declared themselves "allies," revised their language overnight, and repeated claims they knew were untrue while shaming or denouncing anyone who hesitated. The cultural pressure to affirm, to comply, to perform moral purity, became its own enforcement mechanism, often more potent than explicit enforcement.

Proper allyship demanded amnesia. This put parents in a nearly impossible position, for what parent can forget their child? Integral to gender ideology is the adoption of a new name to reflect a new identity. Using an old name is considered akin to an assault, a blasphemy called "deadnaming." In a trans-identified person's self-understanding, they have died to their former self and come back anew to be renamed and re-known. Regardless of how any individual parent navigates this, such an erasure of memory places parents on extremely tenuous ground.

One mother, Jo, spoke with Mittermaier of losing her son Drew when he announced he was trans in his thirties. "And all of a sudden, this person you love and adore hates you. It's not just that they're gone—it's that they hate you."

Drew found a community of friends that encouraged the estrangement. Jo recounted how Drew and others would get a chip—like the kind used in Alcoholics Anonymous—for every year that they didn't talk to their parents. She also spoke of the attack on memory that eerily echoes Mao's attack on the four olds: "Our children have to kill the past. That means they have to kill us, because we represent the past. So do we keep showing up for them to remind them that they have a past, even though that makes them angry?"

She continued, "As a mom, I just want to pick him up and say: 'Come back, we'll help you, you don't have to keep doing this. . . . I understand what you're doing. But come back. I love you.' "[18]

It's the very nature of the parent to be a memory keeper. The parent's memory of the child is longer than the child's memory of themselves. All my life, my parents recounted stories of my third birthday or a funny thing I did as a child—things that I have no memory of. Such stories were amusing but detached from what I carried in the canon of my actual memories. Now as a parent I do the same, knowing my kids don't feel the reality of those stories in the way I do. To me, as to any other parent, those memories are vivid and valuable. The parent can hide away their scrapbooks and use their child's preferred name and pronouns, but unlike the child's new friends and communities, the parent carries the memory of their child in their core. The parent is an existential reminder of an identity that refuses to die.

Those who cut ties with family for reasons like abuse and addiction fit into that longer lineage that seeks not to forget or deconstruct the family but to preserve it, strengthen it, and demand its integrity. Theirs isn't a project of cultural amnesia or existential reinvention. By contrast, what we are seeing now is a tectonic shift in how we understand ourselves, our relationships, our religion. And more and more, it seems a new religion is emerging.

3

THE PSYCHOLOGY OF ESTRANGEMENT

The Empowerment Delusion that underlies modern estrangement recasts identity as a project of radical autonomy, coupled with an intense preoccupation with personal wounds and grievances. The latter part of the redefinition finds ample reinforcement in the therapeutic conception of the self. As this chapter explores, the expanding reach of therapeutic language has made us more fragile, less resilient, and far less capable of sustaining stable, enduring relationships.

In 2022, *Merriam-Webster* declared *gaslighting* its word of the year. Gaslighting is "a form of psychological abuse where a person causes someone to question their sanity, memories, or perception of reality," often to gain control or avoid accountability.[1] "It's a word that has risen so quickly in the English language, and especially in the last four years, that it actually came as a surprise to me and to many of us," said Peter Sokolowski, *Merriam-Webster*'s editor at large. "It was a word looked up frequently every single day of the year."[2]

The increasing reference to gaslighting reflects a broader cultural trend mentioned in chapter 1: a steady rise in narcissistic tendencies from decade to decade among college students.[3] Narcissism as a personality disorder is marked, among other things, by a strong tendency to manipulate others, including by gaslighting. Erica Komisar, a psychoanalyst and parenting expert, believes this rise originates in part from several decades of adults prioritizing their own desires, autonomy, and material pursuits over the needs of their children, leading to a deep insecurity in younger generations: "The repercussions of three generations of self-centeredness means parents are modeling selfishness and emotional fragility to their children. The shift in values to a more self-focused parenting style is contributing to a rise in disorders of the self, otherwise known as narcissistic disorders. These disorders contribute to the relational disconnection and mental health crisis we see in society today."[4]

As these dynamics have intensified, so too has the vocabulary used to name them. Therapy-speak has come to pervade everyday conversation. Some psychologists argue that the phenomenon of therapy-speak is a net positive—an indication that mental health has moved out of the shadows and into the mainstream.[5] For better or for worse, when something is destigmatized, we tend to get more of it. Young adults aged eighteen to twenty-six receiving mental health treatment increased from 18 percent in 2019 to 26 percent in 2022, marking a 45 percent rise.[6] Nearly one in four adults aged eighteen to forty-four sought mental healthcare in 2021.[7] With so many more people carrying a mental diagnosis, it's no wonder we have learned to talk the talk.

On some college campuses, the expansion of mental health diagnoses increasingly translates into formal disability accommodations. Reporting in *The Atlantic* documents a dramatic rise in the number of students at selective universities who qualify for disability accommodations. At the University of

Chicago, that share has more than tripled in the past eight years; at UC Berkeley, it has nearly quintupled over the past fifteen years; and at Stanford, 38 percent of students now receive some form of accommodation.[8]

The expansion cannot be explained by prevalence alone. Accommodations can confer tangible academic advantages, housing preferences, and exemptions from ordinary expectations, creating incentives for students to seek diagnostic status. Whatever the intentions of individual students, the pattern reflects a broader cultural shift in which psychological vulnerability is destigmatized and incentivized.

It's a good thing that those who need therapy seek it. Still, the risks reflected in the rise of therapy-speak and the ease of self-diagnostics are real. Terms like *boundaries, toxic relationships, gaslighting,* and *narcissism* are now commonplace and can be misused to justify avoidance rather than resilience. A challenging friend or relative can be dismissed as toxic. If someone pushes back on my perspective, I can either engage in self-reflection or accuse that person of gaslighting. Therapy-speak makes it difficult to distinguish between genuine psychological manipulation and ordinary human conflict.

As I sat in a café working on this chapter, a teenager next to me discussed her newly released SAT scores with her friend. She had taken and then retaken the test, expecting a higher score—but her score didn't improve. "This is literal trauma," she lamented. Her friend nodded knowingly and agreed the process was deeply traumatic. College entrance exams can be stressful, especially for an eighteen-year-old carrying high expectations and perhaps without a context for actual trauma. Teens using dramatic language is nothing new. I remember complaining with elongated vowels, "Mom, I am dyyying," to convey fatigue after a long ballet class or an arduous exam when I was a teen. But I knew I wasn't dying.

Therapeutic language, however, is just plausible enough to begin to invade our inner world and frame our outer world. The language can shape, reinforce, and freeze emotional states rather than help us work through them. It creates a feedback loop: The more we pathologize ordinary struggles, the more we come to see ourselves as psychologically fragile. We begin to view everyday struggles as insurmountable. We transform temporary conflicts and upsets into identities of woundedness.

Others, especially teens, easily catch this habit—a phenomenon known as social contagion, where emotions, behaviors, or beliefs spread rapidly through a group by observation, reinforcement, and imitation.[9] Andi, a diligent and kind high school sophomore, fell into a period of sadness after a friend transferred to a bigger and seemingly more exciting school. Andi had other good friends, but she missed her old one, and her school and life in comparison felt small. She began to struggle to stay focused; her grades dropped, and her anxiety rose. Soon two of the friends she'd been confiding in admitted that they'd also started struggling with feelings of sadness. Then a third, a fourth, and a fifth. The friend group started to wonder if they were all depressed. Eventually, just as the mood had spread, one by one they snapped out of it. A year later, Andi now laughs about this episode. They refer to that time as "the dark age."

The girls acknowledge that they had a lot going for them to get them through "the dark age." Their parents were engaged in their lives but didn't coddle them. The parents generally listened empathetically but maintained expectations of behavior.

They helped the girls find ways to reframe their problems, seek to learn from struggle, and not allow challenges to discourage them from meeting their duties. What the parents didn't do was dismiss their struggles nor panic and catastrophize alongside their daughters.

Human behavior is highly imitative, and social performance can play a role in how we frame things. The writer Katy Waldman points to therapy-speak's potential to become a class performance: "Think of Woody Allen's Manhattanites, talking endlessly about their shrinks. . . . In the United States, basic mental-health care remains a luxury item."[10] A trend that makes mental instability an aspirational accessory aligns with what Rob Henderson terms a "luxury belief"—an idea that benefits the elite who espouse it but has negative consequences for those without the same resources.[11]

These psychological and social realities play a central role in today's no-contact movement. Therapeutic culture, with its intense focus on personal wounds, trains individuals to see themselves as perpetually harmed and to implicate others from their past as sources of injury. Estrangement thus becomes both a proof of harm and an act of liberation. Like all other luxury beliefs, the therapeutic mindset can look appealing in the movies or on the surface, but in reality, for many individuals and families it's devastating.

When Mental Health Goes Viral

Social media has amplified the reach of the Empowerment Delusion, fundamentally reshaping how we see ourselves and interact with the world. It fosters the fantasy that identity can be self-created and disembodied, while reinforcing the social-hygiene instinct—that our interactions can be perfectly managed through blocking, unfollowing, and muting. Both effects cripple our capacity to struggle with life as it is and learn the resilience that comes from such a struggle.

These dynamics were evident on Tumblr, launched in 2007 and peaking around 2014 as a hub for tight-knit online communities known as fandoms. These groups revolved around shared passions for movies, TV shows, books, celebrities, and other cultural phenomena. Fans engaged in long discussions, created artwork and fanfiction, and developed subcultures that blurred the line between online identity and real life. As Tumblr's influence grew, so did its role in shaping how young people understood themselves, mental health, and social belonging—trends that have only accelerated on newer platforms.

Many users intensely identified with characters and the world they inhabited, sometimes seeing them as extensions of their own struggles or identities. "Fandom comprises such a unique set of behaviors there's an entire academic discipline devoted to studying it," reporter and "internet ethnographer" Katherine Dee explains. "Fandoms are cultures-within-cultures and to identify as a Trekkie or a Browncoat (fans of the short-lived television series Firefly) or Potterhead carries a lot more baggage than just someone who likes a particular television show or book. It is not a stretch to characterize it as something of a simulated nationality."[12]

Over time, fandoms became intertwined with social justice activism, with fans analyzing media through the lenses of race, gender, and queer representation. Dee writes, "Most people I spoke to shared that the first time they were exposed [to] anything related to identity politics (especially queer identity or feminism) was on Tumblr, and almost always within the context of fandom, e.g., representation in a favorite fan property."[13]

For those who weren't in that world, it's hard to imagine how deeply fandoms colonized the mental and emotional space of their participants. It was, as Dee observes, a simulated nationality entirely separate from neighborhoods and communities and physical land and shared living. Instead, it was more of a simulated tribalism built not just on shared loves but eventually on shared hatreds and factionalism.

Erin grew up in the Harry Potter fandom, then became part of the *Glee* fandom. She describes how the TV show sought to represent every category of identity politics imaginable. Fans were so invested that the characters and plotlines felt intensely personal, and the online battles mirrored that same level of emotional investment.

"We would watch the episode. Something inevitably would piss off some subsection. . . . It would just be a bombardment of their fans on Tumblr yelling at each other, fighting or trying to claim that what happened was problematic or that it shouldn't have been represented this way, just nonstop harassment from every side," Erin states. "It wasn't just that there was one side to an issue, but all of a sudden there were 50 different sides to an issue, and every single side had 30,000 people behind it all screaming at you."[14]

Detransitioner[15] Helena Kerschner describes the enormous influence Tumblr had on her gender dysphoria. As a fifteen-year-old with some mental health struggles, Kerschner became deeply embroiled in online communities on Tumblr. "Everything was about social justice, everything was about gender, all the time."[16]

Kerschner had body image issues as many adolescent girls do. The message she got on Tumblr was clear: "If you don't like your body, that's a sign you're trans."[17] The identity issues were tightly woven with social justice issues and Kerschner notes that there were clear hierarchical social dynamics at play "like it was bad to be a cis—not trans—straight white girl. And that's what I was; I was a straight white girl. And I felt that that was very bad."[18] Socially transitioning gave her a new identity and a higher social status that went beyond Tumblr communities. Teachers and other adults who hadn't paid much attention to her before suddenly went to great lengths to affirm and accommodate her new identity. She got a testosterone prescription after one short visit to Planned Parenthood, a prescription that caused her to feel bouts of rage and desires to harm others or herself. Finally in 2018 after a year and a half on the hormone, Kerschner, full of regret, got off it and began to detransition.[19]

For developing minds—especially for those who have painful reasons to seek an escape from their everyday—these immersive online worlds can be a narcotic. Fantasy and role-playing in a virtual world make authoring our own identities seem more feasible in the physical world, reinforcing the Empowerment Delusion. Moreover, online cultures that prize transgressiveness and victimhood make it easy for otherwise-overlooked people to get attention and to be treated as socially significant.

Many young adults who had been formed in the hostile tribalism of online communities in the 2010s were primed to translate those microcosms into the real world. The moral logic of fandoms and identity subcultures—where belonging depends on ideological purity, moral signaling, and denunciation of dissenters—became the moral logic of everyday life. What had begun as virtual performance evolved into social reality. Offline friendships, classrooms, and even families began to mirror the same dynamics of callouts, cancellations, and self-curation that governed online life, sweeping even those who hadn't been in the world of fandoms into this harsh new reality.

The internet had trained a generation to see moral worth through the lens of identity and injury, to conflate emotion with truth, and to regard disagreement as harm. Once social media became the dominant medium of formation—especially during the isolating years of Covid—its norms seeped into the deepest layers of personality. Digital worlds no longer served as escapes from reality; they became the dominant frameworks for interpreting it.

By the early 2020s, the result of this simmering online absorption was a generation of young people fluent in therapeutic and ideological language but often impoverished in the habits that make real relationships sustainable. This environment proved fertile ground for a new kind of influencer culture as online life became increasingly confessional and therapeutic. By the time the Covid quarantine hit, any remaining guardrails to keep people from being absorbed online largely vanished. Social media use skyrocketed as did mental health influencers and accounts. Algorithms turned users' mild interest or curiosity into a portal for endless exposure to highly specific content. A casual click on a post about mental health struggles could lead to relentless targeted posts about mental health issues.[20]

Many influencers flocked to TikTok to share their personal struggles and mental health symptoms. "For teens and young adults who consume this content, it can be easy to relate to the stories shared and identify with the symptoms described," according to Medens Health. "This has led to a growing trend of young people diagnosing themselves with conditions such as anxiety, ADHD, autism, or depression, based on brief, anecdotal information."[21]

This kind of content spread by social contagion, as was the case with so-called TikTok tics. In 2020, medical professionals observed a sudden increase in adolescents, particularly teenage girls, presenting with abrupt-onset tic-like behaviors despite never having experienced similar disorders before. Movement disorder specialists in the United States reported a 60 percent rise in new patients diagnosed with functional movement disorders during the first eight months of the pandemic, with a 90 percent increase in the pediatric population.[22]

Confounded doctors soon realized this phenomenon coincided with an explosion of social media content on TikTok and elsewhere featuring influencers with Tourette's syndrome. By March 2021, TikTok videos with the keywords *Tourette* and *tic* had more than five billion views.[23] Many of the new patients exhibited functional tic-like behaviors (FTLBs), which differ significantly from classic Tourette's. Tourette's symptoms develop gradually, while FTLBs appear suddenly and tend to be more severe. The types of tics seen in these FTLBs also closely resembled those in popular social media videos like involuntary swearing, throwing objects, hitting oneself or others, and exaggerated movements of the trunk and limbs—features that aren't as common in typical Tourette's cases. One notable example was the prevalence of patients with the vocal tic of saying the word *beans*, which tellingly was a particularly common tic in many of the most popular TikTok creators' videos.[24]

Social media doesn't just spread behaviors—it can make beliefs contagious as well. The rise of self-diagnosis led to a parallel trend of "wound diagnosing," wherein young people in pain sifted through their past, often attributing their struggles to parental shortcomings. Like with TikTok tics, plenty of therapist influencers and armchair influencers were eager to feed this effort while growing their platforms.

"If it feels like whispers of estrangement are everywhere lately—in your group chat, at your happy hour, and of course on TikTok [. . .]—it's because the data is staggering," writes a journalist for *Cosmopolitan*. "The rise in millennials and Gen Zers coming forward to discuss their own crises—the hashtag #ToxicFamily has 1.9 billion views on TikTok—may suggest that American families are severing ties at an all-time high."[25]

The *Cosmopolitan* article profiles Jordan, a young woman who was raised Southern Baptist but decided to leave the church—a decision that became a source of conflict with her father. She had several arguments with him about religion and politics until she finally made the decision to go no contact. He continued to reach out, but she maintained the estrangement calling it an "extreme privilege" for parents to have great relationships with their adult children: "I was always hoping [while we weren't talking] that he would take my silence as a cue to get himself together and to apologize to me." The year after she cut contact with him, he was hospitalized. Jordan flew home to support her mom and say goodbye, though he was incapacitated by the time she arrived. Jordan still believes she did the right thing but wishes there had been more time to see if he might have changed.[26]

Jordan's story is placed seamlessly alongside an account of estrangement due to a father's heroin addiction and another because of an abusive mother. These wildly different reasons for estrangement are conflated with little nuance, implying an equivalence. This not only obscures the factual differences but also offers no serious consideration of the underlying psychological, social, and cultural pressures that shape such widely varying causes for cutting family ties. The effective takeaway of such articles for the reader is to simply normalize it all as a broad, unquestioned solution.

This sort of conflation and normalization is commonplace on social media. Scrolling through TikTok, it's easy to find countless influencers ready to share about their "toxic" family.

In one video a pretty young woman with more than nine million likes looks into the camera with the caption "When you reach the age where you realise most of your family members are actually awful people."[27]

In a more dramatic example, a post with twenty-nine thousand likes shows a clip of a young man in a fit of rage, destroying a bedroom. The caption: "How I feel inside because of my family." The scene then shifts to a handsome and confident young man strolling through a school hallway. The caption changes: "Vs how I treat them now after I went no-contact." He bumps into a girl labeled "my family"—she smiles at him, then looks upset as he walks away without a glance.[28]

The barrage of these videos plays into the process of trauma hijacking by reinforcing a new cultural script: Toxic families are a pervasive problem, and escaping them, an empowering solution.

The Barnum Effect

Therapist and online educator Patrick Teahan invites followers to take a free onboarding quiz to determine if they are adult children of toxic parents. I took the quiz and had several of my friends do the same with the guidance that we answer each question honestly.

The quiz begins with a warning: "Please be aware that the

following questions can be activating."[29] Participants choose from five answers for each question, ranging from "I never experienced this" to "I experienced this very frequently."

Here are a couple examples of questions:

> I witnessed (I saw it happening) or experienced (it happened to me) children being physically, emotionally, or sexually abused. (e.g., psychological abuse, hitting, sexually off behavior, exploitation, contempt, harsh punishment, violence, religious fundamentalism, competition with children, extremes in crossing boundaries, infantilization, severe neglect, refusal of medical care, verbal assault, and living vicariously through a child's life).
>
> I witnessed or experienced emotional neglect. (e.g., lack of daily connection, a sense of isolation, raising oneself, not being a priority to adults, not being protected from harmful people, caregivers being more invested with strangers or those outside the family for their own appearance or personal gain).[30]

Many of the questions seem to be worded such that someone with highly abusive parents could score closely with someone whose parents were more normal but who is inclined to interpret experiences with them negatively. For example, the last question could be answered in the affirmative by someone whose parents allowed sexual predators access to their child. It could also be answered just as affirmatively by someone who remembers bitterly times in which Mom gave greater attention to a friend on the phone than a child in the room.

Egregiously the statement "I witnessed (I saw it happening) or experienced (it happened to me) children being physically, emotionally, or sexually abused" lists as examples of such abuse "infantilization" and "religious fundamentalism," terms open to broad interpretation. The quiz doesn't allow for an easy distinction between a survey taker who has endured sexual abuse and one who just has conservative Christian parents.

The Barnum Effect is a phenomenon wherein people believe that vague, general statements about personality are highly specific and personally meaningful, even when they are broad enough to apply to almost anyone. The Barnum Effect is commonly used in horoscopes, personality tests, and fortune-telling.

When applied to pop therapists on social media, the Barnum Effect helps explain why so many young people find online mental health advice so personally relevant. These influencers often use broad, relatable statements like "If your parents ever dismissed your feelings, they were emotionally abusive" or "If you felt like you had to earn love as a child, you were raised by narcissists." Because nearly everyone has had moments of feeling unheard or misunderstood by family, these statements can resonate widely. However, instead of offering real psychological insight, this phenomenon contributes to the growing trend: Young people, shaped by the unforgiving moral ecology of online culture, increasingly label normal family upsets as toxic or abusive. It's a label that is hard to shake, sometimes leading them to cut off relationships based on one-size-fits-all online advice.

After completing the test, my friend group and I came up with toxic family scores ranging from a 25 (manageable toxicity) to a 54 (extensive toxicity). The friend who scored the lowest at 25 said, "I had really great parents and still got 'manageable toxicity,' which I think is BS. There should be a category that is 'not toxic'—aka you had a healthy childhood—and yes, such a thing exists!"

Another who has a parent who struggled for years with substance abuse and was periodically neglectful scored in the "extensive toxicity" range, with the recommendations to get therapy for childhood trauma and join a support group. "I struggled with my history for a while but feel no hard feelings now," she said, noting that the recommendations felt excessive.

One could argue these women weren't seeking out the quiz—I prompted them to take it—which suggests they may not be the intended audience. That's a fair point. The friend who scored higher in toxicity, for instance, has built a fulfilling life—marrying a good man, raising several children, and focusing on her present rather than dwelling on past wounds. Her parents live a town over, and they now share a mutually supportive relationship. Had she struggled in marriage and parenting, perhaps she would have been more inclined to ruminate on the past. At earlier and more impressionable points in life, she could have easily gone down a rabbit hole of defining herself as wounded and her parents as toxic, reorienting their relationship and closing off the possibility of the good—albeit limited—regular connection they now enjoy.

This raises an important question: For those who do ruminate on past wounds, could part of the solution lie in building a meaningful future? When we establish a sense of purpose and fulfillment in adulthood, the emotional grip of past hurts—especially those caused by imperfect but ultimately relatively manageable relationships—begins to loosen.

It's a classic chicken-or-egg dilemma: Are isolated and lonely young adults more likely to reframe their struggles through the lens of blame and childhood trauma? Or does early trauma lead to disconnection and greater struggles in adulthood? As my friend's example shows, people who make happy lives for themselves tend not to feel the need to interrogate their past.

Or is something similar to TikTok tics happening? Are young adults from relatively normal families immersing themselves in online worlds and simply seeing the social capital that comes with identities built on trauma and grievance?

While the Teahan test might not be designed for my friend, it seems well designed to capture vulnerable people and catastrophize their past. This can be an intoxicating road to go down. It's important to underscore that the reason my friend didn't need it was not that she had a trauma-free childhood but that she had learned purpose and resilience. The difference was her—not her childhood. Perhaps if she were growing up now and absorbed in TikTok and other online spaces, such messages might easily have caught her—and kept her—in a more vulnerable place.

Teahan also offers a more extensive evaluation for childhood trauma with sixty yes or no questions. At the top of the quiz is this instruction: "Apply the question to the course of your lifetime. The issue might be resolved but still say yes—it helps with your story."[31] One question reads, "I have a hard time with moderation and can be addicted to things. (Alcohol, food, drugs, sex, media, caffeine)." Others include "I've had or have food, sleep, or energy issues—(exhaustion or busy energy)" and "Growing up, I could be embarrassed or humiliated by my parents." If the participant answers yes to more than ten of the sixty such questions, that means that some childhood trauma exploration or work should be done.[32] Again, the Barnum Effect layered onto the wound seeking of the Empowerment Delusion can easily cause most anyone—from a genuinely traumatic background or not—to internalize these questions and "discover" that they are a victim of childhood trauma or catastrophize and become defined by what genuine wounds they experienced. The justification for no contact is established, as is the felt need to enroll in one of Teahan's courses.

Expressive Individualism

Beneath modern life lie largely unexamined philosophical assumptions about identity, analogous to fault lines beneath a city: mostly invisible yet capable of destabilizing what stands above. We may become so accustomed to the subtle tremors that they go unnoticed—until larger fractures occur. Practices such as going no contact represent some of the more visible consequences of these underlying shifts. Yet these fault lines predate our digital age, reflecting a long evolution in how we understand identity, autonomy, and authenticity.

To see the contrast more clearly, in the medieval world, most men and women became fathers and mothers, and their sense of self was bound up with their duties to each other and their children, to their parents and community, to God and to the Church. Human flourishing and moral character were measured largely by how honorably one fulfilled these roles. At the same time, Christianity taught that identity also transcended social roles and visible structures of obligation, like class or status. It located the deepest identity of the person in an interior life of the soul ordered toward God, not toward self-expression or self-construction.

In *Strange New World*, historian Carl Trueman examines how identity came to be grounded in our inner psychology and a fidelity to the self as defined by personal desire. As Trueman traces, we see early inklings of this in the Romantics of the eighteenth and nineteenth centuries who championed self-expression over social obligation. Freud in the nineteenth and twentieth centuries argued that our psychological identity is shaped by unconscious drives, particularly sexual ones, and that those drives define us. This theory was the precursor to the shift in understanding sexual activity not as what we do but as revealing who we are. By the 1960s, this inward and sexualized sense of identity became a moral mandate for outward expression. The abandonment of external identity markers, combined with Freud's emphasis on sexualized identity, led to the belief that living out one's "true self" was essential to personal authenticity.[33]

Figures like Wilhelm Reich tied sexual liberation to political revolution, arguing that true freedom required the politicization of sex to dismantle social norms, and the power dynamics nested in familial obligation. Through this fusion of liberation with revolution, identity became not just about psychology and sex but about power and oppression. The progression Trueman outlines is that identity becomes psychologized, then sexualized, and finally politicized.[34]

We see this transformation in the common modern preoccupation with the "real me" or the "true self," often in defiance of our obligations or of objective reality. Prior to the rise of expressive individualism, the more common moral instinct favored shaping oneself in harmony with an inherited and intelligible world ordered toward our flourishing. Under the rule of expressive individualism, by contrast, the moral imperative is to shape the world to conform to the sovereignty of one's own will, reinforcing the radical autonomy central to the Empowerment Delusion.

To illustrate the contrast, consider what living a lie might look like then and now. A woman in love with a man other than her husband once would have been considered to be living a fantasy—a lie of emotional infidelity. Correcting course, then, would be to end the affair and be true to her husband. Today a woman in love with another man might easily enough view herself as living a lie in her marriage. Correcting course, then, would be to end her marriage and be true to herself—regardless of the impact on her husband and children or the commitment made in her marriage vows.

It isn't just women who have picked up on the zeitgeist. Brielle, a woman in her late thirties living in Denver, was in a long-distance relationship with Mark, who lives in Arizona. He would visit her monthly and sometimes they would travel together. But she grew worried that something was amiss. He didn't seem to want her to visit him in Phoenix, and she had yet to be introduced to his kids. She soon discovered that Mark, whom she believed was divorced, was still very much living with his wife. He explained that his marriage was as cold as a corpse but too complicated to end. In a letter he described his regret for deceiving her, then went on to say, "I am living in a prison in my own life. Unable to experience real love and desperately wanting to give my children an example of the real me living a full and rich relationship, like I have with you. My time with you has been a quiet protest to this lie of a life I am living." His letter is a perfect encapsulation of the Empowerment Delusion with its laser focus on his victimhood and his need to exercise his autonomy in service of his real, authentic self.

Infidelity in marriage isn't new. What is new is the ease with which the language of expressive individualism allows us to subjugate our duties to one another to the expression of our inner desires, reducing the world and its inhabitants to instruments of our true self. In this framework that true self has the ultimate claim to our fidelity, and it's the last remaining measure of our morality. In the older model the true self can't be defined in isolation from our interdependence and duties but rather is clarified and made whole through the integration of these more external factors into our interior lives.

An essential sleight of hand of expressive individualism is that morality is collapsed into psychological well-being. By this account, the therapeutic self isn't trained or inclined to strengthen or repair relationships amidst challenges; rather, it's empowered to sever them—a mindset that underlies most every movement of social rupture, from the logic of infidelity as authenticity to the logic of the no-contact movement as a means of self-preservation.

Nice with No Mercy

As morality is collapsed into psychological well-being, new moral norms take shape. If identity is entirely self-created and self-expression is our highest moral mandate, then any challenge to one's choices becomes existential.

Three shifts follow from this reorientation. First, love is redefined. No longer is love ordered toward the good of the other but toward the protection and affirmation of desire. At minimum, love now means being inoffensive, to never unsettle another person's self-conception. To love well is to affirm that self-conception enthusiastically. To question it, even gently, is to fail at the most basic requirement of love. At its best, affirmation of another echoes a Christian notion of the dignity of every human being, *if* the true self is understood to be made in the image of God. But once identity is separated from the divine and redefined as individualism, self-authorship, and sexual expression, any objection to behavior can be recast as a hateful denial of that true self.

Second, identity becomes fundamentally unstable. If who we are is understood relationally and through external markers, identity is largely uncontentious. In contrast, identity tied to inner desires works only if everyone goes along with it. The lie at the heart of "The Emperor's New Clothes" is sustained insofar as others agree to affirm it. The ruse is exposed the moment someone names what can plainly be seen.

Third, relationships turn brittle. When identity loses its grounding, ordinary conflicts become catastrophic. Even minor disagreements are felt as profound threats. This fosters a culture of fragility, where individuals demand constant validation. Disagreements, once an expected part of human interaction, are reframed as oppression or even violence.

In sum, love is reduced and weaponized, identity is destabilized, and conflict is catastrophized. As a moral framework, this therapeutic self, replaces resilience with avoidance, and reconciliation with severance. It offers a new vision of the good life, but one that ironically demands total social conformity to the sovereign self.

What presents itself as freedom for the individual increasingly requires submission from everyone else, and many relationships are broken in the process. In 2024 a father whose twenty-year-old transgender child (female to male) had gone no contact with him eighteen months prior took to a popular Reddit Trans forum to ask if anyone there might offer him hope for reconciliation. Upon learning of his child's plan to transition, the father had tried to dissuade the child from the medical course of action. "My son has every reason and every right to go no contact. I did not initially affirm his gender identity," he confides. "Nothing I did afterwards was ever able to make up for the fact that I wasn't there for him when he needed me most. Yes—I realize how badly I screwed this up." He goes on to say he is heartbroken and resigned to the possibility that they might never be in contact again. "He may well have a richer and more fulfilling life without me in it. I have always honored his request for space."

He wonders if anyone there has resumed contact with a slow-to-affirm parent, though he doesn't seem to think he deserves reconciliation. "I can only imagine what a betrayal that must have felt like. I feel like apologizing to the entire trans community on behalf of parents like me who just didn't realize what was really going on or what was [at] stake." To offer context, he explains that he managed and played on his city's LGBTQ soccer team and counts his ex-teammates as some of his best friends. He doesn't think he is a bigot but acknowledges it can be hard to tell.

He gives his reason for not immediately affirming: "I rationalized that the medical risks of him taking T were too great, as I have a family history of thrombosis (blood clots). I tried everything I could to steer him away from medicalizing."[35]

Responses to his query were mixed: "To be blunt, depending on your history with your son (and you admit you fucked it up to a major degree) he might have absolutely no reason to believe you will be become better and be worth bringing into his life again."[sic][36]

Another respondent offers a bit more of a positive take: "Send your son a text or something if you have any avenues of communication you could try to apologize through. If he doesn't respond, well that's how it goes sometimes when someone is pushed to that point by a parent."[37]

"He has no reason to trust me," the father continues in self-flagellation. "He gave me a chance to affirm, and I didn't take it. Every offer I made to affirm from then on was rejected, because (I believe) he was hurt and thought I didn't deserve to know the true him."[38]

"Sorry but it sounds like you'll be waiting a very very long time to hear back," another redditor writes. "Maybe you can serve as a reminder or warning to other parents not to judge your kids for being who they truly are."[39]

What is most striking about this exchange isn't merely the pain of a father grieving a living child; it's the psychological posture he feels compelled to assume. His language isn't that of an ordinary parent who misjudged a situation nor even of someone wrestling with regret. It's the rhetoric of a penitent before a tribunal. He speaks as though he has transgressed a sacred law, as if his temporary hesitation, born of medical prudence and paternal concern, constituted a moral failing so grave that it justifies permanent excommunication.

In his desperation, he takes on the role assigned to him: the repentant heretic who must profess guilt not only toward his child but also toward the entire community. Notice how the framework allows no gradations of human fallibility, no room for misunderstanding or a parent's legitimate fears about irreversible medical interventions. The ideology offers only two categories: the affirming and the damned.

What emerges is the psychology of estrangement elevated to a merciless and fundamentalist religious fervor, demanding total ideological submission. The child bears no obligation to forgive, but the parent bears infinite obligation to repent. And when a worldview requires that dynamic, it's functioning as a mechanism of social control. Estrangement becomes the enforcement arm: a message to the estranged to assume the posture of the ever-imperfect but striving ally and a cautionary tale to those on the sidelines that barely a modicum of mercy will be extended to them.

The Empowerment Delusion has profoundly destabilized identity and the terms of our most intimate relationships. In adopting a god/victim narrative, adherents claim a monopoly on power, and position themselves as the only rightful recipients of compassion. Dissenters may approach as groveling penitents. Meanwhile, the rise of therapy-speak offers language to draw more people into the delusion: Discomfort is pathologized, challenging relationships are toxic, everyday struggles point to childhood trauma, and ideological dissent is framed as psychological violence or genocide. All of this wreaks havoc on our psyches. At any point someone might question my "reality," look askance at me prioritizing my passions over my obligations, or express fatherly concern over a medical course of action, and that person can be publicly condemned. And those who know me best and are most likely to care for my well-being—rather than just being nice—might find that willing my good can be a terminal act.

4

CHOSEN FAMILY

As ideology recasts the family as a social construct and the self as supreme, a new model for family life emerges.

Billy Holder, a carpenter in his mid-thirties, had long sensed he was different. He never felt monogamy was a fit for him and had always wanted to date multiple people at once but with their full knowledge and consent. Early in his marriage to Melissa, the topic of cheating came up after allegations of it emerged among extended family members. Billy and Melissa admitted that they wanted to be open to other relationships but on the condition of total honesty with each other. The couple began to explore polyamory, or living with multiple romantic partners.

In 2014, NBC News spotlighted their polyamorous living arrangement outside Atlanta. Their household consisted of Billy and Melissa, married seventeen years, their nine-year-old daughter Ashley, and Melissa's boyfriend of six years, Jeremy Mullins. They shared financial responsibilities, childcare, and household duties. Ashley viewed both Billy and Jeremy as her fathers, alongside her mother. Meanwhile, Billy had been in a relationship with Lindsey, a slender young woman with blond bobbed hair, for nine months. Lindsey lived separately with her boyfriend, Brian, but Ashley saw Lindsey as essentially part of the family too. "We want to promote the idea that any relationship is valid as long as it is a choice made by consenting adults," Jeremy said. "In this regard, and as in most things, promoting public acceptance is the first step."[1]

For those who practice it, polyamory is considered not a lifestyle choice but an identity. "Life would probably be easier if I didn't feel the need to open myself up to loving more than one person," Jeremy said. "But it's part of who I am, and I feel that my life is enriched by it."[2]

At the time, Billy led a monthly poly meeting where members discussed their experience of being poly and built mutual support. "Monogamy doesn't work for every single person or else there wouldn't be groups like this," Billy said. Another member was asked why so many people were still afraid to admit they were poly. He answered that the social stigma made poly similar to what being gay used to feel like.[3]

Today such unconventional living arrangements—while still not mainstream—are steadily growing in prominence: "Approximately 1 out of 22 people (4–5%) who are currently in a romantic relationship identify as part of a consensually non-monogamous relationship."[4]

Around the time of the Holder-Mullins profile, the term *polycule* was just entering the lexicon. *Polycule* is a combination of *polyamory* and *molecule*—indicating the relationships within a polycule are interconnected like the atoms of a molecule. Among polycules there is an entire vocabulary that describes different relationship roles and dynamics. *Compersion* is the opposite of jealousy. It refers to feeling joy when one's partner experiences love with another partner. A *nesting partner* is a live-in romantic partner. An *anchor partner* provides long-term stability and commitment, similar to a life partner. A *satellite partner* is more independent, often maintaining a separate household.

There are also demarcations by number and how members interact. A *triad* or *throuple* is a three-person relationship. In a *quad*, four persons are in a polyamorous relationship, which may include different configurations of romantic connections. *Kitchen-table polyamory* is where all partners, including *metamours* (the partner of one's partner), are comfortable interacting and socializing together. In contrast, in *parallel polyamory,* metamours don't interact and partners keep their relationships separate. In *solo polyamory,* a person prioritizes autonomy and may not seek co-habitation or deeply enmeshed relationships.

In the decade since the profile of the Holder-Mullins home aired, a number of television shows and video games have featured polyamory. Mainstream dating apps, including OkCupid, Tinder, and Hinge, now let users specify that they identify as poly. Though stigma still surrounds the topic, the needle is steadily creeping toward greater social acceptance for broadening definitions of what constitutes a family.[5] The idea underlying this widening sphere is that family formation hinges on choice—not biology, covenants, or obligations.

Polycules are just one example of a broader landscape of what are called "chosen families" or "found families." The majority of academic discussion on the topic of such new forms of kinship relates to the communities that sexual minorities create. In his 1984 work *A Critique of the Study of Kinship,* anthropologist David Schneider laid the groundwork that kinship shouldn't be universally defined by genealogy. Instead, he emphasized that kinship is a cultural construct, varying significantly across societies.[6]

Kath Weston, another anthropologist, following Schneider's work, coined the term *chosen family* in her 1991 book *Families We Choose: Lesbians, Gays, Kinship.* Weston, like Schneider, challenged the traditional concept of family, which she characterized as involuntary, biological, with set roles and obligations. Weston held that such a model of family life is socially constructed and nested in power differences.[7]

While the chosen-family phenomenon is newer in name, the concept predates it as one long known to gay subcultures. "In the mid-20th century, queer people who had migrated to major cities began forming ersatz family structures that resembled but didn't completely replicate the more traditional nuclear family," writes Emily St. James, then a senior correspondent for *Vox,* in a 2021 piece on rethinking modern family structures. "The creation of queer chosen families . . . stemmed from the fact that gay and lesbian people kept migrating to particular cities. Often they had been rejected by family, but sometimes they had just left. And once they had gotten to, say, San Francisco, they would form close ties with other queer people around them."[8]

The word *family* functioned as a coded way for men with same-sex attraction to identify one another and create a sense of belonging. Saying someone was family signaled that they were "one of us" without explicitly stating it. Over time, *family* as a code word extended beyond gay men to include those who identified as lesbian, bisexual, or transsexual and others, solidifying its role in queer culture. While the stigmas have diminished, the term *family* still holds cultural weight among such communities. It continues to be used both in its original coded sense and as a broader affirmation of chosen kinship.

This coded language is exemplified in the documentary *Paris Is Burning*, which delves into New York City's underground ballroom subculture in the 1980s, wherein Black and Latino gay men gathered to enter a fantasy world of competitive runway-type performances of self-expression and exhibition. Participants devoted to this world often formed households as chosen families. All-male houses established family hierarchies with more experienced members who were called "mother" and "father" and less experienced members referred to as "children" and "siblings." The term *drag family* remains widely used to this day, with many queens having "drag mothers" who mentor them, continuing the lineage of chosen families from ballroom culture.

More recent queer scholarship reinforces this language. The 2020 academic article "Drag Pedagogy: The Playful Practice of Queer Imagination in Early Childhood" examines Drag Queen Story Hour (DQSH), events in libraries and schools in which men dress in drag to read books to children. The authors identify as a key purpose of these events the reauthoring of social conceptions of family: "It may be that DQSH is 'family friendly,' in the sense that it is accessible and inviting to families with children, but it is less a sanitizing force than it is a preparatory introduction to alternate modes of kinship. Here, DQSH is 'family friendly' in the sense of 'family' as an old-school queer code to identify and connect with other queers on the street."[9] The point of drag pedagogy is far more ambitious than the often-cited goal of anti-bullying; its purpose is to deconstruct stable notions of family and to disrupt the transmission of social norms to K–12 schoolchildren. By situating these lessons in children's spaces, the program sidesteps parental authority and inserts a wedge between generations, encouraging children to question traditional family structures. The concept of chosen family was meant not to remain in subcultures but to expand into the consciousness of the mainstream and form future generations that reimagine what kinship can be.[10]

Despite its more revolutionary history and academic genealogy, for many the concept of chosen families need not be sexual at all. In fact, the popularization of chosen families in mainstream culture—seen in TV shows like *Friends* in the 1990s, which moved away from the family-centric sitcom, or in the rise to prominence of Friendsgiving in the 2010s—simply gave language to a well-known reality: Friendships often function as, and feel like, family. The fundamental aspects of familial bonds—belonging, care, love, fidelity, and emotional intimacy—can emerge in relationships that aren't biological or marital. These connections can fill important roles and elicit lifelong devotion. Most people, in some form, have experienced this in their own lives.

This entirely defensible and sometimes crucial reality, in some ways, primed a populace who were already accustomed to seeing family as flexible and chosen to be receptive to more radical reinterpretations of kinship. The concept of chosen families, when detached from its revolutionary or sexualized roots, resonates precisely because it speaks to an important experience: the desire for belonging, care, and emotional intimacy. Yet this mainstream normalization also creates fertile ground for more deliberate cultural interventions—efforts that aim not merely to describe social realities but to reshape them. In time, such efforts influence how future generations understand their obligations and the ease with which they might think they can replace a given family and reconstitute a family of their curation.

Family Privilege and Abolition

In her book *Undoing Gender*, Judith Butler posits that kinship is not about being but about doing and becoming: "Kinship is itself a kind of doing, a practice that enacts that assemblage of significations as it takes place."[11] Butler's concept of gender performativity—the idea that man or woman is not something we are but rather a set of repeated social performances (and hence can be performed by the opposite sex)—naturally extends to the idea of familial performativity. If gender is not a stable identity but something that is enacted, then family also becomes fluid and interchangeable. Kinship, then, isn't given or determined by biology or covenant; instead, it's continually produced, performed, negotiated, and redefined.

Gender theorists like Butler contend that gender is a construct and that, in seizing power over it and reconstructing it according to our will, we can transform ourselves into the gender we perform. Through our power of choice, what we perform becomes our "real" self. Similarly, in seizing power over the family and remaking it according to our will by performing familial functions, we can create a chosen family that becomes more than the performance. The chosen family is made real by our choice to enact it. It follows that the family can also be unmade by an act of will. This is the pattern of cultural revolution: Expose traditional models as artificial constructs, destabilize them, and then exercise our power to unmake and reconstruct them.

The push for chosen family rests on the autonomy to sever ties with the unchosen one. It advances by reshaping the concept of family at its foundation, beginning with the redefinition of marriage. While permanence and exclusivity are the perennial hallmarks characterizing marriage, increasingly these are being questioned, not only as a result of human weakness but as a matter of principle.

Amatonormativity is a term coined by philosopher Elizabeth Brake in her 2012 book *Minimizing Marriage* to describe the widespread social assumption that romantic, monogamous, and long-term relationships are inherently superior to other forms of relationships. This privileging of marriage, Brake argues, is a social injustice, casting a shadow on non-monogamous relationships.[12] "To what extent does its subordination of individual desire to duty and the perceived common good threaten the good of individuals?" she writes.[13] "These constraints are harmful if they prevent people from entering relationships which would be more fulfilling to them or keep them in relationships which cause unhappiness."[14]

In a foreword to another book, Brake references Kim TallBear, an academic in Native studies, who believes monogamy and mononormativity are relics of settler colonialism. Nonmonogamy, Brake writes, can be a liberatory practice. To buttress this point, she appeals to famed communist Friedrich Engels: "If they [monogamy and mononormativity] are an instrument of capitalism, as Friedrich Engels and Emma Goldman suggest, would it benefit us individually and collectively to adopt less possessive norms of relationship?"[15]

Feminists of the 1970s, including Shulamith Firestone, likewise saw family abolition as a means of liberation, freeing women from biological and domestic constraints. In her 2022 book *Abolish the Family: A Manifesto for Care and Liberation*,

Sophie Lewis continues that tradition and argues for a radical restructuring of kinship. Family structures, she contends, are inherently conservative and should be dismantled in favor of chosen families and community-based care. "To love a person is to struggle for their autonomy," she writes. "Frankly, loving one's family can be a problem *for anyone.* It might put extra weights around the ankles of a domestic battery survivor seeking to escape. . . . It might hinder a trans or disabled child from claiming medical care. It might dissuade someone from getting an abortion."[16]

Whether it's framed as family abolition or family privilege (a gentler way to imply family structures are oppressive and perpetuate systemic injustice), the concept is the same: The family is a product of capitalist, patriarchal, and colonial systems that reinforce inequality and oppression. "This definition of a family [those who raised you and who you grew up with] has been provided to us by our culture, our storytelling, and our religious traditions for the past several centuries, and it is officially underwritten by government policy in most nations, including the United States," writes Emily St. James for *Vox.* "Just think of how many TV sitcom episodes have ended with some family patriarch reminding his children—and by proxy all of us in the audience—that family comes first, and your family will never let you down. The unshakable primacy of the family unit is one of the earliest tropes we learn. But it's an idea with profound limitations."[17]

If the unjust privileging of family has been pushed through law and cultural messaging, the corrective is to push the opposite. Traditional structures should be portrayed as oppressive and dysfunctional and alternative structures as liberating and loving, according to advocates of non-monogamy. Even if one isn't exposed to the chosen-family concept in the academy or in subcultures, popular culture has elevated it. For the younger generations there is also a trove of found-family-themed books,[18] and the found-family trope is hard to avoid on TikTok. A young adult immersed in such platforms and grappling with pain or social insecurity can easily find a narrative, an identity, and a direction without ever cracking an academic journal.

Lost and Found

"If you're seeing this, you're either surprised or you're not, depending on how well you know me. But I'm queer, and I'm so grateful for my found family."

This was the caption Greg and Tammy's nineteen-year-old daughter, Alice, posted to her Instagram account the evening that she told her parents she was bisexual. Alice had spent senior year reclusive and increasingly angry, lashing out at her parents and younger siblings often and with little predictability. They had gotten used to walking on eggshells around her. A song on the radio on a car ride could send her into an angry rant about their terrible taste in music. A lost item or a needed change of plans could elicit a tirade of bitter abuse.

The day she came out to her family was during such a tirade. The news wasn't altogether a surprise. Initially her parents had assumed her moodiness was typical teen angst, but the outbursts of anger made them think there was something else happening. Alice had also dramatically changed her look. She chopped her medium-length blond hair into a harsh short cut and dyed it an acidic lime color. She had a new boyfriend and had fallen in with a new group of friends who seemed like misfits. They all dressed similarly in oversize

T-shirts and combat boots. Greg and Tammy learned later that the boyfriend was bisexual and had likely introduced Alice, who longed for social acceptance, into a world of fluid sexuality.

After she screamed her sexuality to them, Alice posted the photo of herself on Instagram with the reference to her "found family." Greg and Tammy had never heard the phrase before, but it struck them as an articulation of the rejection they had all been feeling from her for some time. "It was clear she no longer wanted to breathe the same air as us," Tammy says. It also seemed like she had a new vocabulary to suit her new identity. "More and more it felt like she was repeating some sort of script." Like most of her friends, Alice was very online. "I wish that I had recognized how toxic the online culture was," her mother laments. "It was all new. . . . I underestimated it tremendously."

Alice never explicitly announced that she was transitioning her gender, but at one point she emailed Greg and signed off with a man's name. When her parents did speak with her about it, she said she had known she was queer since grade school. "I can tell you that she had crushes on boys; she was a girly girl. There was no gender dysphoria," Greg told me. Greg is a soft-spoken and gentle man. He began keeping a journal and documenting their exchanges with their daughter in part because so much of it was surreal and at times made them think they might be going crazy. "Another feature of this ideology is that they rewrite the past and falsify it," Greg notes. Keeping a record of emails and texts seemed important so that if Greg and Tammy questioned their perceptions later, they had some tether to reality and a record of how bizarre it had become.

Trying to make sense of it all, Greg and Tammy found

estranged-parent groups and began to realize how many of these kids also seemed to be reading from the same script. Found families and chosen families were celebrated, and families of origin were written off as toxic. For Alice, reinventing her past included recasting her family as "toxic Jesus freaks," as she would tell others. While Greg and Tammy have grown far more devout in response to the pain of estrangement, they describe their family as conventionally religious prior to this. They weren't devout, but they went to Mass on Sundays and sometimes did volunteer work with the church. They weren't much for culture wars nor what anyone would consider preachy about their faith.

Within queer found families, the history of trauma is not just known but embedded in the story of the group, playing a vital role and shaping identity formation. The process of identifying a traumatic past is an expected step for any queer child—trauma will be either discovered or projected retrospectively. According to St. James, queer spaces and discussions of trauma go hand in hand: "And the more that a collective awareness of how trauma operates moves into the American mainstream, the more that queer ideas about chosen family also move into the mainstream."[19]

Because chosen families typically form in adulthood, members lack a long history with one another, a history that functions in traditional families as a means of connection through shared memory. By exchanging their trauma history, chosen family members create a symbolic lineage of shared suffering to bond them to one another.

Queer theory expands this narrative of shared trauma beyond the family, casting ordinary American life as inherently oppressive and traumatic. "The preference for [the term] 'queer' . . . rejects a minoritizing logic of toleration or simple political interest-representation in favor of a more thorough resistance to regimes of the normal," writes Michael Warner, a foundational thinker in the field of queer theory. "For both academics and activists, 'queer' gets a critical edge by defining itself against the normal rather than the heterosexual. . . . The insistence on 'queer' . . . has the effect of pointing out a wide field of normalization, rather than simple intolerance, as the site of violence."[20]

Instead of seeing trauma as something that happens in distinct, exceptional moments, queer theory presents trauma as a systemic and ongoing condition of existing within *any* culture with norms. It need not be limited to heteronormativity; normalcy in general is often described as a source of systemic trauma, oppressing queer-identifying people and threatening their erasure and invisibility.

Trauma Hijacking

The logic that recasts ordinary social expectations as sources of harm creates the conditions for what I call "trauma hijacking" (discussed in the introduction): the ideological co-opting of real trauma narratives to erode trust in the very norms that make stable relationships and moral discernment possible. Trauma hijacking uses egregious examples of abuse to justify responses to far less severe experiences. It amplifies the most sympathetic cases, shifts the blame from perpetrators of harm to the norms themselves, depicts defenders of those norms as oppressors and enablers of abuse, and leverages this moral urgency to deconstruct established social rules.

For example, the genuine trauma of women trapped in violent or coercive relationships draws public attention—books, films, and shows frequently explore these stories with depth and sympathy. But the hijack occurs when abuse becomes the dominant interpretive lens for understanding the structure of marriage. The sleight of hand lies in shifting the blame from individual abusers to the institution of marriage itself, which is increasingly reframed as inherently oppressive to women.

This shift is reinforced by legal changes such as the advent of no-fault divorce, which redefined marriage less as a binding covenant and more as a revocable contract based on personal fulfillment. While no-fault divorce provided a necessary escape route for some, it also introduced a broader cultural message: that marriage is conditional and easily dissolved.

In this framework, those who advocate for the enduring value of marriage can be cast as defenders of an oppressive structure, subtly undermining the norm of lifelong commitment as an archaic, even dangerous, relic of male dominance.

The rhetorical power of trauma hijacking is that it carries the testimony of true victims to justify dismantling norms in the name of aid. But all too often the norm being destabilized turns out to serve as a protective force for the most vulnerable. In the case of marriage, a 2014 National Bureau of Economic Research study found that the strongest predictor of economic mobility for children is the prevalence of two-parent families in their community.[21] Similarly, research from the Brookings Institution found that "children raised in single-parent families are nearly five times as likely to be poor as those in married-couple families."[22] The Heritage Foundation's Robert Rector put it succinctly: "Marriage remains America's strongest anti-poverty weapon."[23]

Given the profound benefits of family stability, the societal consequences of devaluing it should be obvious. But the rhetorical effect of trauma hijacking is difficult to see through.

This dynamic is evident in the no-contact movement, where appeals to compassion are amplified and generalized, often without regard for the wide range of reasons individuals cite for severing ties. Not only are the degrees of severity and legitimacy of these reasons conflated, but the broader aim—undermining the social norm of family obligation—is also subtly advanced under the guise of victim advocacy. Questioning this phenomenon is quickly framed as enabling abusers or offending actual victims. Compassion for the victim is an easy sell; the more revolutionary project of norm destabilization is much less so.

Does the advancement of chosen families—not just as a response to need, but as a new ideal of autonomy over duty—make for healthier social bonds? Not all who are encouraged to find chosen families are satisfied. Brent Hartinger is a gay author who once had a tight-knit chosen family. He was in his twenties the first time he heard the concept: "[It's] hard to overstate how much it resonated with me. *Yes!* I thought. *Forget my biological family, I want to spend my life around people who love and accept me for who I am.*"[24]

Now thirty years later and in his fifties, Hartinger thinks the chosen-family position won the argument in the wider culture—he points to shows like *Friends* and *Sex and the City,* noting how far we have moved beyond even these depictions of chosen family—yet he admits he isn't sure we should have. The idea of chosen families now strikes him as a convenient fantasy until more pressing obligations intrude. Because of this, he believes, chosen families don't age well: "I think about my own chosen family from back in my twenties. At the time, I thought we'd be tight forever. But things changed. Some members of my circle—both gay and straight—had kids and their children became their top priority. In other cases, people changed cities or took in aging parents. We all moved on with our lives."[25]

Besides the impermanence of the chosen family, Hartinger identifies other challenges: Young, moneyed, and attractive people have an easier time finding others than the elderly, poor, and disabled, and rates of loneliness have only increased with the loosening of relational definitions. He readily acknowledges that some situations call for cutting ties and seeking a chosen family. But he objects to the chosen family as a new aspirational model, at the expense of extended family culture. "I'm increasingly convinced the deconstruction of 'family' is also at least part of the reason why America is so messed up," Hartinger reflects. "It's a very strange thing, being old enough to see an obscure fringe belief you once completely identified with and totally championed go on to become a *dominant* cultural belief—and suddenly you're able to see that, along with its essential truths, the concept also contains some real flaws and limitations."[26]

Some participants in forums on familial estrangement share this disillusionment. "I feel like we're always told when we go NC [no contact] that 'the blood of the covenant is thicker than the water of the womb,' that we can choose the people we consider family, those sort of sentiments," writes one redditor on the Estranged Adult Child forum. "I don't have a 'chosen family.' I mean, I thought I did at first—some incredibly close friends that I love dearly, I'd do anything for, that I'd run to tell good news, reach out regularly and catch up . . . riiiiight. The true fact of the matter is that the vast majority of people still value their blood relatives as family over anyone else. You may have chosen them as family, but they sure as hell didn't choose you—they've never needed to choose in the first place."[27]

Another estranged adult writes about losing relationships with people who were part of a chosen family: "In losing these relationships, I also lose my only support system, as well as my ability to [be] around their families and be 'an aunt' to their children. It is a lot to lose in one go, on top of grieving the relationship itself. The other person just loses a friendship—they already have all that other stuff elsewhere. I'm realising that this implicit power imbalance in these relationships has often led me to swallow hurtful incidents and allow my boundaries to be pushed out of fear of losing the relationship."[28]

In a thread titled "Does 'Chosen Family' Ever Work Out?" another woman writes of her experience of the instability of such relationships: "I'm 34 and recently lost all my 'chosen family' to various issues, the biggest one being a major mental health crisis and a divorce. Mostly, any serious crisis or conflict [led] to people disappearing. It has been really hard. It seems like most people who claim 'chosen family' don't actually stick through the hard parts."[29]

Of course, this sense of precarity and abandonment is a sign of a movement hoist with its own petard: A vision of family that begins by dissolving obligation cannot easily produce permanence. When "families" are created by nothing other than individual choice, they are inevitably governed by the same logic of choice, and thus remain vulnerable to being *unchosen* in the name of the very freedom that created them.

To Choose What Is Given

Far from signaling societal injustice, a social norm that recognizes the special significance of family members is a mark of social health. While we should be concerned about the well-being of all people, our obligations are concrete, not abstract. When we are ill, it's our spouse, not a stranger, who sits at our bedside. It's the parent, not someone across town, who knows the child's allergies, fears, and vulnerabilities. Appeals to universal love often become a way to evade the real, demanding work of personal duty. Loving humanity in the abstract requires little; loving the person in front of us demands a lot.

"A child occupies a place of responsibility," Greg says, reflecting on his estranged daughter, Alice. "Even before you are head over heels in love with them and willing to undergo anything to protect them, they are totally dependent on you. So, you give it your all. You keep paying out that willingness to sacrifice and endure anything for this person, and it builds into this innate sense of justice. I'm establishing a connection—not in a transactional way—but it's a connection like none other. . . . It's like with every little thread I tied my heart to you. I don't know—maybe there is a 'you owe me' piece in there, but I never felt that. It was something much more metaphysical. There's a reality. I've been looking into your eyes; you've been looking into mine."

There is a givenness to family life. Parents are given the children who come to them, either from adoption or through their union. Children likewise are given parents and siblings not of their choosing. This givenness can create a sense of rote obligation. Adolescents with friends over might roll their eyes at having to include a sibling. Teens might listen more willingly to wisdom shared by a mentor of their choosing when the same counsel from a parent is reluctantly received. And while, with the exception of arranged marriages, husband and wife choose each other to marry, when the ardor of romance that fueled their initial choice fades, they might at times feel their marriage is more of a given than a choice.

Therein lies the secret to relationships that endure and flourish—to see that there is a choice amid the givenness that invites spouses to remember and renew their bonds in small ways despite the years, the familiarity, and the struggles. Even among siblings, within the obligation is an opportunity to choose to include the other affectionately rather than grudgingly. This combination of givenness and choice can provide a strong and stable environment for the belonging, safety, and significance that every person needs. Relationships that are all one or the other miss something primal. A relationship that is all choice and no duty is unstable. A relationship that is only duty and no choice is impersonal.

In one profile of the Holder-Mullins polyamorous household, with whom this chapter opened, we learn that Melissa has two sons who were fifteen and sixteen when Billy and Melissa sat them down to let them know about their relationship with Jeremy. The older son was uncomfortable but made do, but the younger son didn't take the news well and moved in with relatives in another state.[30] "He left home and never came back," Melissa explained. An interviewer asked if that made Melissa rethink their lifestyle. "I chalk it up to being a teenager."[31] The adults made their choice and so did the son. Freedom from social norms does not abolish consequences; it merely shifts them onto someone else.

5

THE OVERTON CAGE

Sarah Mittermaier noticed a marked shift in her relationships in the year 2020. She and her friends had always been politically aligned progressives, but 2020 was a year of sorting, of which her friend group was a microcosm. Some became newly zealous and militant in their politics, while she found herself unsettled by what seemed like a sudden and unmeasured escalation. Looking back, she sees she was progressive more by default than by deliberation.

The intensity of their politics transformed several friends into walking tribunals. "People started developing prickly personalities, seeking out offense, and then reacting with righteous indignation," she recalls. Conversations took on a strained, almost-performative quality. One friend, for instance, had grown resentful of her aging father, frequently venting to Mittermaier. "He was struggling with needing a cane, feeling depressed about losing mobility," she says. "And she just ranted about how her dad was being 'ableist' [harboring biased views about disabilities] because he was sad about it." The lack of empathy was chilling and increasingly common.

By the fall of 2021, the fractures had deepened. Another close friend, Corinne, announced she wouldn't be attending

Thanksgiving with her family, calling it a settler-colonialist holiday. Corinne's mother, though sympathetic to her daughter's position, pleaded with her to come and suggested she use the dinner as a chance to educate them and share why she believed the holiday to be problematic. Corinne refused her mom's request but opted instead to have a nice dinner with friends, just without a turkey.

Around that time, Mittermaier began noticing the sharp rise in kids—especially girls—identifying as transgender. The swiftness with which the medical establishment affirmed dysphoria, offering interventions with minimal scrutiny, troubled her. She dug into the research, uncovering the lasting and often-permanent consequences of these procedures. But when she cautiously shared her concerns with Corinne, the response was immediate and severe.

"I literally expressed some concerns about puberty blockers and what the implications of those would be, and she iced me," Mittermaier says. "I knew she wouldn't welcome my hesitation about this, but I didn't expect her to disappear." Until then, the two had spoken every day, but that abruptly ended. When Mittermaier reached out, hoping to talk, Corinne's response was decisive: She would no longer speak with her. Every attempt at contact, Corinne declared, would trigger a donation to a trans kids' charity. She added that she might reconsider their friendship on the condition that Mittermaier reeducate herself and recant her concerns.

From shaming an aging relative to avoiding a family dinner or abruptly ending a close friendship, people absorbed the rules of social acceptability from the ethos of the culture and then seemingly enforced those rules overnight. When this new moral logic entered the intimacy of private life, its sudden force caught many off guard. At first, Mittermaier told me, "I had to accept that our friendship was never what I thought it was." A bit later she corrected herself. "You know, I don't think that's true. I think there really was a time when nothing—especially nothing so impersonal—could have come between us. And then something changed, and all of a sudden it was possible to imagine such stupid fractures." Most everyone I interviewed expressed a similar sort of bewilderment—questioning whether the relationship they'd trusted had ever been real or had simply changed beyond recognition.

While the primal need to belong might silence many, Mittermaier felt more strongly about writing and speaking openly. Through her work, she has heard from hundreds of desperate parents trying to navigate this new landscape. "For most of their lives together, these families had never experienced anything that could have driven them apart like this." Most describe extremely strained relationships and a total impasse in communication. Many feel they can't even broach any political topics with their children. "It's like this corrosive acid has been poured over relationships—especially between parents and children. We didn't used to handle conflict this way. And then we all lived through this shift."

What Mittermaier experienced personally others had already been feeling institutionally. Before she began her independent news site, *The Free Press,* and assuming the role of editor-in-chief at CBS, Bari Weiss spent several years at the summit of journalistic prestige as a writer for *The New York Times*. Her resignation letter in 2020, however, shed light on a rapidly contracting sphere of acceptable belief.

Weiss joined *The Times* after the 2016 election. While she shared her new colleagues' sentiments regarding the election—and had reacted to the election results with tears of dismay at her desk at *The Wall Street Journal*—she didn't anticipate the censorious and authoritarian impulses taking hold at the Gray Lady. "The lessons that ought to have followed the election—lessons about the importance of understanding other Americans, the necessity of resisting tribalism, and the centrality of the free exchange of ideas to a democratic society—have not been learned," Weiss wrote. "Instead, a new consensus has emerged . . . : that truth isn't a process of collective discovery, but an orthodoxy already known to an enlightened few whose job is to inform everyone else."

Weiss joined *The Times* with great optimism, but soon found her more centrist views weren't welcome. She describes being subjected to constant bullying by colleagues who disagreed with her while more friendly co-workers were badgered for associating with her. Some staff members posted axe emojis next to her name in company-wide Slack channels without consequence. In her resignation letter, Weiss expressed bewilderment that leaders of *The Times* allowed such behavior while telling her privately that they admired her courage. "Showing up for work as a centrist at an American newspaper should not require bravery."[1]

Voting Booth Estrangement

For many—especially within our most powerful, opinion-shaping institutions—Donald Trump's 2016 election signaled the start of an illiberal era. In response, a similarly illiberal reaction emerged, one that justified and even demanded a moral repudiation of his supporters, including—and maybe especially—family and friends. The personal became newly political with such force that many began to question whether the reaction had eclipsed the original threat.

Under these institutional pressures, the line between private and public life has grown increasingly blurred. Maintaining a personal identity separate from political affiliation now feels nearly impossible. Even those naturally apolitical or conflict-averse were dragged into the fray, as neutrality was recast as complicity: Silence, as the oft-repeated refrain has it, became violence. Political imperatives came to permeate nearly every aspect of life, leaving little room for a fully human existence outside the cultural battleground. For young adults who might not be prone to a politicized identity, most every direction they looked *outside* the home impressed on them the perception that divergent views (and the people who possess them) are indecent and unacceptable *inside* the home as well.

After the 2016 election, feminist author Jessica Valenti wrote for *The Guardian* that shaming and even shunning Trump supporters are vital social tools. She mentioned the experience of then Vice President–elect Mike Pence roundly booed by theatergoers as he attended the play *Hamilton*. "Whether it's Pence at a play or your Trump-voting uncle at Thanksgiving, there are people right now who should be made to feel uncomfortable. In a time when there is so much to protest, so much work to do, the booing is necessary—shame on us if we ever stop." Valenti added, "Being socially ostracized for supporting Trump is not an infringement of your rights, it's a reasonable response by those of us who are disgusted, anxious, and afraid."[2]

The illiberalism moved seamlessly from papers and pundits to families and friendships. In 2016, the *New York Post* interviewed Gary Pollakusky, a Long Island man who lost around a hundred Facebook friends when he changed his profile photo to a picture of him and his wife at a victory party for the president-elect. One person who deleted him had been a friend for more than twenty years and the best man at his wedding. "It's a sad state of affairs if you can't handle a profile pic. This is a friend from college, a friend who I got his first job, as much as I could've done for this particular friend throughout my life, I've done," Pollakusky said. "I like people with differing opinions than myself[;] it makes the world go round. . . . This election so clearly infected his world to a point where he felt the need to delete me."[3]

In those early years of Trump's first term, the political hostility felt acute but still containable—a new cold war waged at dinner tables and on Facebook feeds. Yet as his presidency unfolded, the tension only deepened. Certainly 2020 was an unprecedented accelerant, paralyzing the populace in fear and isolation. The chaos of January 6, 2021, and the relentless rhetoric about "the threat to democracy" hardened partisan animosities into something more dire and punitive. The language of resistance, once aimed at institutions, turned toward neighbors, friends, and family.

In the wake of Trump's second election in 2024, calls to sever ties with Trump voters resurged. *HuffPost* covered the new levels of voting acrimony: "Politics has always come between family members, but there's no doubt that the tenor of these conversations post-Trump has become more intense; many people really feel like they can't accept someone whose morals and values are so at odds with their own. It's the idea that the personal is political."[4]

In response to the 2024 election, Valenti released a video reminding her followers that cutting off Trump-supporting friends and family is entirely right and just.[5] Pundits on MSNBC echoed the sentiment. In response to a question about whether, from a psychological standpoint, people should spend holidays with family members who voted for Trump,

Yale-trained psychiatrist Amanda Calhoun said that we should absolutely reject the notion that just because someone is family, we should feel obligated to be around them: "If you are going into a situation where you have family members, where you have close friends who you know have voted in ways that are against you . . . it's completely fine to not be around those people and to tell them why."[6]

The headlines were reflecting, and likely inciting, voting booth estrangement. An American Psychological Association post-election survey in November 2024 found that 38 percent of respondents planned to avoid family members with whom they disagreed politically over the holidays.[7]

Even for people who felt hesitant to cut contact, social pressure could lead them to do so. One man wrote to the advice columnist at *The New York Times Magazine*, asking how to handle family tensions over his mother's political views. "With the result of the 2024 election, my wife and her family are directing their understandable fury at my mother. My wife's sister said, 'If she voted for Trump again, I'm completely done with her.' I expect that the next time they interact it will not be pretty. But my mother is a member of our family, and an invaluable caregiver to our children. She's pleasant and kind in daily life and moved far from her home primarily for us and her grandkids. And she is my mother, after all."[8]

Though the man appreciated his mom's sacrifices and expressed how his children love her, he felt stuck. "My wife and her family will be channeling their anger at one of the few Trump voters they personally know." His mother meanwhile expected him to intervene and to encourage his wife's family to interact with civility. "She sees her vote as a 'personal choice' and doesn't seem to believe that she should be criticized for it."[9]

Among the people I interviewed, a vote cast for Trump was a common catalyst for estrangement. Others who remain in contact speak of a palpable distance in those relationships. While strong political views and disagreements are nothing new, what seems to have changed is the growing sentiment that political differences are not opportunities to dialogue but moral indictments. People from either side of the divide tell me that they see the people in their lives—lifelong friends and family members—so differently now.

When a Window Becomes a Cage

Joseph P. Overton, a policy analyst at the Mackinac Center for Public Policy, introduced the concept of the Window of Political Possibilities in the 1990s. His key insight was that, at any given time, there exists a spectrum of ideas that are politically viable. Ideas within this window are considered acceptable or mainstream, while those outside it are viewed as too extreme or radical. Policymakers advocating for ideas outside the window can't simply impose changes; rather, they rely on institutions like think tanks to shift public opinion, gradually moving ideas from the unthinkable to the acceptable. After Overton's death in 2003, this concept became widely known as the Overton Window.

Joseph Lehman, a friend and colleague of Overton's, notes that about a hundred years ago women couldn't vote in this country. "Well, now you could not get elected dogcatcher in this country if you ran on a platform of 'women should not be allowed to vote.' That's a huge change, and the Overton Window had to change to do that."[10]

The Overton Window works both ways: Ideas that were once considered radical can become normalized, while once-mainstream views can be pushed to the fringe. "You make the case through persuasion," Lehman explains. This effort involves appealing to logic, emotion, and authority to shift the boundaries of acceptable policy options.[11] Without effective appeals to popular buy-in, policy changes are often unstable and short-lived. Ideas outside the window require substantial advocacy before they become viable.

To understand how deepening political divisions lead to personal divisions in our society, it isn't enough simply to recognize that the Overton Window has shifted dramatically—we must recognize that it has changed metaphysically. It's no longer merely a frame that defines the range of acceptable discourse; it has transformed into a cage. A window helps us to see what is there (even if it is not the totality of what is there), but with the cage, the point is not to see but to be safe. It exists not just to exclude unacceptable or irrelevant ideas but to protect the enlightened from the threat of unacceptable *people.* Now dissent risks social ostracism, and the case for what is politically viable is made no longer through persuasion but through intimidation.

Several parents I spoke with described just such a metaphysical shift—the implications of which will be unpacked further in this chapter. Topics that once were able to be discussed and disagreed over became dynamite. One father summarizes his experience of this shift: "Overnight it seemed the conversation with my [progressive] daughter turned into 'I don't want to hear any reasons *why* you voted that way. I don't want to hear your side of things. I only want to hear you tell me that you were wrong.'" His vote no longer meant he disagreed with her; it now meant he was a threat to her. The recourse, then, was not to reason and persuasion but to penance and submission.

The Collapse of Common Ground

One cause of this transformation from a window into a cage is that the scope of politics has extended beyond its natural boundaries. Traditionally, most citizens believed they shared common ends and simply disagreed on the means of achieving them. For example, we might all agree poverty is bad, but we might disagree on how to combat it. Do we help the poor through a robust welfare state and safety net or through incentivizing hard work, promoting charitable initiatives, and empowering local solutions?

Today, however, our disagreements are increasingly about which ends we should pursue. No longer is the divide about how to get to a shared goal—it's about what the goal even is. Is our goal equality of opportunity or equality of outcome? Should we create a society in which people are free to pursue what is good, or should we maximize individual autonomy and the freedom to pursue what each individual believes is best for themselves? Do human rights extend to the human being in the womb, or is the autonomy of the woman to be preeminently privileged? Is identity defined in ways that unite us, or are we defined into division through politicized identities?

This shift from arguing about means to arguing about ends turns the political into an existential battle of moral tribalism. Issues that once belonged to philosophy, anthropology, and theology have been claimed as political territory and, by implication, are subject to changing political whims.

Progressivism doesn't just argue for different policies—it argues for a different moral order. It deliberately clouds foundational principles with ambiguity, while treating matters of prudence as moral absolutes. Rightly or wrongly, people across the political spectrum sense that this is not politics as usual and that something far more existential is at stake.

All Power, No Agency

This totalizing of the political subsumes individual identity and absorbs it into the Empowerment Delusion—the seductive promise of radical autonomy paired with no internal locus of control. This delusion breeds neuroticism: unattainable expectations colliding with persistent anxiety over ever-present threats.

For example, the trans movement assures adherents and allies that they possess radical liberatory power even as it convinces them they live under constant danger of being misgendered, deadnamed, or denied access to sex-rejecting medical interventions. Or take the broader narrative of systemic oppression: It frames society as rigged to benefit some and to predetermine who succeeds and who fails. In this view, achievement derives primarily from unearned privilege rather than effort, and setbacks are recast as the inevitable consequence of structural injustice.

Yet while this view of the world may seem compassionate and carry some partial truth, at its core this outlook is a form of existential despair. There's nothing empowering about being told you are powerless. In this framework, the way to improve one's life is not by changing oneself but by changing, reeducating, or removing those who perpetuate the systems of power.

I spoke with psychiatrist and scholar Aaron Kheriaty, who sees in this Overton Cage and external locus of control a form of neo-Gnosticism—a belief in salvation through secret knowledge, accessible only to the few who can see behind the curtain. This neo-Gnostic worldview maintains that "there is a good principle and an evil principle, both on equal footing, embedded within the systems of the world," he explains. "Rather than locating evil in the human heart or the will, we strive instead to remake the world."

Therapy or ideologies that say a person can solve their problems by changing the world, Kheriaty says, are doomed. Even if the narrative of overwhelming systemic oppression were true, Kheriaty notes, "if you're only trying to change other people, that doesn't work. Only once you've transformed yourself can you have any hope of transforming others. But in a way that respects their freedom."

For those who are pulled into this Empowerment Delusion, all hope for happiness—both personal and societal—becomes relocated to reshaping social structures through political action. That reshaping turns personal quickly. Friends and family members who don't get on "the right side of History" aren't merely seeing things differently—they are holding up human happiness and will be treated as such.

In an article on estrangement, journalist Allie Volpe interviews Bryan, a transgender female to male whose extended family have welcomed the news of transition with varying levels of enthusiasm. Bryan is committed to not cutting anyone off based on their conservative views. But there is a caveat: "I said to myself that if something happens where my health care is taken away, whether it's because I'm on an Affordable Care Act plan or because the Affordable Care Act stops providing gender-affirming care, and if something actually does happen that's a direct result of Trump being elected, then I will definitely reconsider cutting these people off forever."[12] When the personal becomes political, then the viability of our relationships is outsourced to events and decisions in Washington, D.C., making no contact seem less a choice than an externally forced necessity.

People Will Die

Voting booth estrangement is compounded by a deeper fracture: We no longer inhabit a shared moral or perceptual world. Emotional reasoning increasingly shapes our moral judgments, eroding the capacity for rational debate and mutual understanding.

Social psychologist Jonathan Haidt has explored how moral and emotional reasoning shape political rhetoric. His 2012 book, *The Righteous Mind: Why Good People Are Divided by Politics and Religion,* provides a framework for understanding why appeals to fear and outrage—such as "people will die" rhetoric—are so persuasive. Haidt argues that we don't arrive at political opinions through pure logic. Instead, we often have gut-level emotional reactions first and then rationalize our views afterward. Highly charged rhetoric across the political spectrum exploits this by triggering fear and moral outrage, making people more likely to react emotionally than analytically.

Haidt identifies five primary moral foundations that shape

our judgment: care, fairness, loyalty, authority, and sanctity. Political liberals tend to prioritize the first two—care and fairness—which makes them particularly receptive to "people will die" narratives related to women's healthcare, climate change, or gender ideology. Conservatives, on the other hand, draw more evenly from all five foundations. They value care and fairness but balance them with strong concerns for loyalty, authority, and sanctity, making them more skeptical of appeals to care that ignore trade-offs.[13]

In 2020, the term "Grandma Killer" took aim at those opposing strict Covid lockdown measures and serves as an illustration of this foundational divide. Such rhetoric has strong emotional resonance with left-leaning audiences but didn't work as well on conservatives, who more readily recognized the trade-offs of isolation, including increased risks of mental disorders, loneliness, and learning loss. Without consideration of the trade-offs, the rhetoric of "Grandma Killer" carried a moral urgency and mandate of care for the left that cast dissenters as not merely wrong but immoral and cruel—exhibiting the Overton Cage transformation from bad ideas to bad people.

The same moral impulses that heighten empathy can paradoxically also intensify outrage. Because of this, "People will die" also works in the other direction—not as a warning, but as a threat. One year after the 2024 failed political assassination of Donald Trump, the widely influential conservative Charlie Kirk was murdered while engaging college students in free and open dialogue on a college campus. Millions watched this event with horror. Over the following weeks, the impact of the incident extended beyond the individual involved to neighbors and co-workers, some of whom discussed and reacted to the event both online and offline. Kara, a young professional, was in a corporate meeting when the news broke, interrupting their meeting. Her team leader absorbed the information and then with casual candor said, "Well, we all knew that we would have to turn to violence to right things at some point, didn't we?" Kara knew her boss and several others on the team were progressive. Still, the callousness of the remark and the confident way her boss assumed a consensus around such an inhumane, violent comment shocked her.

In 2025 the Network Contagion Research Institute (NCRI) conducted a survey of more than 1,200 U.S. adults, weighted to reflect census demographics. The report is titled *Assassination Culture: How Burning Teslas and Killing Billionaires Became a Meme Aesthetic for Political Violence.* Some 38 percent of the survey respondents said it would be at least somewhat justified to murder Donald Trump, and 31 percent said the same about Elon Musk. Close to 40 percent said it was at least somewhat acceptable to destroy a Tesla dealership to protest Musk. The report concludes that such tolerance and even advocacy for violence are being normalized: "This pattern builds on a broader trend NCRI identified in two December 2024 reports which analyzed how viral social media narratives were legitimizing political violence, particularly in the aftermath of the UnitedHealthcare CEO's assassination." Such opinions are not outliers but instead part of a rising left-wing authoritarianism that the report's authors call "assassination culture." Part of what is fueling it, according to the report, is a combination of radical ideological commitment and a deep sense of powerlessness rooted in the belief that control over one's life lies largely outside oneself.[14]

In my own experience as a lifelong pro-life advocate, I'm no stranger to believing that there are lives (by the millions) on the line, hinging on policies and votes. Still, it has never occurred to me to cut ties with friends or relatives because they are pro-choice or because they vote for liberal candidates. I don't doubt that there are conservatives who have cut off family or friends to their left or engaged in political violence. But there is a difference in how the animating beliefs of left and right dispose adherents to violence or dissuade them from it. As many noted, the responses to the deaths of George Floyd and Charlie Kirk couldn't have been starker: The former was met with riots, violence, and destruction, while the latter was met with prayer vigils and packed services that Sunday.

There is a logic to the predominance of terminal responses on the left. If what is wrong with the world is systemic, then the reasonable response is to upend the system. If—as Christianity proposes—what is wrong with the world is me, then the logical response is to look within.

Progressivism can foster a "by any means necessary" response to what is seen as structural violence (e.g., capitalism, racism, patriarchy). And some of the cultural policies it most ardently defends in the name of justice—abortion and gender affirmation—themselves require and justify violence. That violence is directed against both civic life and one's own flesh and blood—be it the self or a family member—is therefore not surprising: The no-contact movement is a logical outgrowth of a fundamentally revolutionary movement.

Revolutionary ideology is seductive. Once its logic is absorbed, its conclusions, previously unthinkable, become inevitable. In the analogy of the Overton Cage, it's the ideologues who are imprisoned, not their opponents, an image that captures how ideology narrows, confines, and ultimately isolates those within it.

Even as I write this, I want to correct any interpretation

that this should be viewed through an us-versus-them lens. Lest I, or readers on the right, take any of this as cause for smug satisfaction, two points must be made. First, revolutionary ideology is seductive precisely because it appeals to universal human temptations. Each of us is prone to blame our troubles on outside forces, to see our opponents as evil and ourselves as innocent, to transgress moral boundaries and then dismiss those boundaries as provincial. Second, because of this, the right is by no means immune to the lure of authoritarianism. As polarization deepens, new reactionary voices are emerging on the right, ready to fight fire with fire. A conservative movement that abandons its principles by embracing its own version of identity politics, reducing people to race or sex, or matching extremism with extremism will only mirror the dehumanizing absolutism it seeks to condemn. In civic life and the no-contact movement, there is a powerful pull toward reactionary retribution, but that will only hasten the collapse of both relationship and republic.

The Long March Through the Classroom

Cultural revolutions advance gradually and often imperceptibly at first, until their logic suddenly feels everywhere and inescapable. For decades now, few institutions have been more powerfully situated to shape the future than K–12 education. Because of this formative reach, schools have often become conduits through which emerging activist frameworks are introduced to the next generation.

In 2024, a high school student in South Carolina took to the mic at a public hearing on school book bans. She explained that she had been inspired to speak by her English teachers, for whom she expressed "the utmost respect," and warned of what she described as the dangerous consequences of restricting books in schools. She initially spoke warmly of her parents: "I'm fortunate to have both my parents present and involved in my everyday life. They support me, care for me, and I live a comfortable life. I love both of my parents dearly."[15]

But quickly, her focus narrowed: "Tonight I would like to focus on my father and the concomitantly detrimental effect he has had on my life. He's a conservative, a Republican, and a Christian. For as long as I can remember, he has instilled his political and religious values in me. As a child who unquestioningly admired her father, I took him at his word, and his one-sided, bigoted beliefs became ingrained in my identity."[16]

As an example of his detrimental effect, she recounted a lunchtime in elementary school around the 2016 election. She recited arguments she had heard her dad make in favor of Trump to her classmates, but currently laments having endorsed a man whom she now believes would have her suffer and die. She does not give a reason for this belief but said she wished that her ten-year-old self had been exposed to other political perspectives. Her teachers by contrast, she said, supported her unconditionally and encouraged her to explore other beliefs. "If the classroom is not the place for such discussions, then where? The home? My parents failed me in that area of education—and I can assure you that mine were not the only ones."[17]

Most children push back against their parents' beliefs at some point as they grow up. This can be a normal and healthy way of testing independence and developing a deeper ownership over their beliefs as they enter adulthood. In loving families, this normally unfolds privately with varying degrees of temporary tension. What is new is the moral permission for teens to turn that pushback into a public humiliation performance before a seemingly approving audience of surrogate adult authority figures with little actual responsibility for the teens entrusted to them.

The daughter said she loved her dad. By her own account, he gave her care, stability, and support. He shared his beliefs, but those beliefs were unacceptable, and now maybe he is too.

Part 2

A HOUSE REBUILT

6

REENGAGING RELATIONSHIPS

The path to reengagement, if it opens at all, is rarely linear. It requires the strength to avoid retaliation or defensiveness, the courage and humility to risk rejection more than once, and the prudence to discern what is and isn't possible.

I can't presume to know the specific circumstances of each reader. It's important to acknowledge that family dynamics are rarely simple or one-sided. In many cases, an adult child may be influenced by a totalizing political or ideological framework—but that doesn't mean that their pain is fabricated or that all their grievances are illegitimate. Sometimes what presents as a dispute over politics has multivariate causes, like unresolved familial pain that ideology then gives language to. Sometimes parents have in fact made serious mistakes or caused harm, and reckoning with that honestly is an essential part of the path forward. One of the damaging effects of ideology is that it can make people more fragile in the face of pain, but that fragility doesn't necessarily mean that the wound isn't real. The complexity of these situations requires the deep and humbling work of self-examination: a willingness on the part of parents to ask not only what their child has absorbed from ideology but also whether there are truths in the child's story that need to be faced with honesty and grace.

The central aim of this book is to understand—and help overcome—the ideological forces contributing to the growing phenomenon of family members and friends cutting off relationships. Yet I've also tried to make clear that the cultural currents fueling narcissism and emotional fragility affect us all, not only the younger generation nor the ideologically possessed. Family breakdown didn't begin with Gen Z; its logic has been unfolding for decades. While some divorces are sadly necessary, many are avoidable. And regardless of the reasons, the normalization of divorce has communicated a quiet but devastating message: Family members are replaceable. We can't sit comfortably within a culture that treats divorce casually and then condemn young people for "divorcing" their families. This is not about assigning blame but about acknowledging the ripple effects. Every rupture, however justified, reinforces the same corrosive idea: *You can be replaced.*

While reconciliation is never fully within one person's control, there are steps that remove some of the obstacles blocking the path to reconnection. That work begins with interior scrutiny.

In my early motherhood—amid toddlers, pregnancies, and postpartum exhaustion—I carried a persistent belief that peace was always one fix away. The toddler needed to behave. The baby needed to sleep. I needed to get through the pregnancy. Maybe we needed a bigger house. Definitely, a vacation.

It wasn't a checklist, exactly. More like mental background noise feeding a persistent idea that my equilibrium depended solely on resolving external problems. One day, while I was mentally revisiting that list, the truth of my situation struck me: It wasn't necessarily my circumstances that needed to change.

It was *me*. Yes, there were things to improve around me, systems to adjust or put in place, perhaps more help to be sought. But I also needed to make some interior changes and to meet my situation with greater ownership and a sporting spirit.

While there are far more difficult trials to endure, this simple realization can help prepare us to face them as they come. We may lament the sufferings that come our way, but the path to peace and healing begins not with transforming someone else or our circumstances but with transforming ourselves. This is the kind of radical acceptance found in many recovery traditions, captured in the Serenity Prayer: "God, grant me the serenity to accept the things I cannot change, the courage to change the things I can, and the wisdom to know the difference."

While reconciliation differs from recovery, both can require hitting rock bottom. Some seek to escape the pain of rock bottom by numbing it, further pushing the floor downward. Others might cope by assigning blame to someone who has wronged them, using condemnation as a shield against introspection. A different but also damaging response is believing that we have control over the other person—that if we just say the right thing, send the right article, or defend ourselves sufficiently, we can fix the situation. Still others fall into the reverse trap: believing that the estranged person's actions define and control *us*. In each of these responses, we relinquish either responsibility, dignity, or peace. The work of reengagement requires a reclamation of each.

Surrender

For Kate, estrangement and twelve-step recovery meetings were more than analogous. She grew up with various levels of toxicity in her family of origin: "My dad sort of ignored us, and my mom raged a lot. My dad's family has some significant estrangement. He was one of six kids and only has a relationship with one sibling. There was some rough business with my grandfather's generation. Cutting people off was somewhat normalized in a way that made it feel like a natural, viable option. But it's not natural."

Kate dealt with her difficulties growing up by trying to escape them, mostly through abusing alcohol. She had the courage to come to terms with her addiction and entered recovery as a young adult. There she found enduring help from which she still draws, but initially in recovery she absorbed a message about family that made her intensely self-protective: "I remember there was this wonderful man sharing his addiction story and how he had a revelation that it runs in his family, that this is a family disease." Kate remembers very clearly realizing as he spoke that her parents gave this problem to her. "The truth generally is somewhere in between—your parents did not *give* it to you, but there *is* something with your family at play."

Newly sober and newly married, Kate tried to navigate what her life should look like. "There is this sense I got initially in recovery that I needed to do whatever I could to protect my sobriety. Around that time, I went home to visit my parents, and it was very hard because there were all of these subtle emotional triggers, and I had this sense that my parents were toxic and threats to my sobriety." Kate did therapy for a while, but the focus tended to be on revisiting those wounds and the mistakes of her parents. "The more you're looking at those flaws in someone, the more you're incentivized to erect boundaries with them or to cut them off." She decided to cut them out of her life the way she knew her dad had cut others out of his. At this early stage in her recovery, she viewed her sobriety as a newborn baby that was under existential threat by her family members.

Everything changed when Kate learned she was expecting her first actual baby. "I knew I wanted my child to have grandparents." There was also a practical dimension to reestablishing contact. Kate was in the middle of a work contract that required her to travel monthly at six weeks postpartum. She reached out to her mom, who promptly dropped everything and traveled with her to help with the baby. Perhaps most importantly, her mom didn't demand an accounting from Kate as the price for reentry. "There were not long, drawn-out conversations about what had happened or how it would be now. I really needed her, and she just came. We're in a great place now. I'm ashamed of having cut ties. It was all about me and making sure I was safe."

It isn't a panacea, but many families have found that an adult child's own experience of becoming a parent can serve as a catalyst for healing. The demands of raising a child often invite reflection on the sacrifices once made by one's own parents. Yet that same confrontation with sacrifice can also deepen estrangement—especially when new parents contrast the lengths they now go to protect their child with what they perceive their own parents failed to do.

For Kate, the arrival of her child awakened her to her need. Parenthood also stirred in her a longing for continuity, for roots, for the history and community that come from intergenerational family life. "There is so much strength in numbers," she says. "Good luck doing it on your own. You need that extension across different people, different views—that connection across generations."

Kate's longing for connection wasn't limited to her own

family—it extended to her husband's large, often-complicated family of origin. She knew their long history of disagreements and simmering tensions and the messy, tangled relationships that come with imperfect people sharing life amid differences and old wounds. Yet she saw something deeply valuable in their persistence: People who, despite it all, kept showing up. Kept trying. Kept investing in something larger than themselves. "When we are at an extended-family event, there's no chance anyone is talking politics. All these people have been in each other's lives for decades. They've hung in there."

Even so, those dynamics can take a toll on her. Kate sometimes feels like an outsider for a variety of reasons and carries several hurts from her in-laws—grievances she could easily dwell on. But she's made a habit of talking herself out of that posture. When she feels slighted by a relative, she reminds herself that she doesn't show up at family gatherings for their sake or even fully for her own. She goes for the sake of the next generation and for the enduring connection that might still be preserved. "I don't think people realize that when you cut ties—if you plan to do that unto death—there is an enormous generational impact. I just see the fruits of families who have hung in there."

"I could go no contact," she says plainly. "Based on myself, I would. I have at times felt tempted to say, 'We're not being loved here. We're not coming for Easter.' But I think the devil would like nothing more than me cutting people out." The richness that both extended families add to her own is worth it for her. "My kids get to know their grandparents' Italian cooking and their quirky sense of humor. I can't fill those gaps in for them."

That effort toward family unity has been tested more intensely in 2020 and the years since. Kate watched the escalation from a distance initially, becoming alarmed by the sharp rise in political tribalism. "It felt like all of a sudden people's standards became wholly dictated by politics," she says. The shift first appeared on social media, where longtime friends were posting things like "If you believe x, y, or z, please unfriend me now."

She presumed at first it was mostly just an online phenomenon—until the tension seeped into her real life, straining her close bond with a cousin. "We had made a pact years ago that we're siblings. I love him so much," she says. "But for the first time ever, there was a rift." He let her know that, through another relative, he knew she had voted for Trump and that he was unsure he could move past that. "I pleaded with him and said, 'Look, we can never talk politics, or we can have it out. Whichever you want. But I'm not losing you.'" He replied that he just needed distance for now.

Kate, a sensitive soul, says the rift hurt deeply, but she's choosing not to overanalyze his silence or rush a resolution. "I felt so sad at first. But I've realized that I don't need to know everything right now. I can wait and hope and surrender control over this. You know, you may have to die to yourself to a certain degree to have some people in your life," she reflects. "But the alternative is not what God wants."

With some of Kate's other family members, they've adopted a system: One group thread is devoted entirely to politics. One sister who thinks very differently from Kate frequently posts her political opinions and frustrations there. "Sometimes I'll just chime in with something like 'Well, I disagree.' But I don't engage much with it." Kate lets her and the others vent and reminds herself that she need not try to fix, convert, or control. Then there's a second thread (with all the same people) in which the focus is light: sports, funny memes, everyday banter. "It is sort of how we have navigated how to not ignore our real differences but to compartmentalize them." The politics thread can be engaged or ignored as each person discerns. It's a manifest reminder that we can set aside these things and focus on the personal relationship as separate and more important.

Unity Without Uniformity

Kate has learned how to model high differentiation (introduced in chapter 1)—the capacity to not feel easily threatened by differences and disagreements, even ones that might strike at our core beliefs. I spoke with therapist Rachel Haack, who often works with estranged family members and sees self-betrayal and reactionary anger as core struggles in navigating differences among loved ones: "The ability to stay in relationship with someone who thinks differently from you, without collapsing into excessive people-pleasing or reacting in anger, is the result of developing the capacity allowed by high differentiation."

Unity is the goal, but it shouldn't be confused with uniformity. Difference is natural and to be expected. "You might look at a group of people and see they all look similar—they dress the same; they have very similar beliefs and actions. It is easy to think they must be so united, but there can also be an implicit threat that if you step out of line, you will be cut off," Haack says. "What America is attempting in a pluralistic society is . . . to have lots of different people, views, and religions and have a system that allows for all of that. It's messy and difficult, but it's better than authoritarianism."

Modern American families mirror this challenge in microcosm. The task is to hold freedom and belonging in tension—a balance that depends on high differentiation. When individuals can maintain a clear sense of self while staying in connection with others, families become more resilient, as does the wider society. In fact, the health of the family and the health of a pluralistic society tend to rise and fall together. High differentiation in families can both reflect and reinforce the capacity of a culture to hold together without coercion or collapse.

Haack encourages clients to develop high differentiation by asking themselves three foundational questions. The first question is "Do I know who I am?" In early life, Haack notes, it's natural and even necessary to mirror our parents. "But as you grow, you develop a stronger sense of self, and depending on the dynamics of your family, there may be subtle messages about how loud that self is allowed to be. You might begin to sense that being fully yourself is somehow a problem."

Similarly, parents (often mothers) might also abdicate their sense of self by so identifying with their role as parent that losing contact with their child eviscerates their identity. For both adult child and parent, then, it's important to reground themselves in who they are. Rather than collapsing their identity to maintain harmony or quickly rejecting relationships to preserve autonomy, answering this first question helps a person begin to inhabit an anchored identity that can be both separate and interconnected.

The second question is "Can I manage my own anxiety about difference enough to express my thoughts and beliefs?"

When surrounded by people who disagree, we may instinctively stay silent. At times, silence is prudent and a way to preserve peace. But if we want to grow in differentiation, we must develop the capacity to speak honestly when it's warranted, even when it feels uncomfortable. This doesn't mean always stating our views, but it does mean being capable of doing so without being governed by fear or the need for approval.

The third question follows naturally: "Can I manage my anxiety when others express thoughts and beliefs that differ from mine?" In other words, we must offer others the same freedom we seek for ourselves. If we want to be able to speak without fear, we must also cultivate the emotional steadiness to hear disagreement without feeling threatened.

Haack believes that it's often a signal of something pathological in families and society when we normalize cutting people off because of low differentiation. "You're using splitting as a defense mechanism in order to justify your inability to manage all this." She suggests asking further questions that prompt self-reflection as a way to move toward high differentiation. "What is the harm? What exactly is the threat? If I don't allow this person to express what they think, what does that mean about who I am and what I believe?" Such an examination can help expose any inflated or irrational fears or insecurity in one's own beliefs.

Some years ago, on a work trip with my husband, one of his co-workers started playfully chiding me about my beliefs, knowing that I was conservative and Catholic. I engaged a bit, but he kept it up, and eventually I just smiled and said something to the effect of "Whatever" to end the conversation. His provocations unsuccessful, he pivoted and said, "Wow, you must not really care that much about your beliefs if what I'm saying isn't bothering you." I said, "I care about this a lot, but what I believe does not depend on your assent in order for me to know it to be true."

It's easier to maintain that kind of differentiation with a stranger. With a relative, it's far more difficult. I have to work at it—really work at it. Some relationships make it easier than others, but in the ones where it's hard, every conversation that touches on deep differences demands a choice. There's almost always a higher and a lower road, and over time, the accumulation of those choices determines whether the relationship grows stronger or more brittle.

Exiting the Reactionary Cycle

Some parents are understandably desperate to preserve a relationship with their child. In their desperation they can tend toward over-accommodation, softening or silencing their convictions to keep the peace. Yet this impulse to appease is often the mirror image of the authoritarian child, who demands absolute affirmation of every belief. Both are reacting to the same discomfort: the anxiety that comes from difference. When differentiation is low, that anxiety tends to drive one of two reflexive patterns—either the chameleon, who continually adapts to maintain harmony, or the bully, who demands conformity and can't abide dissent. True differentiation, by contrast, requires learning to stay connected without capitulating and to stand firm without dominating.

"People with a poorly differentiated 'self' depend so heavily on the acceptance and approval of others that they either quickly adjust what they think, say, and do to please others or they dogmatically proclaim what others should be like and pressure them to conform," according to the Bowen Center, where the concept of high differentiation is central. "Bullies depend on approval and acceptance as much as chameleons, but bullies push others to agree with them instead of with others. Disagreement threatens a bully as much as it threatens a chameleon."[1]

More often than not, it's mothers for whom the chameleon instinct takes over. Mothers are more prone to struggle with the question of identity in the face of strained relationships with their children, asking themselves, "What kind of mother has a child who doesn't want to talk to her anymore?" A child's critical narrative can feel like a deep indictment, triggering a highly charged emotional response and creating a feedback loop: The more the parent pleads, the more the child retreats; the more the child retreats, the more the parent pleads. Paradoxically, when a parent grounds their identity apart from their child's approval, they open a pathway to reconciliation. An adult child who once felt burdened by their parent's emotional need might see an opportunity to re-engage as the parent becomes less needy.

Psychologist Joshua Coleman identifies this feedback loop as a common yet difficult-to-name pattern in estranged families, especially among mothers and daughters. A mother's expression of pain, meant to bridge the gap, can be received by the adult child as an emotional burden. That burden might trigger guilt or a sense of suffocation in the adult child. In self-protection, the child then distances herself from the mother, sometimes labeling her as narcissistic or toxic. The mother's hurt deepens, prompting her to escalate the cycle by trying to more intensely communicate her hurt to the child. This feeds the child's need for distance.[2] The antidote is not more emotional disclosure but greater self-regulation, firmer boundaries, and a willingness to accept that healing might be slow or incomplete.

Sarah, her husband Paul, and their daughter Alex were initially caught in this emotional feedback loop. Sarah and Paul had always believed they had a close relationship with Alex and her husband. But after a long visit, Sarah received a curt message from Alex: "I need some space for a while. It was a lot having you here."

Shocked, Sarah pressed for more information. Alex replied that she felt her mother was critical of her appearance, her politics, her lack of church involvement. Alex also said that she felt overwhelmed by family expectations; she had always made a big deal of her parents' birthdays and anniversaries—a tradition Sarah and Paul enjoyed. "I think anniversaries should be the responsibility of the married partners," Alex told them.

Sarah responded defensively. She expressed how hurt she felt and how the request for distance and space was making her cry herself to sleep each night. And she couldn't understand why Alex would coldly end a tradition that had always been meaningful to her. Alex, empathetic by nature, initially felt crushed by her mother's sadness. Her instinct was to comfort and reconcile. But over time, she began to feel emotionally depleted and eventually saw Sarah's pain as manipulative rather than maternal. She pulled away further.

Sarah, in turn, interpreted Alex's further withdrawal as cruel and ungrateful. For Alex, her mother's efforts to explain her pain weren't taken as proof of her love but were clearly experienced as inordinate pressure. Unable to see another way forward, both retreated further into hurt and confusion.

With the help of a therapist, Alex began practicing differentiation. She decided to pull back from Sarah's emotional heaviness and avoid phone calls, but she started sending brief but warm text messages to her mom such as "Thinking of you. Hope your day is a good one."

Sarah also shifted. She sought support from her longtime friends, who gently encouraged her to stop using her daughter as a sounding board for grief. When Alex needed space, Sarah resisted the habit of expressing her hurt and instead texted, "Love you! I'm here if you want to talk. No pressure."

The dynamic eased. The enmeshment gave way to breathing room. Their bond began to reconstitute itself but with a new shape. Only when one or both parties step out of the reactive cycle can healing begin.

Converts or Heretics

Both the one who initiates estrangement and the one left behind are called to work to develop high differentiation. Emotional maturity isn't a one-sided demand. An adult child who can't tolerate a parent's different vote, faith, or worldview and breaks off the relationship is demonstrating low differentiation. But so is the parent who is emotionally needy or routinely tries to argue their child out of their beliefs or self-understanding, hoping to reclaim the connection through coercive guilt trips or constant correction.

Developing high differentiation can be harder based on the real or perceived stakes of the disagreements and differences involved. For example, many adult children might truly think grave harm will come as the result of their parents' vote. Parents, for their part, can truly believe that eternal ramifications might result from decisions their adult children are making. The point is not to trivialize such concerns but to recognize we can hold our beliefs deeply and still understand that the other person simply doesn't. Little good comes from acting as though we have any control over that.

Paradoxically, the more we respect the freedom of our adult kids, the more likely they will be to seek our counsel. My general advice in fraught relationships is to strive to rarely, if ever, criticize or give unsolicited advice to an adult child who lives independently unless absolutely necessary. You can ask questions and open the door to conversation, but then let them be. If they are doing something illegal or abusive, then a correction or an appropriate intervention makes sense. If they are persisting in immoral behavior, then chances are they already know you disapprove. If their behavior infringes on your integrity and life and home, then draw firm boundaries. Otherwise, trust that they are aware of your perspective and that they are more likely to value it the less it's thrust on them.

This posture of restraint and trust requires an inner steadiness that can't come merely from willpower. It depends on a deeper grounding of the self, one that can withstand difference without collapsing into people-pleasing or control. When a person's sense of self is anchored in something higher and more stable than their ideology (most often a religious faith), they are more able to engage across differences without feeling existentially threatened. Of course, this presumes a healthy religious outlook, grounded in a deep trust in providence and the benevolence of God. Religion that is fear-based and coercive will often incline its adherents toward low differentiation. When religion is communicated poorly, without a foundation in love and a conception of human dignity and freedom, it can become very demanding of uniformity and threatened by dissent.

Such fear-based low differentiation isn't unique to religious fundamentalists, though that is often the archetype in the popular imagination. Rather, low differentiation can show up just as readily in seemingly secular belief systems. The abolition of religion doesn't remove our religious impulses; it relocates them. It also distorts them. Progressivism operates like a religion but more akin to a fear-based and controlling one than a healthy one. Highly politicized individuals relate to their ideology with a kind of dogmatic, merciless zeal, treating dissenters from progressive orthodoxies as heretics. Without the supernatural, politics becomes the preeminent human project, one that reduces and absorbs us and erodes a deeper source of unity.

Belief in a benevolent God, by contrast, can serve as a crucial check against the pathological inflation of politics.

This fundamentalist dynamic can be seen in many contemporary expressions of political or moral polarization. For example, after the 2024 election Jimmy Kimmel's wife, Molly McNearney, described on the *We Can Do Hard Things* podcast how she grew up in a conservative family and has since lost relationships with relatives over politics. "I'm kind of in constant conflict. And I'm angry all the time, which isn't healthy at all," she admitted. "When I see these terrible stories every day, I'm immediately mad at certain aunts, uncles, cousins, who put him in power. . . . I wish I could deprogram myself in some way." She recounted sending emails before the election, begging her family not to vote for Trump, only to be ignored by most or met with "truly insane responses." "It's definitely caused a strain," she continued. "I've definitely pulled in closer with the family that I feel more aligned with. And I hate that this has happened."[3]

It's interesting that McNearney was candid and telegraphed

her internal turmoil by stating that she wished she could deprogram herself. At some level she seemed to believe not only that something was wrong in them but that something might be awry in her as well.

Instead of prompting a search to expose heretics, a deep belief in a benevolent God encourages religious adherents to seek converts—to persuade rather than to accuse. By contrast, belief in an ideological "god" often results in the opposite: The impulse is to root out deviation, to shame heretics, to demand conformity, and to seek echo chambers. It generates a brittle uniformity instead of a durable unity.

At the societal level, classical liberalism can operate on a similar principle of high differentiation. By emphasizing individual rights, the rule of law, and the contest of ideas, it assumes that a healthy society can withstand disagreement without collapsing. Just as faith in a benevolent God provides individuals with the internal stability to tolerate difference, classical liberalism provides social structures that allow diverse convictions to coexist. It recognizes that truth and social wisdom emerge not from enforced consensus but from open debate, voluntary association, and the continual negotiation of differences. In cases both of religious faith and of liberal society, the cultivation of stability and resilience depends on a recognition that life is richer and stronger when disagreement is not feared but managed with reason, goodwill, and a common pursuit of the truth.

Assemble a Sounding Board

Kimmel's wife, McNearney, demonstrated black-and-white thinking, which is a hallmark of ideology. An important method of preventing such tendencies in us is to seek out objective feedback when emotions run high, things get confusing, and it's hard to see our own part clearly. One step toward reconciliation can be getting outside feedback from a trusted friend, counselor, or pastor—someone with enough distance to help sort through what's real and what's reactive.

For years, Roger, a widower, thought the way to reach his daughter was through carefully reasoned conversations. A single father of four girls after losing his wife in a car accident, he was used to being the lone adult voice at home and the sole masculine one, and with that came a need for an emotional counterweight.

"When it was both [my wife and me], there was balance," he says. "But once it was just me, they sometimes felt ganged up on. I didn't want that dynamic." So, he leaned on a few trusted women, friends of his late wife affectionately dubbed "the godmothers," to serve as guides. He aimed to stay approachable, to keep the lines of communication open, and to run things by the godmothers when he felt he might be out of his depth.

His oldest daughter, Rebecca, had always had a passion for underdogs. In high school, she was outraged at the snide comments made about an openly gay student in her class; in college, she became a loud voice for climate change. When she told Roger that she was a lesbian, he wasn't altogether surprised. A year later she declared herself non-binary.

Rebecca, a smart teen, had gone to a prestigious and progressive college—an environment that Roger believes radicalized her. While she had always been drawn to social justice, in college the emotional force behind her activism took on an entirely new ferocity. "Suddenly it didn't seem like her beliefs and her politics were coming from compassion anymore but from vengeance," he says.

Their relationship grew strained. "It felt like she'd been given a script and that having a tortured relationship with your dad was a part of that script," Roger says, echoing something many other parents have said. She began sending him long texts filled with grievances. Sometimes they were about their family, sometimes broader accusations of systemic oppression. "There were a lot of half-truths," he says. "Some grounded in reality, some not." At one point over a school break, after hearing tirade after tirade about white men, Roger calmly repeated back to her some of her recent statements and then said, "You know, it sounds like you really hate men." That set her off. She felt like he had backed her into a corner. She went no contact.

Though Roger was hurt, he decided to take stock of what he might have done to contribute to this rift. He came to see that every one of his arguments, no matter how calmly and logically he presented them, seemed to her like a threat. "I learned that debating wasn't going to get us anywhere. I had to let go of the need to explain or reason."

He shifted strategies. He reached out and said plainly that he loved her very much. He stopped defending himself even when she made what he thought were unfair accusations. Instead, he listened and found places to ask for forgiveness. "It wasn't easy, but that's the long game."

With fraught relationships there can be a tendency to hear the other's hurt and feel defensive and want to solve it or avoid entering into it. The term for the latter such behavior is *relational bypassing.*[4] It can take the form of pat answers, defensiveness, or premature advice, keeping us emotionally distant. Validating the other's emotional experience is an important piece of moving forward.

Roger sensed that he needed to avoid bypassing and simply start listening to his daughter without any defenses up. That long game of shifting strategies has borne fruit slowly. Though Rebecca lives far away, they have gotten back in regular touch. She texts him, asks questions, even says she loves him. "I think deep down she knows I'm on her side and that nothing she does will ever change that."

He's also made peace with the occasional volatility. Holidays can still feel like emotional minefields. Sometimes she goes back into no or low contact. "My mom was like that. She was volatile but loving. I've accepted that there will always be some of that in Rebecca too." Everyone in the family is learning to be present but also have boundaries and the ability to step away if things intensify.

Although it would be easy for Roger to write off all responsibility for Rebecca's radicalization and volatility, he continues to try diligently to claim responsibility for his part as well where it's warranted. He leans on trusted friends like the godmothers for feedback. "Sometimes I ask, 'Am I seeing this right? Do I have blind spots here?'" It helps to have outside voices, he says. Through this feedback he has become more aware of how his own tendency to raise his voice has contributed to the tension in his family. "I've been reactive in the past. I like to think I've approached all of this in a measured way overall, but I can think of times when I got frustrated and yelled."

Roger recognizes that though things seem reconciled now, it could look different in six months. Part of the peace he has gained comes from striving to do the right thing as best he can. Doing this, he believes, can help him avoid the spiral of constantly questioning himself if she cuts him off again. "If you focus on doing the right thing, you can put your suffering into context. It doesn't derail you."

Know the Script

"It took less than a year of unrestricted internet access to turn me from a happy, loving kid who obsessively researched niche neurological conditions for fun, into a 12 year old who obsessively researched ways to kill herself because her parents refused to affirm her transgender identity."[5]

When Maia first told her mom that she identified as transgender, she could hardly speak. "There [were] so many things I wanted to say to my mom that day," she recalls. "But the words swirling around in my head kept forming a barricade at the base of my throat—and they wouldn't come out."[6]

Maia's parents' reaction wasn't what she wanted. They didn't affirm her new identity. They panicked, argued with her, and took away her internet. "As an adult, I now understand my parents' panic and their impulse to not affirm. I frankly don't know if I would have been able to handle the situation better than they did." Though she understands now, at the time it felt like betrayal. "I felt that a war was being waged against me." She says she needed someone to help slow down her thoughts, to assure her that everything would be okay so she could get to the bottom of why she felt this way.[7] "There is no arguing or debating your kid out of an identity crisis. This will only further entrench them in it, and the transgender identity will become the thing your adolescent will feel the existential need to protect at all costs."[8] Maia doesn't downplay the real distress she felt but recognizes that her parents' panic and arguing only made her want to transition more desperately.[9]

Though she didn't initially think she was suicidal, she began to be afraid of what she might do to herself after watching activists online speak of how a lack of gender affirmation by parents leads many kids to commit suicide. "I adopted a belief system as a young child which convinced me that my parents who were only trying to protect me, literally didn't care if I lived or died—simply because they refused to affirm an identity I had adopted during a time of adolescent confusion."[10]

Maia, now a detransitioner and back in relationship with her parents, believes their refusal to affirm her trans identity was an act of love. "[It] was ultimately in my best interest," she says. "It didn't prevent me from transitioning and sustaining harm as a result—though, had they affirmed, I would have been hurt by this far worse."[11]

Like many young people today and Rebecca in this chapter, Maia had absorbed an ideological script—a powerful narrative framework that dictated how her story was supposed to unfold. It told her that parental concern was violence, affirmation the only acceptable response, and dissent a form of rejection. The script framed her identity crisis in absolute terms, leaving little room for nuance or dialogue.

Not all parents recognize when their child is living within such a narrative. Without that understanding, their efforts to show love or express concern can unintentionally reinforce it. In Maia's case, her parents' panic and defensiveness confirmed the script's central message: They were opponents of her true self rather than allies in her search for it.

What can parents do instead of getting pulled into the script? The goal isn't to out-argue them, as Roger tried, and it's certainly not to tell them they have bought into a script.

The former doesn't work, because an ideological script isn't developed through reason nor will it be defeated by it. Pointing out the presence of script-like thinking won't work either, because it's insulting and hardly anyone is persuaded through being insulted. In fact, most people become more radicalized through such antagonism.

The only way to help break the script is to respond in a way that effectively undermines its power by refusing to play your part. Here are four practical steps for navigating a scripted dynamic:

1. *Recognize the script for what it is.* Your child is operating within a worldview that flattens complexity into good versus evil, victim versus oppressor. Within that frame, your concern can easily be misread as hostility. They will also have responses ready. Seeing the script clearly helps you stop taking things personally.

2. *Refuse escalation and instead opt for curiosity.* These frameworks thrive on emotional reactivity. Arguing, defending, or trying to prove your goodness confirms the very narrative you're trying to disprove. Instead, stay calm and be genuinely curious. Curiosity slows emotional reactivity and can foster deeper thought in the other, eventually weakening the script. One adult child, Kim, who experienced parental tension over her identity confusion told me that what kids often most need in these charged situations is to be seen: "What they often most need is for parents to pull back and become curious, asking things like 'How long have you been carrying this?' Instead of trying to fix them, see if they will let you bear their burdens."

3. *Affirm a deeper identity.* While curiosity lays a good foundation, eventually you will need to show your hand. Unconditional love doesn't mean unconditional agreement. Continue to show up with patience and warmth, even when that love seems ineffective. The script thrives on panic, escalation, and rejection. Remaining measured refuses the action-and-reaction cycle. Over time, consistent peace, presence, and affirmation of love dismantle the lie that your care is conditional or controlling. "Too often parents think they need to fix their child, but that can reduce the person to a problem," Kim told me. Her family never disowned her. They never affirmed her lifestyle either. What they did affirm was her life.

4. *Seek outside wisdom and support.* You don't have to navigate this alone. Find mentors, counselors, wise friends, or faith leaders who understand these dynamics and can help you stay clear, centered, and emotionally regulated.

By recognizing the script and choosing to respond with steady, unconditional love rather than capitulation, confrontation, or withdrawal, parents can begin to rewrite the narrative, opening pathways back to connection.

The Return

Yet even as parents work to reopen pathways to connection, one of the hardest questions remains: Is the relationship truly over—or is a season of silence an act of panic or a cry of pain disguised as self-protection? One father I spoke with described this confusion vividly: After the 2024 election, his daughter demanded no contact. Believing he was respecting her boundaries, he backed away only to learn later that she was hurt by what she perceived as his failure to try to reach out. Moments like this reveal the emotional and moral complexity of estranged relationships. For many parents, the hardest part is not the silence itself but how to interpret it: whether it signals finality or simply pain.

Attachment expert Adam Lane Smith warns that going no contact can be driven by a misguided desire to manipulate or reset a relationship but it's a strategy that can easily backfire. "No contact only works if you never want to see that person again," he explains. "If you're just starving the connection that you're experiencing, what you're doing is actually driving them away and treating them like an enemy."[12] He explains that when you cut someone off and experience the anxiety, anger, or stress that often accompanies no contact, your body releases cortisol, the stress hormone. Over time, your nervous system starts to associate that person with the feeling of stress, even if the goal was reconciliation. When you think about or see that person again, your body reacts as if they're a threat.

In effect, no contact teaches the body to stay in fight-or-flight mode when it comes to that relationship. That physiological pattern then makes emotional reengagement feel unsafe or impossible, and the other person perceives that distance as rejection, reinforcing the very disconnection you hoped to repair.

Smith cautions that attempting reconnection afterward can appear unstable. "Using no contact to try to bring a person back into your life? Not going to work," he says. What he advises instead is to "learn to regulate yourself and your own nervous system, build stronger friendship relations that are helping you co-regulate . . . and then have a clear discussion with the other person about the role they'd like to share in your life." Smith's advice is disarmingly simple: "Don't go no contact unless you never want to see them again."[13]

While a warning against going no contact may fall on deaf ears to someone who is firmly convinced it's necessary, it serves as a cultural reminder of how extreme such a decision truly is. Using it as a temporary tool makes reconciliation far more difficult. This reality presents those on the receiving end of no contact with a predicament: when to respect boundaries set and when to continue to reach out.

Beyond the physiological cortisol association that links the other person to stress and danger, another dynamic further entrenches the separation: Once we've declared someone irredeemable, we often feel compelled to keep reaffirming that judgment to ourselves. We replay old conflicts, amplify past wrongs, and rehearse our grievances as a way of maintaining the moral clarity that justified the cutoff in the first place. Over time, the story ossifies, and the possibility of reconciliation feels like a threat to the fragile peace we've built on our own righteousness.

In this way, no contact not only severs the relationship but also creates a psychological and moral need to protect one's narrative. The longer no contact persists, the more it reshapes memory and identity. What might have begun as a reaction to pain or confusion can calcify into a worldview that resists forgiveness and forecloses growth. Because of this, those who are on the receiving end of no contact must walk a careful line of expressing a desire for reunification while being willing to let go if it becomes clear that reunification is truly not the goal.

There isn't a concrete formula for exactly how to respond

given that it might not be obvious whether the other person is hoping for reconciliation or is dead set against it. A standard recommendation is to write an amends letter, an example of which we will look at in the final chapter. Its purpose is to take moral responsibility where appropriate in a way that isn't defensive nor accusatory. A good letter avoids justification or pleading and names and owns specific actions, acknowledging their impact and expressing genuine regret. It recognizes the other person's pain without presuming to interpret it. The focus stays on accountability and growth—what you've learned and what you hope to do differently—while releasing the other person from any obligation to respond.

Finally, lasting reconciliation means respecting the freedom of the other. In the parable of the prodigal son, a young man goes to his father to demand his inheritance be given to him to do with as he wills. The father, a reflection of God's benevolence, respects his son's freedom and complies with the demand. The son takes his portion and goes into a *chōran makran,* which translates to "a great empty place" (a land of alienation and commodification),[14] where he squanders his inheritance and eventually hires himself out to feed swine. Having hit rock bottom, he realizes the rich abundance in his father's home and the bankruptcy of his current life, so he returns home.

As he is returning, the father sees him from far off, signifying that he is waiting and watching for his return. He runs to meet him. This is a small detail in the story, but it's significant. It shows a lack of bitterness and an eagerness to restore the relationship. Had he needed a grand demonstration of repentance, he wouldn't have run. Had he shared the calculating spirit of the older brother, he wouldn't have run. That the father runs to his son as soon as he realizes his son is turning homeward reveals a freedom from the corrosive human responses to division: defensiveness, rumination, self-pity, and hard-heartedness. There is no shaming lecture, no relitigating of the past, only an embrace and a rejoicing in the restoration of his sonship.

For parents navigating estrangement, the father in this parable offers a blueprint. He doesn't celebrate his son's departure into the *chōran makran* nor chase after him. He doesn't lick his wounds and recount his grievances. His posture is one of readiness: watching, waiting, and tending to those still in his care.

Reengagement will look different in every family; it might never follow the tidy arc of the prodigal son's story. Some children may not return for years; others may never return in this life.

At the end of part 2, we will consider what it means to live without closure, without such a joyous ending. But between now and then, we will explore the personal and collective need to reorient our understanding of family, authority, and disagreement as bulwarks against the fragmentation of the age. Each of the three is reconceived by ideology to be damaging: The family is oppressive, authority is identical to authoritarianism, and disagreement is a threat. Yet each of the three, properly understood, serves as an essential antidote to what most ails us: Family humanizes, authority stabilizes, and disagreeing well civilizes.

7

FAMILY IS HUMANIZING

Far from being a structure of domination, the family is where our most human needs are met. It's in the family home where dependence is met with duty, and duty is softened and propelled by affection and intimacy. Modern ideologies often depict family ties as constraints to be overcome, but in truth, they are the bonds that dignify both the person in need and the person giving care—and each of us moves into and out of either category throughout life.

Once the family is reduced to a battleground of power, it becomes disturbingly easy to recast abandonment as virtue. What follows is one of the clearest and most heartbreaking examples I've encountered.

Anne, a recently widowed mother and grandmother, sat down with me to discuss her thirty-year-old son, Michael. The conversation was punctuated by nervous laughter and some understandable trepidation about sharing what is naturally private. She and her late husband raised five children, four of whom still live nearby, remain active in their churches, and maintain a close connection with Anne.

Michael lives several states away, in Philadelphia, where

he's resided for more than a decade after marrying a woman from that area. Michael was always gifted, Anne told me. His youth was marked by academic achievements. During his college years, the tragic illness and death of a girlfriend shook Michael's faith to its core. While he remained connected to the family, his presence became more reserved. The family knew Michael had started moving leftward in his politics, so they avoided political conversations altogether. Interactions were limited because of distance, but visits—when they happened—were warm and pleasant.

As is the case for so many other families, the year 2020 calcified those differences. Anne's late husband was battling pancreatic cancer at the time, and in 2021 Michael made the trip to visit his father in their family home in St. Louis. He knew his mom and dad were vaccinated and assumed his siblings were as well. At the start of his visit, he discovered several had chosen not to take the Covid vaccine. He abruptly ended what was to be a weeklong visit, packed his things, and caught a flight home. "He was very stubborn, and we didn't fight him on it," his mother recalls. "But my husband was devastated. He asked, 'Will I ever see Michael again?'" Anne relayed his concern to her son. He told her that he understood the concern and acknowledged that this was likely the last time he would see him but reiterated that he was unwilling to visit his father under the same roof as people who hadn't received the shot.

Months later, Michael returned for his father's funeral. He was polite, even kind, and rejoined the extended family at their large reunion the following year. Things seemed to improve. But when the 2024 election season came around, tensions flared again, this time publicly. Along with many others, Michael took to social media the morning after the election, clearly distressed by the results. He expressed a suspicion that his family had voted for Trump and vented his disgust and anger toward them. Later that day, Anne's phone registered an incoming call from her son.

Having seen his post that morning, Anne looked at the phone with dread. "I picked up, but I was hoping this wasn't what I thought it was."

"Who did you vote for?" he asked.

"I don't think I need to share that with anybody, Michael," she replied.

"Then I'm going to assume you voted for Trump, and I don't think I can move on from that."

What followed was an excruciating exchange. Anne describes Michael as not quite disrespectful, but his words were cutting. He compared her to the worst kind of people, lumping her in with bigots and dictators. She tried to explain her stance: that she didn't like Trump but voted pro-life. "You shouldn't have voted at all," he insisted.

Realizing the conversation was going nowhere, she told him, "I love you, Michael."

"I love you too, Mom. Goodbye."

He left the family group chat shortly afterward and hasn't responded to texts since.

Her other children are a mix of sad and angry. Some feel he owes the family an apology—especially after shaming them publicly online. But Anne sees it differently and told her children, "Our faith tells us to forgive. You may not completely trust him without an apology, but you accept him back if he is ever willing to return."

Despite the pain, she focuses on the good. She has four children nearby and six grandchildren she sees often. The various kids and grandkids have her over for family dinners;

Anne babysits the grands regularly. "I count my blessings," she says with deliberation. "And I wait in hope."

A Command and a Warning

To restore human wholeness and reclaim a clear-eyed vision of family—its true meaning and indispensable role—we must first measure the modern threats against a deeper, enduring understanding of its significance. Nowhere is this contrast more striking than in the command to honor one's parents, whose observance carries lasting personal and cultural consequences, shaping whether society is generative or declines into degeneracy.

From the earliest records of human thought, the family has stood at the center of debates about society, virtue, authority, and human flourishing—and at least since Plato, people have understood that the family is a force that limits the power of politics. Is the family a given—a pre-political institution that arises organically from the facts of our embodiment and procreation? Or is the family a social construct—a malleable arrangement shaped by economics, ideology, and custom? The stakes of this debate couldn't be higher. If the family is a natural and necessary institution, it deserves protection from external intrusion. If it's only socially constructed, it can be redesigned, even dismantled, in the name of progress.

It's no accident that many of the world's enduring civilizations placed the family at the center of moral and civic life. In Confucian thought, family piety is the cornerstone of social harmony. Aristotle likewise believed that a just city could be built only on rightly ordered households.

The Old Testament elevates family even further by enshrining familial piety in the Ten Commandments, following immediately after duties to God. The Torah doesn't command children to love their parents; it commands them to honor them. As Rabbi Jonathan Sacks writes, "The Torah is a book of laws, not feelings."[1] According to the Talmud, the commandment is practical: Help them; speak respectfully; stand when they enter a room. There are also specific examples of things from which a son or daughter should refrain, such as sitting in a parent's designated seat, contradicting them in public, calling them by their first name, and shaming or humiliating them.[2] Even if the relationship is strained, the obligation remains.

It also is the only one of the Ten Commandments that is accompanied by a promise. Exodus 20:12 states, "Honor your father and your mother, that you may have a long life in the land the LORD your God is giving you." This promise carries an implicit warning: A society that abandons this mandate won't flourish. Old Testament scholar Dennis Prager notes that many people read the second half of the command as a reward. "But while it may be regarded as a reward, the fact remains that it is a reason: if you build a society in which children honor their parents, your society will long survive. And the corollary is: a society in which children do not honor their parents is doomed to self-destruction."[3] Why would societal stability depend on this command? Prager suggests that family unity is among the best antidotes to totalitarianism. "One of the first things totalitarian movements seek to do is to break the child–parent bond. . . . Even in democratic societies, the larger the state becomes, the more it usurps the parental role."[4]

In the Talmud, honoring one's parents is likened to honoring God, as parental authority is seen as a bridge to divine authority.[5] Accordingly, to dishonor one's parents carries not merely familial and social repercussions but spiritual ones. Parents are owed reverence—not because of their moral perfection, but because they, in cooperation with God, gave their child life.

That parents are imperfect is a given, and the reality of imperfect parents doesn't weaken the law; it reinforces it. A child who learns to honor a flawed parent gains the moral grammar to honor other forms of authority: flawed teachers, traditions when they feel inconvenient, and ultimately God. Though God isn't imperfect, our perception of him is, and honoring imperfect persons in our immediate sphere can scale up and out by habituating us to separate our emotions and desires from our duties to society and to God. To collapse our duties into our desires in the name of liberation is to unlearn the very conditions of human dignity, religious commitment, and social cohesion.

In neither the Jewish nor the Christian tradition does honor of a parent mean enabling abuse, obedience in all things (or obedience in adulthood), or pretending that harm didn't happen. In such cases, honor might look like forgiveness, respectful distance, and prayer, not closeness. "[The Bible] does not demand what may be psychologically or emotionally impossible," writes Prager. "But it does demand that we show honor to our parents. And it makes this demand only with regard to parents."[6]

Preserving this relationship reverberates well into the future. Rabbi Sacks writes, "The family—man, woman, and child—is not one lifestyle choice among many. It is the best means we have yet discovered for nurturing future generations. . . . It is where one generation passes on its values to the next, ensuring the continuity of a civilization."[7] And if we fail to honor our parents, we are failing not only them but also our children. The commandment underscores that history itself is familial and that the preservation of the family is for the sake of what has been and what is to come.

In an age of irreverence, Old Testament commandments might seem uncompelling, until the pathologies that flow from our dismissal of them cast them as prescient. Anne's story is one I've heard versions of time and again: formerly close and well-functioning families rent apart over the course of the last five years. While Anne's story is a personal tragedy, it isn't merely that. Michael's future children won't know their grandmother nor aunts, uncles, or cousins if this persists, nor will he have the consolation of a shared history with his siblings through the inevitable crises of life. Their story is also a microcosm of a deeper civilizational disorder. The family as a pre-political institution means it exists *prior to* the state rather than as a creation of the state to be revoked at will. For many families now, the political has invaded and decentered the familial and now claims a higher personal loyalty.

"I Did Not Consent to Be Born"

In the politics of estrangement, not only is the fourth (or, if you're Protestant, fifth) commandment rejected, but it's also inverted in several ways. In a conversation on family estrangement, *New York Times* bestselling author and neuropsychologist Rick Hanson and his son, Forrest, outline a view that is typical in no-contact forums. In Forrest's words, "One way or the other, a parent makes the choice to have a child—a child does not make the choice to be born."[8]

Rick concurs: "You inflict consciousness on unsuspecting

flesh; you owe it a lot."[9] He goes on to ask questions that introduce some complexities to estrangement. But the framing of the conversation reflects a common thread among those who have severed ties with their parents: Parents make the decision to bring a child into the world, they argue, and their child didn't consent to that decision. Thus, any obligation in the relationship is one directional and entirely on the side of the parents—not on the child and not even on the adult child. Implicit in this script is that one's own life is not a blessing but a burden. The response to one's life, then, is not gratitude but grievance. Parents have power, so the duty in the relationship is theirs and theirs alone.

The idea of parenthood as the nonconsensual infliction of life is gaining traction, and so are its troubling implications. In a short documentary for *The New York Times,* filmmaker Iris Zaki explores the tensions between three adult daughters (Zaki and two friends), who have chosen to remain child-free, and their mothers, who struggle to understand that choice. In it the daughters swap mothers and sit down one-on-one for candid conversations. One mother speaks to Zaki of how motherhood reshapes a woman and helps her to grow in ways that are hard to anticipate. By way of example, the mother says it makes women less spontaneous and pushes their needs aside.

Zaki smiles and says, "This just reinforces why I'm not interested in it." She explains, adding that it traps women in a "traditional, feminine role." When the mother gently suggests that this perspective might be a bit selfish, Zaki reverses the charge. "Having a child can actually be seen as selfish. We see it the other way around. Because I see this world for what it is. It's only getting worse." Zaki tells her that to bring a child into this mess is to place a burden upon that child. "It breaks my heart. I always tell my parents: 'You never asked me if I wanted to be born.' Honestly, that's the biggest reason I'm child-free."[10]

This exchange captures the reigning moral filters of our time of autonomy and victimhood. It doesn't matter if something is good—if I didn't consent to it, then it's an assault on my autonomy, thereby victimizing me. By this logic, even the most foundational objective good—being—is recast as harm, privation as good, and parenthood is recast as something selfish. This inverted moral grammar makes us not just ambivalent toward but repelled by the activities that meet our deepest human longings for belonging, significance, permanence. The sacrifices of family life, and suffering itself, make no sense through this lens.

It's certain and obvious that parents have grave duties toward their children and that children begin life with little capacity for practical reciprocity. The mistake is to view this asymmetry primarily through a lens of power, where consent becomes the sole criterion for evaluating it. This reductive framework renders the parent-child dynamic as inherently fraught. The problem is parental duty isn't grounded in guilt over the nonconsensual nature of the relationship. Parental duty is grounded in gratitude for having participated in something quite grand and for the vulnerable and needy life entrusted to one's care.

Framing parental obligation as a unilateral exercise of power strips human relationships of spiritual depth and upends the meaning of family. It also obscures the reality that honoring one's parents benefits not just the parents but the child, who, through maturity, is invited into the goods of reverence, service, and awe.

Vulnerability is a weakness only if our measure is power; if our measure is love, then it's not a weakness but an invitation to service and reverence. But all of that is hard to see in our prevailing framework of materialism and individualism. Instead, children are taught to fixate on autonomy, seeing their own existence as an imposition, and their origin story as life inflicted on unsuspecting flesh. It's hard to imagine a more mechanistic and resentful formulation of the meaning of life than to cast it as a form of nonconsensual assault.

This nihilistic approach to life is socially sterile and surely contributes to the reality that young adults are increasingly opting out of parenthood altogether. If the choice to have a child is a selfish one, a burden to your progeny, then why do it? If the act of bearing children exposes you to lifelong scrutiny and potential condemnation, then why take the risk?

Parenting is tiring, physically and emotionally. It's hard work, and its benefits can be realized more longitudinally than immediately and maybe not even then if estrangement is normalized. It's challenging enough to try to sustain the sacrifices of family life amid a culture that supports and honors it. But it's nearly impossible when the meaning and purpose of it are obscured.

Once we can no longer perceive the good of family life, the duties that once animated that life—sacrifice, service, forgiveness—begin to feel intolerable. What was a vocation of love is flattened into rote obligation and we lose the very ability to form habits of life that make family harmony feasible. The result is families functioning poorly or young adults rejecting parenthood altogether.

A 2025 piece in *The New Yorker* confirms this cultural diagnosis: People are opting out of parenthood. The demographic decline is alarming and undeniable, and it shouldn't be seen as merely a conservative concern. "For most of human history," Gideon Lewis-Kraus writes, "having children was something the majority of people simply did without thinking too much about it. Now it is one competing alternative among many." While there are multicausal explanations, he claims one cause is threaded throughout: "The only overarching explanation for the global fertility decline is that once childbearing is no longer seen as something special—as an obligation to God, to one's ancestors, or to the future—people will do less of it."[11]

In her essay "We Have Been Subverted," conservative Somalian-born writer and activist Ayaan Hirsi Ali describes the dismantling of civilization using Soviet-inspired tactics, which unfolds in four stages.[12] This four-stage framework she learned from former KGB agent Yuri Bezmenov, but his insights only gave formal structure to the pattern of subversion familiar to her because of its impact in Somalia. The four stages are demoralization, destabilization, crisis, and normalization.

The first stage of demoralization takes the longest period of time and is meant to undermine a society's ideas, institutions, and structures. Old ways of thinking, unifying symbols, and old heroes are systematically discredited as a means of making what is obviously good for us seem bad. "Demoralization of the family is probably a familiar concept to us all. It involves promoting ideas that weaken the bonds between members of the family, promoting narcissistic individualism over family unity, creating financial stressors that discourage family formation, acrimony between the sexes, and the replacement of parental authority with the state."[13]

Once society is weakened through demoralization, destabilization follows. Civic life fractures into volatile political and identitarian tribes and the social fabric unravels.[14] The same logic that fractures public life also moves inward, colonizing the private sphere and pitting family members and friends against one another: men against women, women against men, parents against children, children against parents.

Crisis marks the third stage of subversion. At this point, society crosses a tipping point where things that are good for us—and foundationally so—are treated instinctively with suspicion and cynicism. Isolating, abandoning, opting out, all seem like entirely reasonable acts of emotional sophistication.[15] As Hirsi Ali notes, at this stage subversion advances on its own, erupting eventually in a series of crises that expose the depth of the rot.[16]

Therapist Rachel Haack observes in the rise of estrangement a lunging toward the crisis and normalization stages. "Even in religious spaces, this narrative is gaining traction. I've seen pastors and religious influencers online emphasize the importance of cutting off parents as a show of strength in one's marriage—turning what was once a biblical passage about the prioritization of the marital bond into justification for total cutoffs. It's become a black-and-white interpretation: Leave and cleave means sever and discard. But that was never the spirit of the text. Prioritizing your marriage doesn't require abandoning your family. It requires maturity, boundaries, and balance—not estrangement."[17] And to the point of the promise and warning embedded in the fourth commandment, if we can't support the good of familial unity, how can we hope to support civilizational unity?

The fourth and final stage, normalization, occurs when the subversion is so culturally and institutionally supported that it no longer seems subversive at all.[18] At that point estrangement might be met with a shrug because family life would be broadly understood to be optional, predictably harmful, and entirely subordinate to political allegiances.

Individualism, Tyranny, or Interdependence

Against this tide of subversion, twentieth-century figures like G. K. Chesterton and Christopher Lasch defended the family as the foundational institution of a free society. Chesterton wrote, "Without the family we are helpless before the State."[19] Lasch warned that as the family weakens, individuals become more vulnerable to manipulation by bureaucracies and therapeutic culture.[20] Without the moral formation and rooted identity provided by the family, we become atomized, anxious, and easily controlled. These thinkers, and many others, pushed back against deconstruction to reclaim the idea that the family isn't a creation of the state; it is its precondition, limiting the state and protecting individuals from isolation. When the political is prior, it quickly metastasizes to become total, eventually consuming every space and redefining every relationship.

Philosopher Hannah Arendt also saw the connection between the health of the family and the health of civic life with piercing clarity. In her book *The Human Condition*, Arendt draws a vital distinction between the private and public spheres of life, arguing that the private realm of the household concerns the necessary parts of life such as eating, sleeping, reproduction, and survival. These are the conditions that make human life possible, and they are inescapable. The private sphere functions as the ground where durable human bonds are formed and where persons become capable of meaningful public life. In the domain of the private, necessity governs daily routines, and relationships are hierarchical.

By contrast, the public realm, Arendt claims, is where individuals transcend necessity and emerge as equals, engaging in speech and action to shape a common world. True civic freedom, she argues, is possible in this space only if the private realm of necessity is protected. It's the shelter of the private sphere that allows people the stability and rootedness necessary to appear in the public as free participants. When the two realms are confused—when the private is politicized or the public is burdened with the needs of the household—both are undone. Intimacy becomes transactional and conditional, and freedom among equals becomes impossible, for the public realm can't meet needs that are familial. In such a collapse of categories, neither genuine intimacy nor authentic public freedom can survive.[21]

We see the consequences of this collapse in the confusion surrounding identity. The family is organized to sustain the existence of its members and by extension affirm that existence. Tenderness is a particularly familial means of doing this—it's an intuitive sensitivity to the needs and vulnerabilities of another person. The gaze of parents toward their baby silently proclaims, *It is good that you exist.* There is nothing to fix, only something to behold and cherish.

As a child grows, tenderness should be joined to truth. Parents offer the unconditional affirmation that grounds a child's being while introducing the boundaries, expectations, and moral realities that shape character. This combination of unconditional belonging with the steady disclosure of truth forms the basis of a stable identity. Without it, the self has no place to stand.

When we reject the importance of daily sacrificial love in the home, we don't eliminate the human need for it. Instead, we shift that need into the public realm, where it can't be met rightly. This dislocation is visible in the rise of identity politics. People define themselves by their wounds and insist on unqualified affirmation from all. But as Arendt foresaw, removing the goods of intimacy and necessity from the private sphere doesn't liberate us—it distorts us, destabilizing the very idea of a shared, free civic life.

This is what happens when politics becomes total. The family ceases to be a sanctuary of love and becomes a theater of ideological purity tests. A son refusing a visit with his dying father hasn't simply made a political choice; he has allowed politics to colonize his home and his humanity. What remains is neither family nor polity but a barren landscape where nothing is sacred, no one is free, and the conditions for human dignity are destroyed.

Preservation of the family is the antidote to the two societal extremes of radical individualism and totalitarianism. But the two extremes aren't really opposed so much as mutually reinforcing. Extreme individualism disregards the bonds that restrain the rise of totalizing power, while totalitarianism, in turn, intensifies isolation by usurping and devaluing those bonds. The family forms the first line of resistance to both, grounding the individual in love, duty, and belonging before any totalizing state or isolating ideology can lay claim.

Re-Moralizing the Family

To counter demoralization, we must recover a moral vocabulary that restores meaning to family bonds. We need to start by clearly exposing the problems and pathologies that are demoralizing us and, as Haack urges, re-moralizing the family: "We need language like *loyalty, forgiveness, responsibility,* and *repair.* Because if we want a future where families can thrive, we need more than boundaries. We need wisdom."[22]

For many in my generation (Gen X), the idea of re-moralizing the family might evoke awkward memories from the 90s of televangelists or figures from the Christian Coalition touting family values. Former vice president Dan Quayle's 1992 ham-fisted condemnation of the television sitcom *Murphy Brown* illustrates how such moralizing was refracted through media. Quayle was discussing the problem of fatherlessness and stated, "It doesn't help matters when prime-time TV has Murphy Brown—a character who supposedly epitomizes today's intelligent, highly paid, professional woman—mocking the importance of fathers, by bearing a child alone, and calling it just another lifestyle choice."[23]

He was referring to a storyline in which the character of Brown, a single, successful journalist, decides to have and raise a child on her own. Quayle's comments were widely derided. Critics accused him of being out of touch and attacking a fictional character instead of addressing real-world problems.

Three decades later that scuffle seems quaint. One mother I interviewed mentioned that her daughter's anxiety was exacerbated after watching all four seasons of the popular Netflix show *13 Reasons Why* about a teen girl's posthumous release of the thirteen reasons (and persons) responsible for her decision to commit suicide.[24] Some critics objected that the show glamorized revenge, valorized emotional woundedness, and depicted the raw landscape of teen suicide, sexual assault, and trauma with unflinching detail. But these critiques were largely met with a collective shrug—they were both true and yet irrelevant to a culture that seemed to have given up on the possibility of wholesome media content for adolescents.

The accelerated moral decline as reflected in these two shows in some ways creates new opportunities. While Quayle's "family values" rhetoric was easily mocked in the nineties, for many young adults today family life is experienced not as a stifling old-fashioned imperative but as a foreign country—or even a lifeline. Gen X may recoil at talk of re-moralizing the family, but a growing contingent of the youth is instinctively returning to it, seeking stability in the very places their culture taught them to dismiss.

Here again the pandemic in 2020 served as an inflection point: While for many families it was a time of unraveling, other young adults moved to the countryside, baked sourdough, planted gardens, and took up knitting. Though some of this can be superficial, there are deeper stirrings as well. Easter 2025 saw a record number of conversions among young adults to Christianity, many of whom now gravitate toward pre-boomer forms of Christian liturgy.[25] This isn't yet a mass cultural return, but it is a sorting. Some members of Gen Z are drifting further into the atomization and nihilism of the age; others are clawing their way toward meaning. Neither group should be entirely lionized nor dismissed.

What is increasingly clear is that, for the vast majority, the cultural rot was absorbed passively, through the ambient culture that shaped their imagination. The implicit rejection of older moral frameworks cleared the path for the ideological grammar of the Empowerment Delusion in which power and woundedness define the self.

To re-moralize the family is to clearly unmask the causes of its subversion while also confidently putting forward a positive and grounded vision of why it's our most fundamental humanizing force. The desires that the Empowerment Delusion attempts to address are not themselves delusions. Our longing for autonomy masks a deeper longing for freedom, rightly understood. The insistence on self-definition reflects a hunger to be known as singular and irreplaceable. Our fixation on wounds expresses a real desire for recognition and healing. These desires are not wrong. But when filtered through ideology, they are endlessly inflamed and never fulfilled.

The problem is not our longing but the lens through which we evaluate and direct it. If I were to sit down at the finest chef's table in Paris and evaluate the meal before me solely through the lens of utility, I would be blind to most of what is actually before me. "Will this satiate my hunger?" is the wrong question to ask. The years of apprenticeship, the precision of technique, the aesthetic vision, the passion and craftsmanship poured into that creation—all would be rendered invisible by the reductive lens of mere biological need. Through the wrong filter, the meal becomes indistinguishable from a McChicken.

The modern mind also applies the wrong filter when it looks at the family. We have come to see it through a utilitarian, power-oriented, and therapeutic lens rather than a human one. "Does this relationship still serve me? Has it been rocky? Does it enhance my well-being?" we might ask ourselves. Such a reductive filter applied to family renders invisible the history, the struggles, the sorrows and triumphs, the lineage of sacrifice that make each relationship and life possible.

South Korean–born philosopher Byung-Han—an insightful diagnostician of our current ills—observes that our age is ruled by "the aesthetics of the smooth," a world of frictionless surfaces. To illustrate the aesthetics of the smooth, he points to iPhones, Brazilian waxes, and Jeff Koons's sculptures. In the aesthetic of Koons, there is "no disaster, no injury, no ruptures, also no seams." Seams would indicate effort, a tension in holding things together. The smooth has no such interruption, no sense of history or labor; it offers nothing to resist our will, nothing that asks for patience or contemplation. And because it offers us no resistance, it also excludes beauty. Beauty arises only where there is otherness—something that unsettles us, stops us, and draws us beyond ourselves.[26]

The family, too, involves a sort of friction, a long history, the capacity for injury, and the potential for a depth of love—all of which can expand our souls. It isn't made for the aesthetics of the smooth. Family relationships are marked by imperfection and obligation, by the friction of one will against another and the call to extend and receive forgiveness. Family life demands endurance, but it isn't a demand that makes sense according to a calculation of utility. It makes sense for the cultivation of our humanity.

Gratitude is the posture that allows us to perceive this reality rightly. It disposes us toward reverence. To be born into a family is to live in the tension of dependence and inheritance. Of course, I didn't choose to be born. Neither did you. It's not a clever question to ask. It's like asking if the greatest Parisian chef has made something that will satiate your hunger—maybe, but you're missing the point.

To re-moralize the family is to recover a moral vision rooted in gratitude for our lives and reverence for all that had to unfold, without our effort and without our consent, to make our existence possible. Gratitude restores a sense of duty and awe toward those who came before us, inviting us to recognize that we are heirs long before we are agents. Against the aesthetics of the smooth, gratitude reengages us with the roughness of reality in a way that exposes the boredom of the seamless.

Family Ecology as an Affirmation of Being

Besides speaking the truth about the deeper and humanizing vision of the family against the aesthetics of the smooth, an essential piece of re-moralizing the family is to forward a compelling and rooted vision of family in our particular homes and communities.

I sat down with Kristen, a thirty-six-year-old wife and mother who neglected in her own family to see the importance of family history. "I read a book on family life that talks about having photos up in your home of ancestors.[27] At the time I didn't have any. My mother-in-law had even made a collage of photos of my husband, Sam, and also his great-great-grandmother, great-grandmother, grandparents, et cetera, and I had it put away in the linen closet, seeing no value in it." Kristen was struck by the book's suggestion and began to wonder if honoring family history might provide a highly relevant context for their family now and into the future. She took the collage out of the closet and dusted it off; it now hangs on their wall along with photos of Kristen's own great-grandparents, who met in Boston after emigrating from Spain and Ireland and went on to have ten children.

From this experience, Kristen began to consider that while our lives aren't strictly determined by our ancestry, we are undeniably shaped by it. Our family histories can ripple through generations, influencing how we relate and respond to one another. For Kristen, what she once saw as a personal flaw—her choleric tendencies—became, through family context, part of a broader picture. "Sam now finds my emotion in an argument endearing," she says, laughing. "His family is all northern European—German, et cetera. When he doesn't show emotion, I now understand that doesn't mean he doesn't care about what I'm saying. It could, and I can ask to clarify, but it's not usually the case." Hanging old photos won't cure all that ails us, but it can serve as a bridge—a small but meaningful way to better understand one another and to weave families more tightly together. It's one way to begin remoralizing the family through concrete acts.

I've seen a similar effect in the way conversations can be subtly redirected. In my extended family, political and religious differences run deep. Over the years, those differences have left us either hardened or painfully raw, depending on the season. Many of us grew weary of discussions that never seemed to lead anywhere but division. I noticed that our family gatherings (surely by the intention of some) increasingly became focused on our shared history. Some took care to tell old stories of relatives long gone; others, especially the younger adults, leaned in—asking questions, pressing for more detail, trying to chart the terrain of lives that came before them. Piece by piece, we began to reassemble a shared narrative, renewing old affections and reaffirming a common identity based not on agreement but on belonging and a sneaking sense of providence.

Every culture must find a way to hold together past, present, and future, and the primary vehicle for that continuity is the family. The family isn't merely a private arrangement or social convenience; it's a transgenerational institution in which individuals learn who they are, where they come from, and what they are for.

Inculcating and safeguarding the traditions that shape a family culture may require only small, repeated acts of intentionality—but such efforts are far from insignificant. They often take simple forms: old stories, yearly camping trips, holiday rituals, shared meals, and daily habits. Our own family practices include all the above, as well as something seemingly trivial: inside jokes. My husband and I never kept baby books or scrapbooks, but we did keep a journal—aptly named *The Funny Things Book*—where we recorded the moments that made us laugh together. Whenever one of the kids said something amusing, we wrote it down. Eventually, they began searching for humor in the everyday, eager to see whether a moment was worthy of being added to the book. Now and then, one of them would shout, "Let's go through *The Funny Things Book*!" and all would squeal with delight as we revisited and laughed together at those small, shared memories. Now, years later, all six children—spanning from teens to adults—are delightfully funny, from slapstick to dry wit, and genuinely eager to be together. Human beings are naturally drawn to fun. It's a kind of social gravity; it pulls people toward one another.

Laughter can be a barometer of the moral atmosphere of a family. The bonds of family can be forged by the affection that accompanies laughter. But when laughter disappears, it can be an early sign of deeper division. One woman I spoke with, whose extended family had fractured because of political differences, described this warning sign: The precursor to estrangement was that laughter had entirely evaporated. She remembered gatherings years before where everyone had laughed freely. Over time, as political tensions flared and the social environment grew more polarized, those gatherings became minefields, leaving everyone too anxious to abandon themselves in the way that allows freedom and space for laughter.

Identity, whether familial or national, is transmitted through shared memory and a living culture. Pope John Paul II had this insight when Poland's national identity was under assault by the Communists as it had been earlier by the Nazis. He knew that totalitarian regimes seek to erase a people's memory, language, rituals, and sense of place in order to remake them in the image of the new state. In response, he championed the revitalization of Polish culture—its history, art, religious traditions, and familial bonds—as a way of safeguarding the soul of the nation. Likewise, today, as the concept of personal identity is fractured and politicized, the antidote is found not in ideological debate alone but in the recovery of family culture: shared meals and activities, inherited stories that are peculiar or heroic or hilarious, modeling intergenerational care, and having rituals and religious commitments that ground a person in something deeper than their latest self-perception. Just as a nation remembers itself through culture, a person remembers who they are through the living traditions of the home.

For author Wendell Berry, family and community are moral pillars necessary for any society that hopes to endure: "Community, however, aspires toward stability. It strives to balance change with constancy. That is why community life places such high value on neighborly love, marital fidelity, local loyalty, the integrity and continuity of family life, respect for the old, and instruction of the young."[28] His vision pushes against the grain of our culture's elevation of autonomy, which often frames fidelity, obligation, and generational continuity as threats to personal freedom. But Berry understands what many are now beginning to rediscover: that the family is the moral ecology in which virtues are grown, tested, and handed down. When estrangement severs these bonds, it doesn't merely end a relationship; it unmoors a person from the very structure that teaches what it means to belong and to be themselves.

To re-moralize the family, then, isn't to retreat into tradition for its own sake—it's to reclaim the human need that safeguards *individuals* from disintegration.

One way to grasp the spiritual and civic importance of family and place is through analogy: The body is to the soul as the home is to the family and as the land is to the community. Just as the body provides a material form through which the soul is made visible, the home gives tangible shape to the life of the family; it shelters, grounds, and expresses the shared life within. Likewise, land is not just a resource but a medium through which community life takes root and is sustained. As persons become fragmented by the disembodiment that comes from an increasingly ideological and virtual world, so too family fragmentation can make home seem not like a haven but like a hellhole, and a community severed from its land loses its identity. In each case, the visible form isn't incidental; it hosts, protects, and reveals something hidden that makes human life meaningful. In an age of disembodiment, individualism, mobility, and technology, reconnecting these dots is an existential necessity.

The physical realities of body, home, and land impose limits—and not as burdens to be overcome, but as the very boundaries that make love, cooperation, and coherence possible. A body locates and defines a person; a home gathers the scattered elements of life into a center; land offers continuity, memory, and belonging. All three demand stewardship and self-restraint, yet they offer in return a profound richness: connection, rootedness, and meaning.

Revolutionary projects displace concrete, embodied love with ideological abstractions. The worth of a new human life is weighed against data sets and models of climate change. A dying father becomes a symbol in a broader political cause. Dostoevsky captured this displacement through the words of a medical doctor in *The Brothers Karamazov,* who proclaims that the more he loves humanity in general, the less he loves man in particular.[29]

Estrangement feels like an amputation because something native to us has been severed. The modern ideal of autonomy insists we are whole on our own, but our bodies and our souls tell us otherwise. From the moment of birth, we cry out for connection. In death, we cry out again. It's no wonder that, in an autonomous and fearful society, we increasingly avert our eyes from both. Birth and death speak to our poverty, what we owe one another, and the limits of our lives. Through those experiences, we come to know that our lives are smaller and more mysterious than we thought, and that knowledge reorders us. Reverence becomes the only tenable response.

These kinds of reorientations toward truth in thought and practice gently loosen the grip of tribalism and lessen the totalizing pull of political ideology. In reconnecting with family history, we begin to see the person who came before us reflected in the person sitting beside us. In that connection, something unspoken is affirmed: *It is good that you are.* Josef Pieper puts this simply, that to love someone is to say, "It is *good* that you exist."[30] In this light, the family is not merely a social arrangement but a metaphysical affirmation. It's our first school in the truth that life isn't a burden; it's a gift. Not just life in the abstract, but *your* particular life. When a family is functioning rightly, it teaches this truth again and again in the most personal ways—across diapers and dinner tables, during chores and arguments, in hospital rooms and funeral homes. It's an invitation into the limitless mystery that extends before and beyond us and the surprising realization that we are each smaller and nobler than we thought.

8

AUTHORITY IS STABILIZING

"Question authority." Timothy Leary's countercultural slogan captured a spirit of rebellion in the 1960s, but its consequences reached far beyond its milieu. A healthy skepticism of power is both wise and arguably an ingrained American value. But there is a profound difference between questioning authority in a particular instance and rejecting the very idea of authority in principle. The former guards against tyranny; the latter invites it. When legitimate authority is dismantled, it leaves a vacuum—one that is rarely left empty for long.

The great irony of our time is that by rejecting authority, we've made ourselves more vulnerable to authoritarianism. We tend to confuse the two, as if authority is just domination in disguise. Blurring the line between authority and authoritarianism has led to a deep cultural suspicion of all authority—and, in turn, decades of permissive parenting endorsed by experts alongside an undermining of parental rights in law and policy.

True authority, as its etymology suggests (*augēre:* "to cause to grow"), is generative. Its role is not to control but to cultivate. In healthy families, authoritative parents offer structure and love in tandem. In healthy societies, parental authority is seen as something to foster in culture and policy. The absence of such authority doesn't produce freedom—it leads to degeneracy, cultural sterility, and fragmentation.

To see why authority is stabilizing rather than oppressive, consider how it unfolds in the life of a family. New parents begin with near-total control over their infant's life—they decide where the baby goes and sleeps and what and when the baby eats. Yet while they hold control and technically have parental authority, they don't yet possess the sort of hard-won authority associated with wisdom. It would be laughable, for example, if brand-new parents began pontificating on parenting from a place of their parental "authority." As children grow, this dynamic should reverse: Parents ought to gradually relinquish control while gaining moral authority, ideally leading to adult children who are independent but still value their parents' wisdom and guidance.

This natural progression from control to authority can be disrupted in three general ways: Parents fail to live in a manner that earns respect, they fail to parent children to be respectful, ideological forces discourage the younger generation from offering respect, or (and most often) some combination of the three. The first (parents failing to live worthily) is real but isn't the central focus of this book. My concern is primarily with the cultural and ideological pressures that erode familial honor and distort the parent-child relationship, though I address all three disrupters insofar as they bear on practical solutions.

When the personal and social expectation to honor one's parents is weakened or rejected, a strange inversion occurs. Instead of being treated as elders to be respected, parents are regarded as problematic figures to be corrected. Adult children step into the role of disciplinarian—educating, criticizing, even scolding their parents, and, in some cases, severing ties entirely. When parental authority collapses, the child often ends up imitating the very authoritarianism they claim to reject.

As we've seen, this inversion of the parent-child dynamic didn't appear overnight. It's the culmination of decades of cultural drift: parenting philosophies that reduced parenting to a therapeutic role, the civic evisceration of parental rights, a dogmatic rejection of authority throughout culture, and a sharp decline in family stability.

The result is a generation of young adults who are often ill-equipped for independence and resentful of their parents. Many parents now live in quiet fear of estrangement, tiptoeing through their relationships to avoid rupture. The urgent question, then, is how we might restore a vision of parental authority that is earned, humane, and built on mutual respect.

"I Am Terrified of Losing Contact"

Catherine and her husband, David, are accomplished professionals—she, a physician, and he, an engineer. They raised their three kids in a warm and welcoming home with progressive values. So, when their middle child, Monica, began bringing home friends who identified as queer or transgender, it didn't seem unusual. "She was the social justice type," her mother recalls. Monica had always been drawn to causes and people that she felt needed protection.

In her third year of college, Monica began spending a lot of time with a fellow student, Quinn. A year into their friendship, she came home beaming—he had asked her to be his girlfriend. At a family meeting shortly after, she revealed what was news even to her: Quinn was a woman who identified as a man (although she simply said a "trans man").

Even though they had always been supportive of Monica's trans friends, this romance gave Catherine pause. "It wasn't our dream situation," she told me. "It made us a little anxious, but we liked this person, and she was happy. So, we supported them."

That support turned into a kind of family project for Catherine, David, and Monica's older brother and younger sister: learning how to affirm a transgender partner, navigating pronouns, and adjusting expectations. As the family was settling into this new rhythm, the 2020 quarantine began and Monica, like many others, became withdrawn.

Monica was once a sociable, energetic child. She had some struggles with friends in high school, from which the family thinks she never fully recovered. A therapist at the time floated the possibility of borderline personality disorder. Now as the lockdown continued, Quinn suggested Monica see a new therapist—one who had previously supported Quinn in transitioning. That therapist, Catherine believes, failed to explore deeper issues such as Monica's past struggles with mood disorders. "When I raised concerns about Monica's depression symptoms, the therapist laughed and told our daughter we were out in left field." Eventually, Monica discussed with her therapist a sense of struggling to see herself as a grown woman. The therapist replied that she was wondering when that might come up. With her encouragement, Monica told her family she was trans.

"I was completely unprepared for that. I was fine with the trans boyfriend, but when she said it about herself . . ." Catherine trailed off. "She told us that she never felt uncomfortable as a girl but just could not see herself as a woman. The therapist said that the fact that she had never before questioned being female was probably just because she was raised in a progressive home without sex stereotypes." Catherine and David realized that the absence of previous signs of gender dysphoria could be dismissed whether the parents are conservative or progressive. Conservative parents raise their kids in an environment that makes such exploration of identity unthinkable, and progressive parents simply don't foster an environment that requires their children to confront sex stereotypes, leaving their identity unexplored. "Anything can be interpreted to support a course of gender affirmation."

Despite her reservations, Catherine said to David and to Monica's siblings, "We will celebrate this." But privately, she began researching. What she found—concepts like rapid-onset gender dysphoria—only deepened her unease. "We encouraged her to pause before starting testosterone. But it was clear we weren't going to have an impact."

Monica seemed determined, so Catherine and David let her know they would support her emotionally but didn't feel comfortable paying for medical transition. This news introduced a level of strain to their relationship. "She felt we were denying her existence and did not love her if we didn't support this in every way." As an unspoken but clear threat of estrangement loomed, Catherine and David decided to contribute some financial support out of fear of losing their daughter entirely.

Things deteriorated further when their younger daughter, Jaime, grew suspicious of her parents' loyalty to Monica. Though not queer herself, Jaime had also immersed herself in a queer community in college and saw herself as a staunch ally. Her suspicion culminated in a message to her parents while several states away at school: "I am sorry to have to say this but because you did not immediately and fully affirm [Monica], I am going no contact." Her parents were devastated and tried to discuss further but received a sharp email with Jaime's boundaries: She would allow them to send her one email per week but no more. She also included in her boundaries that Catherine and David seek therapy and sever ties with any so-called transphobic friends or communities online.

Her parents complied with the email limit and remained respectful and cautious. "We stuck to the rules," Catherine says. "We just didn't want to lose another child." They hadn't quite lost Monica, but the relationship was tenuous despite them quieting their concerns and giving financial support. Though Monica remains in touch with them, the relationship is conditional. "As long as we don't ever talk about the gender stuff, it's generally easy and can be warm and fun," Catherine explains. "I don't have illusions that I understand all of this. I think she wants connection. I think she's angry. And I think there's a lot of cognitive dissonance."

When David's brother died, he sent a message to Jaime expressing his hope to regain connection. "Family is so precious," he wrote in his grief.

Two days later, her reply came: "Please don't contact me again. You're my parents in name only." Jaime maintains that her position is in honor and support of Monica.

With the medical interventions, Monica, once athletic and active, began struggling to walk even normal distances. Her brother asked her if she thought her physical struggles might be connected to transitioning. Monica erupted, "You've been talking to Mom, haven't you!"

Catherine learned from this that she wasn't hiding well her concern for Monica. She now tries to maintain silence and even enthusiasm in or out of Monica's earshot. "I know the line. And I know the cost of crossing it." She is torn between an instinct to protect her daughter and an instinct to protect her relationship with her daughter. The two goals feel at odds. "It is hard to see my daughter with a beard. I don't want to see her health decline. But my highest value is to keep the connection."

Catherine's therapist is skeptical of this parenting strategy and told her, "The only way to guarantee you won't be estranged is to give your children everything they want." Catherine takes this not as a prescription but as a warning that she has chosen an untenable path. While she admits she might not have the right strategy, she repeats several times that she is terrified of being cut off again. Her only hope lies in a societal change that makes people realize how wrong this all is. "I think there's going to be a shift. This era of child medicalization is going to end. And so will this wave of estrangement. I just hope that when that happens, maybe she'll see that I wasn't the enemy. I was just her mom."

The Authoritarian Child

Many parents feel that silence and affirmation are the only options for staying in contact with their adult children. These tenuous relationships don't just invert the traditional parent-child dynamic—they echo a dysfunctional version of it. Imagine a child walking on eggshells around an unpredictable parent, fearing their rejection or rage. Now reverse the roles. The toxicity becomes unmistakable: The authority these adult children wield mirrors the very authoritarianism they claim to oppose.

To reengineer a culture, what is now must first be undone. Cultural revolutions, by their nature, don't merely shift external structures—they unsettle the foundational identities within the family itself. Each member is, in some way, unmade. For men, this often takes the form of emasculation—not the loss of machismo or some other caricature of masculinity; rather, they lose the strength that comes with virtue and become enslaved to their vices. Medieval philosopher Thomas Aquinas describes the effeminate man as one who is unwilling to endure what is arduous for the sake of what is good.[1] An effeminate man, then, is one who is passive or hedonic—which tends toward predation.

The unmaking of one sex inevitably contributes to the unmaking of the other. As men grow either passive or predatory, women often respond with self-protection that can lead to individualism and hostility. At the same time, traditional maternal virtues—such as tenderness and nurturing—are increasingly pathologized and misdirected toward society at large or misdirected toward their wounds. By way of example, one woman I've known for years never became a mother but now in her sixties still seems consumed with recounting the hurts of her childhood—none of which were extreme. Once as she spoke again of them bitterly, I realized her wounds had become her child—something she felt compelled to nurture and feed and protect.

In short, as men grow soft, women grow hard. Children, meanwhile, become prematurely powerful. With adults stripped of moral authority, children are left without clear models to emulate or firm boundaries to respect. In this vacuum, kids often respond with rebellion and control, pushing boundaries to see if they exist and stepping into roles of miniature authoritarians.

What begins as a private, familial disorder soon becomes a cultural one. Slowly but pervasively, the very concept of parenthood is redefined. Parents are depicted as ignorant or oppressive, in need of correction and discipline, while children are treated with undue deference. Youth becomes idealized and dogmatically followed. Because this disorder bleeds into the collective, even healthy and high-functioning families can be affected simply by the milieu in which their kids are raised.

This dynamic of youth authoritarianism doesn't stop with conservative households, whose parental authority is often swiftly recast as authoritarianism and then assumed by the kids. As Catherine's case illustrates, progressive parents who raise their children with progressive ideals may find those very ideals turned against them if they fail to keep pace with the ever-shifting standards of ideological purity. What was once celebrated as enlightened parenting can, years later, be judged as retrograde by children who have advanced further along the arc of "History." Such parents can find that, ironically, the values instilled at home become the lens through which the parents are eventually condemned.

From Therapy to Estrangement

As parental authority has been rendered suspect and the inner life of the child elevated as decisive, therapeutic frameworks increasingly step in as the primary lens through which family relationships are interpreted. While therapy can be deeply beneficial, it can also, unintentionally, provide ammunition for estrangement through a phenomenon called reappraisal.

A 2024 study found that when individuals are asked to reflect on their relationships with parents, their recollections and emotions about those relationships can change, even without suggestive questioning.[2] This phenomenon of reappraisal can lead to distorted memories, introducing emotional distance unnecessarily and potentially causing long-term family conflicts or severance. "We all have childhood amnesia in early years, because we're constantly producing new neurons. This leads to complications around what we think we remember, and what actually happened," says the study's lead author, Lawrence Patihis. "For example, imagine that someone experiences positive emotions with their father during the first 11 years of their life, but this changes at age 16 when he divorces their mum. What they don't realise is that this negative re-evaluation of their father will subtly change the memory of their relationship with him when they were younger."[3]

In one of the experiments, some participants were asked about recent times when their mothers presented a positive characteristic, such as warmth or competence. Others were asked about recent times when their mothers presented a certain negative characteristic, such as coldness or incompetence. The participants' current emotions toward their mother were significantly altered by this practice, and how they remembered feeling in childhood was changed too.[4] For example, people remembered feeling more or less happiness toward their mother in their youth depending on how they reappraised her now.

In the conclusion of the study, the authors point to the potential for unintended harm, pointing out that for over a century, therapists have prompted clients to discuss their experiences with their parents without measuring possible side effects such as "lowered evaluation of parents, worsened current emotions towards parents, and contaminated memories of childhood emotions towards parents."[5]

Patihis suggests reappraisal's effect on memories can be minimized by making sure clients and therapists are aware of this tendency and strive to ward against it. He argues that such discussions with patients should be part of informed consent.[6]

Parenting theories grounded in the belief that authority is inherently corrupt often produce emotionally dysregulated children and parents who feel powerless. In the vacuum created by this abdication of authority, therapy culture and social media step in as surrogate guides—ones that can (unwittingly or not) reframe young adults' emotional connection to their parents or even their memories of their experiences with them. TikTok psychologists focused on helping young adults identify childhood harm with little professional or personal accountability can also do this; once the algorithm targets someone as even mildly interested in childhood wounds, a barrage of content will prompt them toward reappraisal. In this pattern, parental authority is first surrendered, then pathologized, and finally replaced by ideologies that aren't oriented toward family preservation.

Cultivating True Authority

After decades of gentle, permissive parenting shaped by therapeutic notions of the self, many are beginning to see the need for a recalibration. Developmental research affirms what common sense is reclaiming: Children thrive under authoritative parenting, a model that combines emotional warmth with consistency and structure.[7]

The ancient Greek philosopher Aristotle understood that

virtue is found in the mean between two extreme vices. Courage, for example, is the mean between rashness on the one hand and cowardice on the other.[8] As Goldilocks would say of the three bears' chairs, one is too hard, the other is too soft, and one is just right. Similarly, according to clinical and developmental psychologist Diana Baumrind, the two extremes of parenting styles are authoritarian and permissive.[9] The just-right mean between the two is authoritative.

Researchers later argued that these three categories of parenting[10] can be understood by examining how parents balanced responsiveness and demandingness.[11] Responsiveness in parenting is characterized by a lot of empathy and acceptance. Responsive parents engage in active listening and are openly supportive. They are involved in the details of their kids' lives and strive to provide guidance. They tend to be warm parents, attuned to their children's emotions. Demandingness in parenting is characterized by clear boundaries of behavior and high expectations of responsibilities. Parents with high demandingness tend to set rules, prioritize structure and self-control, and discipline in a consistent manner.

Authoritarian parents tend to have low levels of responsiveness and high levels of demandingness. These parents value control and are quick to restrict freedom. The authoritarian places much emphasis on obedience, discipline, and force to curb behavior. There isn't much attention to or affirmation of the child's emotions and desires in an authoritarian household.

An example in literature of authoritarian parenting is Mr. Gradgrind from *Hard Times* by Charles Dickens. Mr. Gradgrind famously runs both his household and his school with rigid, oppressive rules. He crushes imagination and individuality in his children, demanding total obedience and emotional restraint. He well represents the authoritarian parent: high control, low warmth, and little room for emotional development.[12]

Permissive parents, by contrast, show high levels of responsiveness and low levels of demandingness. These parents tend to be indulgent and allow their child an excessive amount of freedom, often deferring to the child's impulses, desires, and actions. The child is consulted about most decisions and given extensive explanations for family rules. Permissive parents are more like friends than authority figures.

Mrs. Bennet from Jane Austen's *Pride and Prejudice* gives flesh to the idea of a permissive parent. Mrs. Bennet is indulgent and driven by feelings, and she often lacks boundaries with her daughters. She is more concerned with her daughters' short-term fulfillment than with their character or long-term well-being. She exemplifies the permissive parent: emotionally invested but ineffective at guiding or correcting behavior.[13]

Neither extreme establishes true parental authority. Kids raised by authoritarian parents tend to become rebellious. Though the parents might have a veneer of control, they won't likely gain authority with time. Never having had much of an emotional connection or a deeply embedded sense of being beloved, older children of authoritarians can easily distrust that their parents have their good at heart.

Children of permissive parents don't generally fare better. They tend not to have much self-control and easily feel defeated in life without the competence and capabilities born of instilled discipline and habits of virtue.

In contrast to both authoritarian and permissive parents, authoritative parents combine responsiveness with demandingness. They set clear yet reasonable boundaries and expectations while being attuned to the emotional tenor of their child. The child can generally meet the parents' expectations with effort, and the parents are generally warm and responsive to their child's needs. Authoritative parenting is also marked by the parents' ability to regulate their own emotions and provide a good model of self-control. Age-appropriate independence and responsibilities are emphasized. Authoritative parents affirm who the child is but also set standards of conduct that must be met.

Authoritative parenting is the steady exercise of real authority for the sake of a child's maturity. Translating that principle into daily practice requires knowing how children actually grow, and here several lines of psychological research converge. Albert Bandura's work on self-efficacy adds a crucial psychological backbone to this approach. Bandura makes clear that self-efficacy isn't a vague sense of affirmation or self-esteem; it's highly task-specific with a focus on developing confidence primarily through mastery of real tasks.[14]

Psychiatrist Kevin Majeres, who teaches at Harvard, offers a similar framework. He describes three steps that help a child become genuinely growth-minded: connection, confidence, and consistency. First, the parent joins the child in the moment of difficulty—through eye contact, warmth, and validating the struggle at hand. This connection regulates the child and opens the door to learning.

Second, the parent expresses confidence in the child's ability to master the specific challenge before them. The parent helps the child identify what skill this setback is giving them the opportunity to learn and affirms that the missing skill can be learned through practice.

Finally, the parent practices consistency by resisting the impulse to rescue the child or accommodate the child's perception that the struggle is too difficult. Consistency also means modeling and upholding the very ideals the parent wants the child to internalize. Ideals are the animating "why" behind the skills. An example Majeres offers is that the why behind striving not to be a picky eater is to be healthy and to be grateful for what others have done for us. We show gratitude by eating what is offered. Consistency is what allows those ideals to take root. "It's how children internalize the ideals and values and beliefs of their parents," Majeres says.[15] Even when inconvenient or frustrating, steady follow-through embeds principles more deeply than words ever could.

This framework can help all parents at any stage—from parenting an anxious young adult to parenting a small child throwing a tantrum. Each needs some age-appropriate version of connection, confidence, and consistency.

Eli Lebowitz of Yale has developed the SPACE program (Supportive Parenting for Anxious Childhood Emotions), a parent-centered intervention for children and teens struggling with anxiety. Unlike conventional therapies that focus on the child, SPACE teaches parents to examine their own behaviors: which responses, however well intentioned, are actually enabling fear or dependence and can be replaced with supportive, confidence-building practices. Lebowitz's approach follows a similar framework to Majeres's and reflects what is needed in estranged or at-risk family dynamics. SPACE helps parents communicate understanding of their child's discomfort or anxiety without validating fear or other harmful patterns. Parents also learn to set clear expectations, boundaries, and standards, demonstrating authority without panic or threat. And finally, this program helps parents develop consistency over reaction, removing accommodations that enable anxiety, reinforcing coping skills, and fostering self-trust and resilience in their child.[16]

Parents are like a mirror, according to Lebowitz. The child looks into their parent-mirror to see who they are. "And when what you see reflected back to you is a child who is weak, who's helpless, who's vulnerable, who can't deal with things, that's what you start to believe about yourself. But if you look into the mirror of your parents and what you see is a strong, capable, competent, resilient child, that's what you start to believe about yourself."[17]

By looking beyond behavior to growth opportunities, parents teach children to embrace challenges, develop competence, and internalize a desire to improve. Both permissive and authoritarian parents are focused on outcomes, not lasting growth. Permissive parents don't want their children upset, so they inevitably become indulgent, removing obstacles from their children's path and not aiding the learning of new skills. Authoritarian parents emphasize performance, achievement, and success, but without the emotional connection, they tend to raise kids who haven't internalized the why behind their efforts. The children end up with skills but no lasting ideals, except flaccid ones like keeping the parents happy or perhaps looking good for others. True authority, however, is generative: It prioritizes growth over outcomes, equipping children to become independent, resilient, and capable of propelling themselves forward, guided by internalized values rather than external pressures.

Defending Parental Rights

In addition to cultural and personal forces, parents today face unprecedented challenges to their authority from legal and institutional trends. Over the last century, the U.S. Supreme

Court repeatedly affirmed that parents have a fundamental right to direct the care and upbringing of their children, including religious upbringing. Those rights come from God—not the state—and are protected by the Constitution. Cases such as *Meyer v. Nebraska* and *Pierce v. Society of Sisters* recognized that parents have the right to direct their children's education and upbringing without undue state interference. Later rulings, including *Wisconsin v. Yoder* and *Troxel v. Granville*, reinforced the primacy of parental rights in matters of moral, religious, and personal care.

Despite the reality that parents have these rights by nature and enjoy strong legal protections, parental authority is being steadily eroded. In schools, parents are often denied transparency regarding curricula and its implementation and are left unaware of the work of destabilizing their children's innocence and understanding of bodily meaning and human anthropology. In many districts, schools are protagonists in the process of destabilization—introducing the concepts, encouraging "exploration," providing "supportive" counseling without consent/notice, and facilitating children's rejection of their sex and adoption and expression of a chosen identity.

In some states, minors can freely access abortion and mental health services without parental knowledge or consent. In all states, minors can access sexually transmitted infection (STI) testing and treatment also without parental knowledge and consent—although the ages vary. In many states, minors can access contraceptives without parental knowledge and consent.

The appeal to "harm" is now the chief rationale for excluding parents from LGBTQ-related decisions at school, often framed by the exaggerated claim that disclosure would lead to children being kicked out of their homes. But the deeper justification has shifted toward child autonomy—an asserted right to make major, sensitive decisions in secret, with confidentiality used to override parental authority. This pattern traces back to earlier policies on STIs and contraception, where weak evidence and inflated "public health emergency" claims were used to remove parental knowledge and consent requirements on the assumption that teens would avoid treatment if parents knew. Yet no research shows that sidelining parents actually improves children's health. Instead, it establishes a precedent of cutting parents out on the thinnest of grounds.

Many parents I spoke with expressed feeling caught between two worlds: a time when schools and medical communities were trustworthy partners, and a present reality in which institutions appear to shepherd children into a cultlike ideology while parents are cast as adversaries. One father summarizes the tension sharply: "We raised our kids for the culture that we were raised in, not the culture that they were being raised in."

Defending parental authority requires both awareness and action. Parents need to exercise their rights, insist on transparency in schools, and participate actively in their children's education and social development. They also need to not be afraid to make a change in favor of homeschooling or alternative schools when their rights aren't respected. Joining forces with other parents and engaging with parental-rights organizations are critical measures. Because legal protections for parental rights are deeply enshrined in American law, parents can approach these challenges with confidence, knowing that protecting their children's upbringing is not a concession from the state but a preeminent duty entrusted to them.

Park Bench Parenting

When society fails to honor and protect the role of parents, children suffer across communities and generations. If we are to rebuild a culture in which children thrive and families endure, we must recover a public understanding of parental authority as necessary and good. This means resisting ideologies and institutions that undermine it and instead cultivating norms, laws, and policies that support the vital role of mothers and fathers in forming the next generation.

Any parent at any age can be a part of this restoration. Younger parents can model parenthood deliberately among their peers. Older parents and grandparents can and should strive to serve as mentors to younger generations. If their children and grandchildren aren't receptive, mentorship can happen in churches and neighborhoods, among friends, and in school communities.

For the first twelve years of motherhood, I wrangled my kids weekly to a local moms' park group every Friday afternoon. There, mothers gleaned from one another advice for marriage, potty training, summer reading, discipline issues, and how to feed growing families on tight budgets. The group was a homeschooling community so persisted with park days well beyond the preschool years. This longevity led to a vast range of mothering experiences intermingling, from newly minted grandmothers to young moms with one toddler. Mentorship happened naturally while moms sprawled on the grass and sat on park benches.

Even for parents dealing with more dire questions and issues than meal planning and weaning, these sorts of intentional communities can be of crucial aid. Family therapist

Ron Taffel concludes as much about the overwhelmed parents he has encountered who'd seemingly lost all control: "What most overwhelmed parents of out-of-control kids need—just as much as psychotherapy—is a strong, vibrant community that includes *other parents*. Parents need help and encouragement in authority building."[18]

Beyond mentorship and community, reclaiming parental authority requires intentional, not accidental, parenting. Accidental parenting takes two common forms. The first is a reactionary form: Parents simply don't have a unified plan for how to go about setting boundaries and consequences, so they parent on the fly. This usually leads to inconsistent parenting that depends on who is home at the time or the mood of the parent in charge. It's a recipe for chaos. "Here's how to have a terrible child," warns clinical psychologist Jordan Peterson. "Imagine your child will whine and complain when they want something. If you want to have that happen all the time, then vary the amount that they have to whine and complain before you capitulate unpredictably. That's what a slot machine does. It rewards intermittently and variably. . . . What the child learns is if they're persistent enough, you will cave."[19]

The second form of accidental parenting is to passively accept what passes for the wisdom of the day without critically evaluating whether it makes sense and contrasting it with what successful parents do. This sort of accidental parenting I call "diet pill parenting." Rather than doing the daily hard work of healthy living, it's easy to be persuaded to just pop diet pills or inconsistently graft onto varying diet trends that claim to address the symptoms of unhealthy living. In the same way, if kids are acting out, they might not need a therapist or a trip to Disneyland. They definitely don't need an iPhone to calm them. What they need is the long-term, consistent work of structure and presence to restore relational health. To achieve this, parents need a unified, well-thought-out family vision and the will to commit to it. "You want to have a sense in your household of how you would want the relationships and the household to operate," Peterson says. "And that's what allows you to detect deviations from that."[20]

Many modern challenges compromise our ability to provide basic structure and emotional presence for our kids today. Permissive parenting has eroded our confidence in setting standards and sticking to them. Financial realities and social expectations can make daily parental presence challenging. Modern mobility and the attenuation of mediating institutions such as churches and community groups often leave parents isolated, not only struggling to advocate for their kids alone but sometimes even contending with the very institutions that should serve as allies.

Though the parenting landscape is daunting, there is hope. Parents are increasingly distrustful of the surrender and usurpation of their authority. From grassroots parents' rights movements to the desire to address skyrocketing rates of mental health pathologies, a return to the basics looks to be happening. Grassroots movements like MAHA (Make America Healthy Again) show how parents are mobilizing around medical freedom, dietary health, and the broader well-being of their children, asserting control over decisions that were once ceded to institutions. Across the country, families are participating in school-board meetings, joining advocacy groups, and demanding transparency in curricula, policies, and programs that shape their children's most intimate beliefs. Rising concerns over youth mental health and social media exposure are also prompting parents to turn away from gentle parenting and return to foundational practices: setting clear boundaries, enforcing consistent structure, prioritizing parental presence, and reengaging with more human (and less screen-based) activities.

While these trends could be dismissed as fleeting or nostalgic, the parent-child bond is deeply human. There can be a tendency to overlook ideologies that target us, only to become fiercely protective when those same ideologies affect our children.

For many families just starting out, skepticism of institutions and experts is a default setting as they navigate the pressures of modern culture. Several young parents I spoke to are seeking to carve new pathways for their families. Max and Hope are in their mid-twenties and married with a toddler and a baby on the way. I asked them how they think of developing parenting skills both now and as the kids grow. Max says that he filters the numerous "expert" parenting voices: "I . . . try to evaluate the source, assuming many might have an agenda or just be trying to sell a book or program or something. If something resonates with us, we look to see if the writer has a philosophy undergirding his or her suggestions." Hope adds, "We also seek friendship with parents who are a few steps ahead of us and seem to have well-behaved and happy kids." Other young couples echoed both their skepticism about the numerous theories and their desire for community and mentorship.

Ironically, their awareness of the erosion of expert authority is accompanied by a desire to have authentic authority and to live as intentional parents. I think of these young couples and their Gen Z peers who have structured their lives so differently. Some seek a return to foundational things like community, mentorship, and the wisdom of grandparents over passing trends. Others are deeply invested in progressive, destabilizing narratives that challenge traditional social and familial norms. It mimics the broader divide in society that increasingly seems unbridgeable.

The family is clearly affected by this polarization, and its own internal divisions reverberate outward, reinforcing the very dynamics that produced them. Political factions begin to treat one another like "toxic relatives." Communities retreat into ideological echo chambers. Dialogue dies. Forgiveness is a relic. The perception of our common humanity fades. And the emotional logic of estrangement becomes the political logic of civil conflict. But the family is also the seedbed of solidarity, and that logic scales up too. As we strengthen the family and restore healthy parental authority, we form more stable human beings who can move into the world and change it exponentially.

Parents are awakening to the cost of silence and surrender. Many, like Catherine, are beginning to find hope in signs of societal change. But parents can't wait for society to change. They can maintain or reclaim their moral authority—an authority that ought not vanish even if it's unwelcome. As one father told me, "They might leave . . . but they know where home is and what a welcome awaits them." Authority is stabilizing, for children at any age, and it's the best long-term strategy for enduring relationships and a more unified civic life.

9

DISAGREEING WELL IS CIVILIZING

Ask people how they handle political disagreements today versus a few years ago, and most will tell you the same thing: They don't. A meme has recently made the rounds, capturing the transformation. The first GIF shows a man flushed and belligerent with anger, pointing his finger, straining to win an argument. The caption reads, "POV: How I used to argue with people 10 years ago." The second shows a cool, detached figure merely lifting his eyebrows, widening his eyes, glancing away with a bored air of superiority. The second caption says, "How I argue with people now." The contrast is instantly recognizable, and it reflects a new consensus: There's no point even trying to discuss disagreements anymore, much less argue them to the death. People across the political spectrum tell me they feel this. In one sense, the second response may be preferable to the first. Avoiding arguments is wise if it's in service of preserving the relationship. But the more accurate interpretation of the meme—and why it touched a nerve—is that it reflects a general feeling that we are inhabiting different realities and have given up on one another altogether. Whether we are belligerently arguing or simply slipping into cool contempt, the underlying reality is that we have forgotten the discipline of disagreeing well.

When both parties are oriented toward discovering truth, disagreement is deeply civilizing. It trains us to listen, to refine our own thinking, to see from another vantage point, to lower our defenses, and to let truth, not ego or tribal loyalty, be the goal. When we enter disagreement with the hope of discovering what is real, the exchange elevates everyone involved and is one of the highest marks of personal and civic maturity. Families, friendships, and nations thrive not by suppressing conflict but by cultivating the courage and skill to engage it.

When that will and skill to disagree well are lost, we either fight to the death or dismiss the other as hopelessly wrong and unworthy of engagement. Eventually, we even bureaucratize interpersonal conflict. In February 2022, a Tulane University freshman, May, received a message from the division of student affairs in her inbox that read like a legal order: a notice of no contact between her and her former roommate. It was official and final: no communication, no social media interaction, and no third-party contact whatsoever. "It was like a bad breakup," May later said.[1] The no-contact order (NCO) ended with a warning that any violation could result in suspension and conduct charges.

May hadn't been violent or threatening. She and her roommate had simply not gotten along, and May found her to be manipulative and unkind. The tipping point? May had told a mutual friend she didn't like her roommate—a confidence that traveled back to the roommate, who promptly posted a note to May to move out immediately. A few days after May changed rooms, she was served with the NCO. The roommate had informed the university she feared for her safety. May was stunned: "This person used a system that is supposed to do good in the world and used it against me."[2]

Originally designed to protect victims of sexual violence, no-contact orders have quietly expanded far beyond their original intent. As *The Wall Street Journal* reports, they are now used for everything from roommate disputes to stolen bagels. "Schools hand [NCOs] out like candy." David Karp attributes this to an increasingly fragile and conflict-averse generation, among other causes like helicopter parents and litigation-wary institutions.[3]

Part of that fragility in students stems from a digital upbringing. Today's students are fluent in online boundary setting practices such as blocking, muting, and unfollowing. That fluency doesn't translate into real-world maturity. "This generation of college students grew up in an echo-chamber world where they could block or filter out voices they disagree with," says Caroline Mehl, co-founder of the Constructive Dialogue Institute. "They're bringing online communication norms to the real world."[4]

Another administrator notes how often students today view their peers with black-and-white thinking, as either helpful or hurtful, with no middle ground. Tolerance for differences, he observes, is severely diminished and sensitivity to conflict heightened, leading to real anxiety in students.[5]

Tools such as no-contact orders, once meant to address the reality of our vulnerability, are now used to amplify our perception of that vulnerability by inflating what threatens us to include dislike, discomfort, and disagreement. In doing so, they often exacerbate the very emotional instability they were meant to mitigate.

The Authoritarian Blind Spot

This mindset isn't confined to college campuses but rather signals a broader generational shift in how conflict, especially ideological conflict, is approached. A viral video captured a young woman conducting an interview of her eighty-two-year-old grandfather. She begins by asking his name and age, what party he has historically voted for, and for whom he voted in 2024. His responses are somewhat sheepish, but he says he has voted Republican and for Trump.

She says she suspected as much, then asks, "Can you see after all of these questions . . . if I continue to have a relationship with you without absolutely any change in your behavior how I would be enabling fascism?"

He protests that he doesn't ask her to change what she believes to suit his needs, then asks, "Shouldn't we both look at ourselves and change what we can?"

She responds that she will now give a summary of her thoughts and asks him not to interrupt her. "I spent years educating you. If you truly, unconditionally loved me, your politics would reflect that. You wouldn't have spent the majority of your life voting my rights away. That is *not* unconditional love," she says, her voice and emotions intensifying as she speaks. "Allowing a relationship with you would allow you to believe that there are no consequences for the way that you vote. . . . These are my boundaries." She continues in a resolute voice. "We have fascism in this country because we allow fascism in our homes. We allow it in our communities. . . . Your politics have real-world consequences. Your inability to see my point of view, to change—your change is necessary."

She goes on to challenge what she sees as hollow gestures of atonement. "You cannot go to church and ask God for forgiveness," she says. "I'm the real person you negatively affected, and I don't forgive you. Not until your actions change, until you are really ready to hear me." Her voice turns frantic. "I don't understand how you cannot see that your support of the system affects our relationship. . . . You understand. We've had talks. I know you get it. You have to change. I don't care how old you are. Like I don't care. I seriously don't care."[6]

The video encapsulates the authoritarianism that replaces true authority, as discussed in the last chapter. It also reflects a logic that is increasingly familiar: To hold conservative views is a form of personal assault. If a friend, parent, grandpa, or other loved one is the source of that violence, no contact becomes the reasonable response. How can you disagree civilly with someone who is assaulting you?

That logic isn't new. It traces back to mid-twentieth-century Freudian-Marxist critical theorists like Herbert Marcuse and Theodor Adorno, whose ideas seeped into mainstream progressive thinking. In his 1965 essay "Repressive Tolerance," Marcuse argued that what passes for neutral tolerance in liberal societies often serves to entrench unjust power structures. If dominant voices are permitted to speak freely, he suggested, they reinforce oppression. Genuine liberation, therefore, might require "liberating tolerance"—that is, tolerance for progressive movements but intolerance toward regressive ones. Speech deemed oppressive need not be answered; it may be suppressed.[7]

This moral reasoning seeped beyond academic theory into the cultural reflex. Today its influence can be seen in the casual labeling of political opponents as fascists or nazis. The inflation of these terms has had real consequences. If opponents are branded fascists or nazis, then stopping them by any means necessary is responsible. At the very least cutting them out of your life makes sense. Who would go back in time and be friends with nazis?

Groups like Antifa, short for anti-fascist, for instance, have adopted the logic of Marcuse and Adorno quite literally. In cities across the United States, activists operating under that banner have justified property destruction, physical intimidation, and civic rebellion as necessary forms of resistance. The rationale is simple: Fascism must be confronted by any means necessary, and those categorized as fascists forfeit the protections of liberal order.

Conservatives, too, indulge in dehumanizing language—dismissing opponents as "commies" or "libtards"—and at times flirt with illiberal impulses of their own, including calls to stretch constitutional powers in service of preferred ends. Such excesses should be resisted. The point is not that one side is uniquely immune to authoritarian temptation but that certain frameworks make authoritarianism easier to justify.

Yet much of the modern psychological literature has historically treated authoritarianism as a predominantly right-wing phenomenon. As accusations of fascism are increasingly leveled against conservatives, there is a persistent blind spot toward the authoritarianism on the political left. In his 1996 book *The Authoritarian Specter,* social psychologist Bob Altemeyer suggested that left-wing authoritarianism (LWA) is like the Loch Ness Monster: People claim to see it, but there's no solid evidence it exists.[8] Altemeyer was adamant that authoritarianism was a right-wing phenomenon, famously claiming that LWA was "as scarce as hens' teeth."[9]

Altemeyer's perspective gained academic traction in 2003,

when social psychologist John Jost and colleagues cited it approvingly in their influential paper "Political Conservatism as Motivated Social Cognition." Echoing Adorno's F-Scale (a test to determine fascism) as well as Altemeyer, they argued that authoritarianism is inherently tied to traits like tradition, resistance to change, and support for hierarchy—features they believed applied only to the political right.[10] As a result, for decades, scholars marginalized or dismissed serious inquiry into left-wing authoritarianism, while they pathologized even mainstream conservative thought.

More recent research has challenged the long-held assumption that authoritarianism is exclusive to conservatives. Social psychologist Lucian "Luke" Conway began laying the groundwork for this shift, and a landmark 2022 study led by Thomas Costello of Emory University, "Clarifying the Structure and Nature of Left-Wing Authoritarianism," built on that foundation.[11] Their work reveals left-wing authoritarianism to be not only real but also measurable and politically consequential.

Costello and his colleagues developed and validated a robust LWA scale, identifying the distinctive traits of left-wing authoritarianism. Like its right-wing counterpart, authoritarianism on the left involves dogmatism, black-and-white thinking, and support for coercive control, but it channels those tendencies through progressive and seemingly opposite aims. Whereas Altemeyer and Jost and his co-authors identified things like adherence to tradition on the right, LWA traits include the elevation of transgressive behavior and disregard for tradition. While a feature of RWA is support for hierarchical structures, LWA encourages anti-hierarchical aggression. And more recent claims that a robust defense on the right of free speech is a fig leaf for bigotry and a symptom of fascism are contrasted with the rise of censorship as a sign of authoritarianism on the left.

According to the Costello study, higher scores of LWA were positively associated with increased support for political violence. RWA scores, in contrast, didn't show a significant relationship with support for political violence.[12] Not only is LWA real, but it also arguably carries a greater threat of violence than its right-wing counterpart.

Insights from Conway's work yield a striking additional conclusion: There is a profound asymmetry in self-awareness. The *higher* individuals scored in LWA, the *less* likely they were to recognize authoritarian tendencies in themselves. In contrast, right-leaning respondents were significantly more willing to admit to authoritarian inclinations. The authors attribute this inverse correlation to a psychological blind spot—rooted in the leftist belief that their values are inherently anti-authoritarian.[13] This moral self-concept functions like a kind of purifier, baptizing all actions, no matter how coercive, as being in service of liberation or justice. The result is that denial of LWA is not merely an academic oversight but a deeper failure of introspection among those most prone to it.

This also reveals a critical point: that the anti-fascism professed in principle is often not a principle at all. True principles apply universally; they constrain our allies as much as our enemies. When anti-authoritarianism becomes selective, used only to target political opponents, it ceases to be a principled stance and becomes a tribalistic weapon. In that sense, the refusal to recognize authoritarianism on the left is not just a blind spot but a strategic evasion, one that erodes the very moral high ground it claims to occupy. If there is a consistent principle to be teased out on the left, it's more akin to the principle of Marcuse's "Repressive Tolerance"—that authoritarianism isn't inherently wrong; it's wrong only based on who is exerting the power.[14] Morality, then, hinges on identity, not act.

Conway notes that authoritarian tendencies exist on both ends of the spectrum. But he also points out the significance of progressives' reluctance to recognize authoritarianism in themselves. "A party that denies the problem," he writes, "also won't address the problem. Right now that party is the Democratic Party."[15] The authoritarian blind spot makes self-correction increasingly difficult. But paradoxically, it may offer hope for a sharp moral reckoning (which I will discuss later).

Certainly, there are bad actors on the right who invoke values like free speech, debate, and constitutionalism while acting in ways that contradict those very principles—censoring dissent or compromising fidelity to the Constitution when it suits their purposes. Many are also guilty of turning a blind eye when the bad actions are at the behest of "their guy." But it's important to distinguish between hypocrisy and ideology. Hypocrisy is the failure to live up to one's stated principles. Ideology, by contrast, rewrites the principles themselves.

What we see on the left is not merely the inconsistency of the hypocrite but a coherent ideological framework—one with academic pedigree—that justifies discrimination, censorship, and even political violence as moral goods when they are directed at certain sorts of people. This is the logic of Marcuse and Adorno, echoing Marx's prescription that the dictatorship of the proletariat is the remedy for the dictatorship of capital. That logic is also reincarnated in Ibram X. Kendi's assertion that "the only remedy to past discrimination is present discrimination. The only remedy to present discrimination is future discrimination."[16] The implication is that discriminating based on skin color is not necessarily racist or intrinsically wrong but rather can be entirely morally justifiable depending on the identity of the people involved. This isn't hypocrisy. It's ideology.

Such group-based morality also tends to cause more of the very thing it claims to oppose. As the left reduces people to racial categories, the right begins to mirror this logic in reverse, developing its own reactionary identity politics. Emerging authoritarian tendencies on the right, amplified by provocateurs who traffic in an especially ugly version of identity politics as entertainment, illustrate how easily unjust provocations can cause people to abandon their principles and become the very thing their opponents had long been saying they were. Such reactionary dynamics further entrench both sides, end discussion, accelerate hatred, and fracture us both personally and civically. But recognizing how this cycle works gives us the clarity to resist it and to step back from the fight to the death, preserving our principles while refusing to be dragged into such spirals.

We Become What We Consume

What we attend to shapes our souls. Jason Baxter, director of the Center for Beauty and Culture at Benedictine College, holds that wonder is the process through which we become like what we see.[17] I think the inverse is also true: Outrage is the process through which we become like what we hate. The pleasure of feeding our outrage is addictive, keeping us in constant contemplation of what we despise. And in that fixation, we are gradually shaped by what holds our attention.

Focused on the perceived ills of "those other people," we

slowly take on their contours. They are stupid and hateful, so we become stupid and hateful. We become what we consume.

Beneath the ideological fervor of our civic and familial polarization lies something more primal to which every one of us is susceptible: contempt. Unlike principled conviction, contempt clouds judgment and impairs self-awareness. It widens the fractures within families and makes disagreements terminal. Once contempt takes hold, curiosity and dialogue wither and relationships break under the weight of moral certainty.

While away for a book event in 2022, I sat down to the planned dinner in a parish hall in the time between Mass and my talk. I chatted affably with a couple at my table until the husband got up to get wine. The wife's countenance shifted, and she seethed, "Why weren't you wearing a mask in Mass?" Taken off guard, I let out a nervous laugh, which she imitated with condescension.

I asked why she felt threatened by me when I was at least ten feet away from her in Mass but now at dinner felt safe although I was unmasked and just two feet away from her, passing dishes and sharing conversation. She rhetorically asked me for my scientific credentials, then answered that she was vaccinated and trusted the experts' policy decisions regarding sitting to dinner. The appeal to the vaccine and the experts didn't make up for the absurdity of the situation. Nothing about sitting to dinner gives a vaccine a new power it didn't have moments before. Nor does a respiratory disease lie dormant when people share a meal.

The remarkable disruption introduced to all our lives beginning in 2020 understandably left people anxious and isolated, and an obvious enemy is an intoxicating palliative. In such a climate, our natural suspicion of the powerful and the profiteers can easily turn into an obsessive suspicion of the person next to us.

That distrust of neighbor often signals something deeper: a collapse of trust in thought. We no longer believe we can reason clearly, observe accurately, or discern truth from falsehood without a mediator. In the wake of crisis or conflict, irrational policies that once would've been met with scrutiny instead become untouchable—because to question them is to risk being seen as one of *those people*. And for many, that social or moral taint feels worse than surrendering their capacity for thought. Better to parrot the consensus than to stand alone or align with an out-group.

What replaces personal discernment is a kind of outsourced cognition: expert thought as a substitute for thought itself. The subtle transaction is this: Seduced by contempt or fear, we forfeit trust in our "lyin' mind" and entrust reality to a priesthood of experts who promise certainty. We think we are elevated by the association, but it is, in fact, profoundly diminishing. Contempt and fear close the mind and block dialogue.

Divide and conquer is a perennial strategy for good reason. Fostering in citizens an unhealthy *suspicion* of one another often leads them to have an unhealthy *faith* in the powers that be. Identity politics habituated us to this. The turmoil that started in 2020 put it on steroids. This kind of tribalized contempt isn't new. Racism, anti-Semitism, and misogyny are ancient and recurring evils. But in recent decades, mainstream discourse rightly recoiled from such forms of bigotry. What is striking and troubling is how quickly tribalism can reinvent and reconstitute itself.

According to renowned marriage researcher John Gottman,

the foremost sign of an impending divorce is contempt.[18] He identifies a common form of contempt in marriage: when spouses roll their eyes at each other.[19] Both personally and civically, contempt often reveals itself first in the impulse to dismiss rather than engage—to discount another's stated arguments without serious consideration.

Long before 2020, this shift toward open derision was already surfacing, notably during the rise of the Tea Party in 2009. The movement's stated concerns—ballooning national debt, unchecked government spending, and bailouts for corrupt financial institutions—echoed long-standing themes of small-government populism. Yet the media and cultural response frequently ignored those arguments, choosing instead to pathologize the movement itself. A friend of mine, a devoted Obama supporter, unintentionally captured the tenor of this shift when he remarked, "Let's be honest. They're just mad that there's a Black man in the White House, a woman as Speaker, and a gay man in Congress."

His words marked, for me, the moment when ideology went viral. The comment struck me as so blatantly unjust and represented the mainstreaming of interpreting dissent as hatred and a growing willingness to ascribe the worst possible motives to half the country. In fact, his opinion was proclaimed in (and maybe derived from) *The New York Times* in a 2010 essay diagnosing the real reasons behind conservative objections to Obamacare: "A woman (Nancy Pelosi) pushed the health care bill through the House. The bill's most visible and vocal proponents included a gay man (Barney Frank) and a Jew (Anthony Weiner). And the black man in the White House signed the bill into law. It's enough to make a good old boy go crazy. Hence their anger and frustration . . ."[20]

Such rhetoric is a fallacy, and it erodes the ground for honest debate. The question is no longer what is true but who is worthy of taking seriously, who is dangerous, and who is allowed to speak.

This impulse is embedded in a broader academic framework known as standpoint theory. Rooted in feminist scholarship beginning in the seventies,[21] standpoint theory was initially presented as a call for epistemic humility—a reminder that knowledge is shaped by one's social location and that marginalized voices can illuminate blind spots in mainstream discourse. But standpoint theory now functions as a kind of rhetorical caste system.

Under this regime, the emotional safety of the "less powerful" becomes a moral trump card. The more claim you have to a grievance identity, the more weight your claims are presumed to carry. And because suffering now confers discursive power, there's a perverse incentive to magnify injury. The consequences are devastating, as this framework fuels contempt. It also ignores a fundamental aspect of the human condition: that suffering doesn't automatically confer insight or clarity. Pain can just as easily obscure as illuminate. In moments of deep anguish, people are often less able—not more—to see their situation clearly. Suffering and contempt can distort perception, heighten emotion, and narrow the field of vision.

If we want to disagree without division, we must rediscover the courage to say, "Your experience matters, but so does your argument." We must hold firm to the belief that truth isn't the property of any one group. It's a common good, and we access it not through identity but through reason and by resisting contempt.

We must also recognize contempt as a harbinger of an irrational society. Gottman identifies contempt as uniquely corrosive—it communicates disgust, superiority, and a lack of respect, eroding the very possibility of reconciliation.[22] If we wish to rebuild a culture of shared reasoning, we must learn to resist the reflex to sneer, mock, and assume the worst of those we disagree with.

While I have highlighted several examples of contempt from the left, conservatives likewise must be vigilant to avoid contempt. Contemptuous pejoratives employed against the left are terminal to restoring reason and dialogue. If we want to oppose identity politics and ideology, we can't reduce the other to an avatar of a system that we want to defeat. Each person is far more than what positions, political identities, or slogans they espouse, and we don't know what wounds or injustices have led them to such beliefs. Just as contempt in a marriage signals its collapse, a culture that normalizes contempt for the other half of the country is one on the brink of civic disintegration.

We all need to attend less to what angers us and far more to our loves. That means not watching CNN or MS NOW or Fox News every night nor scrolling our favorite hate-feeds dunking on those idiots on the other side. There is no need to ride the roller coaster of the daily news cycle that moves faster than anyone can keep up.

We also need to attend to what we love in one another. With the people in my life who disagree with me most, I try to be most intentional about meditating on their good qualities. Most of them have a great many. Some are especially thoughtful; some are funny and great storytellers; others model for me an inspiring devotion to a craft. Turning our attention to the things that are lovable in others helps us not reduce them even in our imagination. And it disposes us to act with greater affection toward them.

In his book *Love Your Enemies*, Arthur Brooks argues that

the key is not to disagree less but to disagree better. Competition, he observes, benefits us across nearly every sphere of life by fostering excellence and warding off complacency. We recognize this instinctively: A sports victory feels hollow if it's achieved through cheating. Competition drives companies to improve, innovate, and stay alert, preventing stagnation. As Brooks notes, in business it's the mediocre leaders who hate competition and have no drive to improve.[23] Applied to ideas, this suggests that the competition of ideas in the form of rigorous, well-structured disagreement is not a threat but a tool for growth, both individually and collectively.

Spell-Breaking

A friend once told me a story of a woman who shared an article on social media that she believed condemned a policy from an administration she despised. But someone pointed out it had been written during the tenure of a previous president whom she admired. She quickly deleted the post, but the moment left her unsettled, like waking from a trance, she later said. I don't know whether the story is strictly true or more of a parable, but it resonates. We all know the pull of confirmation bias—the ease with which we accept what flatters our beliefs, and the reflexive suspicion we reserve for anything that challenges them. These uncomfortable moments of self-examination and awakening don't happen often. But when they do, they reveal something critical: The spell of ideology isn't unbreakable.

Earlier in this chapter, I mentioned a sign of hope related to the blind spot toward left-wing authoritarianism. While psychologist Conway writes that the blind spot makes it difficult for those on the left especially to admit even obvious examples of their authoritarianism, he also notes that "on the positive side, this means that liberals in the United States do still have a built-in aversion to authoritarianism. If one can tap into that aversion, it could make it easier to defeat authoritarian tendencies on the left side of the aisle."[24] When left-leaning individuals are able to overcome the blind spot and recognize authoritarianism on their own side, they are often deeply disturbed by it—precisely because it violates the identity that they hold most dear. Such individuals demonstrate a loyalty to principle, not ideology: Their commitment to fairness, curiosity, and human dignity outweighs their commitment to partisan conformity.

In recent years, a growing number of thinkers on the left have broken ranks with their side, alarmed by a turn toward ideological conformity and censorship. Figures like Bari Weiss and Bill Maher exemplify this shift; both have defended classical liberal values like free speech and open debate, even as they face backlash from former allies. Glenn Greenwald and Matt Taibbi, once stalwarts of the progressive press, now criticize the collusion between government and media to suppress dissenting views, especially around Covid, national security, and tech censorship. J. K. Rowling, a self-described liberal feminist, has been vilified for defending biological reality and women's rights in the face of gender ideology. A few longtime progressives that I know personally have denounced the illiberalism and groupthink that now dominate much of academia and media. These figures haven't necessarily all moved rightward; rather, their fidelity to liberal principles has brought them into conflict with a left that continually narrows the demands of ideological compliance. Progressivism by its nature is always advancing—doggedly moving the goalposts in service of "History" with a capital *H*. In this sense, dissenting liberal figures who break ranks may be more accurately described as faithful to classical liberalism, not ideologues in service of progressivism.

What about deeply entrenched progressives—people like the granddaughter at the beginning of this chapter who confronted her grandfather over his support of Trump? Reasoned arguments will likely fall flat. Something deeper needs to occur. Kier Adrian Gray is a former social justice warrior from Canada who was once as militant as the granddaughter interrogating her grandfather. She now writes candidly about her journey out of ideological possession and the dangers she sees in leftist identity politics. She describes her former militancy: "The white supremacist capitalist cisheteropatriarchy was my all-consuming enemy and I was going to overthrow it, with the help of my like-minded friends."[25]

At the height of her zealotry, Gray was consumed by hostility and paranoia, constantly scanning people, books, media, and interactions for signs of oppression. That suspicion infected everything. "There was a sinister foundation of hatred underneath much that appeared innocent at first glance . . . and I became an expert at uncovering it."[26]

If friends or acquaintances said something Gray found offensive (and her list of offenses was ever growing), she would correct them. If they protested or defended their meaning, that reaction served as further proof to Gray of their guilt. "I was so convinced I was right that I considered the mere act of disagreeing with me tantamount to bigotry."[27]

There was no curiosity, no room for dissent, and suspicion and denunciations were regular occurrences in her social circles. Because of this, friendships in her social circles were highly unstable.

In an essay, she reflects on the purge mentality that defined her world. "The right looks for converts," she writes. "The left looks for traitors."[28] Gray readily admits in retrospect that she had to shut down her ability to think critically. "I avoided taking in any media that would challenge my beliefs, and I thought that this made me dedicated and superior."[29] She didn't know how to win arguments, but she knew well how to shut down conversation by impugning the motives of an interlocuter. Her most frequent accusation was of bigotry of one sort or another.[30]

Looking back, Gray is perplexed by how long she stayed in this mindset, despite how suspicious and angry it made her. She sees now that it was a self-fulfilling prophecy: "The more miserable and isolated I became, the easier it was to believe that I lived in a sinister, oppressive world that was actively working against me. This was a profoundly helpless belief to hold, but it was comforting in a strange way: it allowed me to take zero responsibility for my well-being. My problems were everyone else's fault, just as their problems were mine."[31]

A few moments stand out in her memory. "A friend read my Instagram profile aloud to me, starting with 'white settler.' I remember physically cringing when I heard this; why was my race the most important thing for people to know about me? Wasn't this what white nationalists believed?"[32]

One day a thought came to her, and she wrote it on a yellow sticky note and placed it on her bedroom wall. It read, "How do I contribute to my own misery?"[33]

This moment of self-examination served as a turning point for Gray. She began to admit, if only to herself, that she didn't want to live that way anymore. Her behavior started to shift. She started exploring forms of spirituality. She took up gardening. Over time, she made new friends—people who hadn't known her during the height of her ideological extremism.[34] With them, she began to speak honestly. She shared the doubts about progressive positions that her former self would have considered intolerable. And slowly, that honesty gave her the courage to speak more publicly.[35]

To facilitate that spell-breaking process in our friends and other loved ones, we can be the sort of friend or family member who they can trust won't be triumphalist if they begin questioning their beliefs. In order to do this, we have to actively resist the reactionary contempt spiral. We need to see the good in them, attend to it, and reflect it back to them. In so doing, we become the type of people that care about *them*, rather than winning an argument.

Ultimately, self-examination is a gateway to the sort of humility that can break the spell of ideology. It can't be imposed externally but needs to well up within the person. A parent or friend must respect that such transformation in a loved one takes time and neither strive to extract it nor obsessively look for signs of it. Most people can tell when someone is doing that, and it feels manipulative and makes the relationship seem conditional. Efforts like barraging someone with perfect articles to read or slyly bringing up a point favorable to one side are rarely effective and can work against this process, which needs to happen internally. Generally, our loved ones know what we think, and regularly reminding them isn't helpful. What people embrace freely, they tend to embrace more deeply.

Rules for Restoration: Logic, Language, and Love

Beyond removing obstacles to interior conversion, we can cultivate a deeper fidelity to the truth. Ideology thrives on lies, distortions, and seductive half-truths; resisting its pull requires an unwavering commitment to what is real, even when it's costly or inconvenient.

My mother-in-law, who is something of an etiquette expert, is fond of saying that the rules of etiquette aren't for preening socialites but exist for the sake of charity—to make others feel at ease. Similarly, I would say the laws of logic aren't just tools for academicians; they, too, are for charity. They serve as guardrails to keep debate fair, to prevent manipulation, and to ensure that disagreement can take place without devolving into dehumanization. They are indispensable if we want to preserve any meaningful form of dialogue.

The ad hominem fallacy, for instance, isn't just a logical error; it's uncharitable. To dismiss someone's argument by attacking the arguer is to refuse to justly engage their ideas. It's a fallacy inherent in the rhetoric around identity politics, wherein the identity of the speaker signifies more than the argument itself. It's a form of contempt.

Other classic fallacies like the straw man (misrepresenting someone's position), appeal to emotion, false dichotomy—all undercut the conditions necessary for a good-faith exchange. The fallacy of a false dichotomy is a common feature of ideology stemming from dialectical materialism. Examples are myriad: "Do you want a trans son or a dead daughter?" "Either you're actively anti-racist or you're complicit in white supremacy." "Trust the science or you're endangering lives." "If you're not affirming, you're not loving." Learning and internalizing the rules of logic can keep us from mirroring such fallacies and render us less susceptible to their manipulative power.

Fidelity to truth also demands discipline and accuracy of speech. Josef Pieper's *Abuse of Language, Abuse of Power* offers a profound diagnosis of the mechanisms by which language, when corrupted, becomes a tool for manipulation. He warns that when language is twisted into propaganda or demagoguery, it's not a minor deviation but a profound moral disorder. The abuse of language is the precursor to the abuse of power: Once words are no longer bound to reality, they become weapons used to shape perception, suppress dissent, and seduce people into submission.[36]

Pieper's remedy for a propagandized society is not political but philosophical: a radical recommitment to truth and the integrity of language. Truth, according to Pieper, requires more than factual accuracy; it requires a habitual devotion to reality. The abuse of language erodes the conditions for trust and freedom. Pieper insists that the love of truth—however inconvenient—forms the core of a free and virtuous society.[37]

Finally, fidelity to truth calls us to more than winning arguments, saying true things, or electing better leaders. It requires a deeper allegiance to the truth about the human person—an allegiance that moves us to resist contempt and honor their dignity, even in disagreement, conflict, or estrangement. Our animating force must be love: a love that is willing to be guided by what the moment truly demands. Sometimes that means speaking hard truths; other times, remaining silent. It may require risking the loss of a relationship or pursuing it with new humility. Above all, it asks us to see the person in front of us as a fallible human worthy of care—and to examine ourselves with the same honesty we ask of others.

10

CARRYING ON WITHOUT CLOSURE

"It hits me like a deep grief. Small things can trigger it. It is gripping and sometimes overwhelming and paralyzing," a mother confides to me as she reflects on her estrangement from her adult son. "A child is gone, and there's no path to do what comes naturally as a mother to support and protect the child, and that drive, that instinct, that basic nature of being a mother . . . it's just an assault on it. I say to myself, 'He's not dead, he's not dead.' Even when it feels like he is. I can reassure myself with that, but on the other hand, I'm not sure when I'll ever see him again."

The grief of estrangement, particularly when a resolution doesn't look to be on the horizon, is no small thing. Greg, the father from chapter 4, says there were months when tears became part of the daily routine. "Every day, we were crying. The pain is staggering—and there's no closure," he told me. "When somebody dies, there's a kind of linearity. It's over, you grieve, and eventually you move forward. But this isn't like that. It's a big, jumbled mess. It flares up, dies down, and then your hope gets reawakened."

In any conflict, there's only so much each side can control, and that control ends where the other person begins. As I noted in chapter 6, reconciliation may come slowly or not at all in this lifetime. Many of the parents I spoke with are living in this uncertainty. Yet genuine peace is possible when they've honestly examined their part in the breakdown, expressed remorse where warranted, and extended a sincere desire to rebuild the relationship. Once they've done that, it becomes easier to release control over reconciliation and avoid the chaotic spirals that can plague people in the wake of family estrangement.

True healing requires avoiding the two extremes of being racked with guilt or consumed with blame. Guilt and blame can be helpful catalysts in a certain way—guilt can prompt necessary reflection and correction, and blame might be useful in gaining clarity on the limits of one's responsibility and control. But both are easily consuming in unhealthy ways and can obscure rather than reveal the reality of one's situation.

The Gray Rock Method

Amid division, each party must do the hard work of examining whether a relationship is truly toxic or merely strained. This can be a fraught endeavor. As we've seen, past wounds and the ubiquity of pop therapeutic language make it easy to pathologize the other and difficult to see clearly. But there is a meaningful distinction: A toxic relationship isn't simply painful or challenging—it's marked by patterns of manipulation, control, coercion, and confusion. When such dynamics are present, it becomes essential not only to reject those behaviors within oneself but also to disengage from them when on the receiving end.

Disengaging from manipulative behavior doesn't always

require cutting off the relationship entirely. Boundaries can be drawn without resorting to total rupture. One adult daughter I spoke with has, at times, considered going no contact with her mother. The reasons would be familiar to many: chronic criticism, an impenetrable victim narrative, and unpredictable outbursts. Just after the birth of their second child, the daughter and her husband called to share the joyful news, send photos, and invite her to the hospital to see the baby. Her mother didn't answer. Instead, she sent a curt message accusing them of snubbing her because she hadn't been invited into the delivery room for the birth (though she had never asked to be). Her mother left town without seeing the baby or speaking to her daughter and refused to take her call for weeks.

This daughter reflects on how easily, in her vulnerable postpartum state, she could have turned to TikTok or other platforms, where a wealth of "pain porn" accounts might have filtered her experience through the lens of #ToxicParents and funneled her toward severance. Instead, without even knowing the term, she adopted the strategy of gray rocking—a way of dealing with manipulative or emotionally volatile people by making yourself emotionally nonreactive so they lose interest in trying to provoke or control you. "I just learned the term *gray rock*," she told me with a laugh. "I thought, *That's what I have been doing for the last twelve years!* I used to try to give my mom a different perspective. I used to expect her to improve or have healthier reactions, but now I just treat her with kindness but don't expect too much nor engage too deeply."

She visits her, takes her to appointments here and there, meets her occasionally for lunch, hosts her for holidays, but keeps emotional and physical engagement minimal. She trained herself to let what used to be triggering roll off her back. She offers no alternative perspective when her mother spirals into suspicion or self-pity, nor does she pursue greater closeness. The daughter has a full and flourishing life, and her emotional needs are met elsewhere.

From the outside, their relationship shows no sign of this emotional distance or of a history of struggle. Her mother seems unaware that what she now receives is not intimacy but duty. This unspoken emotional boundary—quietly, consistently maintained—has made the relationship more stable. The daughter interacts with her mom cheerfully but no longer responds to provocations, and she is quick to extract herself if her mom escalates. She simply doesn't expect or hope for a healthy perspective from her so is no longer frustrated by her limitations. "I really could have justified going no contact at various points, and I would not judge anyone who does. But I am so glad I did not. I think it is good for me to not be consumed by past hurts and to be present for someone who is unpleasant. And I think it is good for her to not be totally alone."

From the parents' perspective, several interviewees shared that they've also had to learn the discipline of not taking the bait when their adult child becomes emotionally volatile or seems to be provoking a fight. One mother described her turning point as the realization that peace comes not from controlling the relationship but from mastering her own responses. "I simply ignore any and all provocations, and they seem to have become less frequent now." Self-control in challenging relationships can simply mean refusing to let someone else govern our inner world.

While accepting this sort of limited relationship is short of the ideal of full reengagement and closeness, many feel it's infinitely preferable to either full estrangement or the exhausting struggle to force a relationship that simply isn't possible. Still, there are no guarantees that even this limited arrangement can be forged.

End with an Olive Branch

Natalie, another estranged mother, is learning the difficult art of surrender in what now feels like a final rupture with her daughter, Helen. During college, Helen began drifting away from her Christian upbringing and into progressive activism. Natalie admits that she and her husband were unprepared. "We were pretty naïve," she says. What started as ideological disagreements—on abortion, feminism, and gay marriage—gradually widened into a deeper chasm, one that included a growing disenchantment with church life altogether.

Natalie carries deep regret about how they responded in those early years. "We didn't listen well. We didn't see it coming, and we thought it might be a phase," she reflects. "One of her criticisms, of me especially, was that I didn't ask enough questions, that I didn't seem curious."

But Natalie was more curious than Helen realized. Helen had started a blog to air her frustrations with conservative Christianity and discuss the need to resist it. Natalie read every post. "It was painful. She's a great writer—strong and articulate. Not someone you push back on easily. I'd describe her tone as that of a zealous evangelist for an anti-Christian progressivism."

Before Covid, they were finding their way. "It was not particularly comfortable, but we were in relationship," Natalie says. During Covid lockdowns, however, Helen's blog took on a new tenor. "She was posting pretty regularly about it, and it was striking how fearful she was. It just wasn't how we raised the kids with more of a sense of peace." Christmas 2020 became a flash point. Natalie and her husband hosted several extended family members in addition to their immediate family. Helen criticized her parents for not adhering strictly to Covid rules by exceeding the number of guests that was deemed safe at the time. "She called very upset and said, 'I'm disappointed in you.' I just can't imagine saying that to my parents." Her mother found the correction not just jarring but full of hostility.

Once the vaccine became available, Helen asked her parents if they were going to get it and became irate when Natalie said that she and her husband had decided to opt out. This news for Helen was the tipping point. She made it clear that she wouldn't be seeing any of the unvaccinated and told them to please cancel their planned visit. Helen cut all contact from there. Natalie sent cards and letters, but they were returned.

After a couple of years, Natalie heard from a family member still in touch with Helen that she would be open to hearing an apology from her mom. Natalie reached out. She tried to write a letter without defensiveness, laying down her faults and regrets. "I tried to avoid referencing context to steer clear of shifting blame."

Dear Helen,

I often think back to a time in your life when you were becoming an adult—discovering who you were and forming your beliefs and values. Looking back, I now see more clearly what my role should have been: to offer steady love, to stay open in communication, and to be very respectful of the young woman you were becoming.

Helen, I fell short in all of these. I see now that I failed you in many ways. Instead of listening with curiosity to you, I withdrew. I wish I had just sat and listened, asked questions and affirmed my love for you. I let fear and pride get in the way. And over time, instead of fighting for connection, I allowed distance and disappointment to settle in. That has been one of my deepest regrets.

I am so sorry for the hurt I have caused you. I would handle it all so differently now. Thank you for hearing me out.

I love you,

Mom

Helen hasn't yet responded. Natalie has come to terms with the fact that she can't control the outcome. A raw and recent source of pain is knowing that Helen is now married with two small children whom she might never meet.

Natalie realizes for so long she defined herself by things other than God, including, naturally, the love of her family. She has found new comfort in her faith and the relationship she has with her other adult children. "This experience in some ways has drawn the rest of us very close." Two of Helen's siblings have also left the Christian faith they were raised in but still can express gratitude for what it gave them and how they were raised. One sister who was particularly close with Helen seems bewildered at her treatment of their parents: "They just approached it all so differently. Helen was so angry about being raised with conservative Christian beliefs. The others are no longer Christian, but they aren't angry." Of course, she notes, the other siblings aren't as political as Helen, which Natalie believes may have contributed to her more severe approach.

The estrangement is now almost five years in, and the

struggle is still difficult, but Natalie no longer ruminates as she used to. "The most repeated question I have asked myself over the years is 'What if you really are the problem?' That is getting less and less."

Though Natalie has regrets, she feels peaceful knowing she has sincerely accounted for what she should have done differently, and she has found a freedom and surrender in owning that and speaking it. When I asked for what further advice she would pass along, she simply said, "It's in that apology I sent her. It's who I should have been and how I should have shown up."

Rethinking Strategic Shunning

A common theme in these conversations is how decisively 2020 served as an acceleration point. In a 2025 *New York Times* essay adapted from his memoir, David Litt reflects on the escalation of contempt, rethinking it from a progressive perspective. The essay's title raises a question that, just a decade ago, might have seemed unthinkable: "Is It Time to Stop Snubbing Your Right-Wing Family?"[1]

Litt's essay is part reflection, part confession. He tells the story of his evolving relationship with his wife's brother, Matt Kappler, a man he first met in 2012 and with whom he had almost nothing in common. "He lifted weights to death metal; I jogged to Sondheim," Litt writes, also contrasting his ivy league degree to his brother-in-law's electrician's license.[2] Litt and his brother-in-law had an amiable but not close relationship, though Litt clearly saw him as too other (and from the tone of his description, perhaps he also saw him as too inferior).

The breaking point came in 2020, when Kappler decided

against getting the Covid-19 vaccine. Litt, like many others on the cultural left, saw this not as a personal choice but as a civic affront, and he decided he had an obligation to begin treating him coldly on the rare occasions he saw him. He believed, at the time, that being unfriendly to the unvaccinated was the only way to help them "mend their ways."[3]

He wasn't alone in thinking this. Litt cites a 2021 *USA Today* column bluntly titled "It's Time to Start Shunning the 'Vaccine Hesitant,'" which advocated for social exclusion as a public health tactic.[4] The *Los Angeles Times* went further, suggesting public mockery of some who die unvaccinated as a kind of "teachable moment."[5]

Litt began to rethink his treatment of Kappler when he started surfing—a hobby at which Kappler excelled. Litt, needing a surf guru, asked Kappler to join him. It reset their relationship and soon became a habit. "It helped that in the ocean, our places in the pecking order reversed. Matt's a very good surfer—one might call him an elite—and I am not. According to surfing's unwritten rules, he had the right to look down on me. But he never did. His generosity of spirit in the water made me rethink my own behavior on land."[6]

In 2020 and the years following, there was a tacit understanding on the left that political disagreement, particularly with those coded as holding out-group beliefs, was grounds for moral condemnation. Such people were not just wrong but inferior. Estrangement, then, was not only justified but also sanctified as a moral imperative. Political purity, in effect, trumped kinship.

It's a sharp diagnosis of the pandemic years and of a broader moral realignment in American life. The politics of estrangement thrives on the illusion that coercion can replace persuasion and that shame can substitute for reason. Some are only beginning to reckon with the relational wreckage left in its wake.

One perceptive social media commentator responding to Litt's piece explains why this coercive strategy failed so profoundly: "Libs thought that other people were invested in social approval and in-group membership to the same degree that they are; their theory of mind couldn't account for how little their disapproval mattered or even, paradoxically, worked as a motivation for the oppositional."[7] In other words, they assumed that belonging was universally mediated through group consensus—and that dissenters would fall in line if the in-group signaled disapproval loudly and persistently enough.

This was a tactical misstep. It was also a profound failure of imagination: the projection of one psychological profile onto a vast, pluralistic nation. The disapproval of the chattering class didn't merely fail to persuade their perceived inferiors; it came across to half the country as insufferable, mimicking the social dynamics of an adolescent girl at the "in" lunch table. The result was not persuasion but predictable repulsion. The more they were shamed, the more resolved the dissenters became.

Now, as the power to coerce wanes and the emergency atmosphere recedes at least temporarily, ruptures among families and friends in many cases persist. It's one thing to post a quiet retraction in a newspaper. It's much harder to admit to a lifelong friend or relative that you shamed and shunned them over a pack of partial truths and social pressure.

This refusal to examine one's own complicity has cascading consequences. The issue is no longer simply who was right about masks and mandates, school closures, and the firing of the unvaccinated. It's about how we define persuasion, how we handle difference, and whether we can still function as a pluralistic society. The stakes are civilizational.

While there are signs that some, like Litt, are beginning to reckon with the fallout of ideological division, the comments section on his piece indicates that many still have no appetite for introspection. The most upvoted response—endorsed by nearly 4,800 readers—delivers a blunt rebuttal saying that no, it is not time to stop the snubbing and that this isn't about tax policy but about an embrace of dehumanization and the cheering for "policies that cage children, strip bodily autonomy, demonize the poor, and erase entire communities from public life. And now we're being asked to make room for that at the dinner table? No." The path, this commenter says, is repentance and change.[8]

Another comment in the highly upvoted category reads: "I will continue to shun people who knowingly support cruelty, corruption, and dangerous incompetence."[9]

One popular comment said that unless Trump voters are asking to atone for this sin, they are not good people. "My life is too short to waste time trying to find 'small moments in common' with them."[10]

An another said plainly, "Do not normalize evil."[11]

No society or relationship can endure when one side denies all culpability, clings to tribalistic black-and-white thinking, and insists on interpreting the other in the worst possible light. It might be only a comments section, but each of these comments was upvoted by the thousands, and there are hundreds more of them—it reveals a real and troubling psychology. It's hard to imagine any of those commenters preparing to un-shun their conservative friends and relatives. And frankly, who would want to reconcile with someone who regards them with such unyielding contempt?

How Dysfunction Fuels Dogma

The complexity of personal estrangement defies easy categorization. There is often a spectrum of culpability on both sides, yet online echo chambers tend to flatten that complexity. Forums for estranged adult children can be quick to label all estranged parents as toxic narcissists. Meanwhile, support groups for estranged parents may too readily dismiss their children as entitled or emotionally unstable. In my own experience and in conversations with therapists—outside of cases of abuse and addiction—estrangement is rarely a simple story of villain and victim. Most fall into a murky middle: imperfect people, strained relationships, missteps, and miscommunications. That said, genuine pathology does exist. Some parents do exhibit toxic narcissistic behavior, and increasingly, clinicians are identifying the same in adult children. Yet the progressive injection of cancel culture into family dynamics, combined with a left-wing blind spot toward its own authoritarian impulses, has made ideological estrangement far more commonly instigated by the left, though that can swing the other direction as the ideological winds shift.

Litt's case captures the political dimension in isolation, but others' clinical experiences show how often those politics are fused with deeper psychological pathologies, making reconciliation far more challenging or perhaps not possible. One of those clinicians is psychiatrist Hannah Spier, who has seen a marked rise in adult children cutting ties with their parents in recent years. Her clinical work has brought her face-to-face with a pattern of emotional immaturity among young adults, many of whom exhibit traits associated with Cluster B personality disorders: borderline, narcissistic, histrionic. In conversation with me, she notes how behaviors once written off as adolescent rebellion are now stretching well into adulthood. "Slamming doors and yelling 'I hate you'—that might be developmentally understandable from a fourteen-year-old," she explains. "But when it's a twenty-three-year-old doing it, the damage is real. The parent is no longer in a position of authority, yet the tantrums remain."

Spier's clients, mostly young women, often come from homes where attachments didn't form well. "Either the parents were over-permissive, or they outsourced parenting, believing that kids simply did not need their presence as much as they do. The parents often didn't give them a coherent value system. They said, 'Whatever you want is right.' And 'Follow your truth.' But that kind of permissiveness creates confusion, not confidence."

"If you have a stable identity, you don't think about it as much," Spier explains. "It's just who you are, so you're not as prone to feel attacked. You can be with a person and disagree and not crumble." Spier says that the underlying issue for such patients isn't primarily ideological but, for them, the draw of ideology is almost irresistible.

"They are desperate for an identity, and what they often find is ideology. Ideology offers clarity, identity, and a moral righteousness." According to Spier, in such cases the ideology is secondary to the pathology. "If you're so set on hating half of the country, that is a sign there is some underlying issue; you are too sensitive to ideological possession. When people cannot talk and disagree about politics, it is because that's become their identity, so disagreement feels like an attack."

While this militancy can sometimes stem from severe attachment disorders, it's also the case that today's political and cultural climate can inflame even moderate identity insecurity into full-blown pathology. "Birds in a high predation area—they're high in neuroticism. Similarly, during Covid, trait neuroticism went up as people sensed they were constantly under threat." Spier observes that, even before the pandemic, girls were already being conditioned to feel perpetually unsafe. A pornified adolescence, the erosion of sexual boundaries, and the cultural narrative of men as inherent predators have left many young women living in a constant state of alarm.

One of the most challenging dynamics Spier sees is what she calls "lavatoric transference"—when all a young person's anxiety, hopelessness, and shame get poured onto the parent. "They dump it all on you. And if you respond, you're validating the behavior. Parents need to resist the urge to fix it. Don't chase them or fight with them. Just repeat, 'I'm here to talk when you're ready.'"

Spier notes that she sees many young adults who tend to villainize their parents, often engaging in rigid, black-and-white thinking. Part of her therapeutic work involves helping them develop a more integrated view of people—to be slow to idealize or to villainize others. "Understanding is the antidote to hate. For most adults that is a normal thing, but it is completely novel to them."

For many of her patients, it's a very long road to shift into a more mature way of thinking. It's not that reconciliation is impossible, but it usually comes after some kind of crash. "I tell parents to have faith," she says. "When the child's life starts to fall apart, that's when you might get a window. But you need to be ready. That's when you start 're-parenting.' Reward insight. Encourage small steps when they make them. Show up when they want connection. But disengage when they want drama."

Still, Spier cautions against a simplistic diagnosis and stresses that though she is seeing a sharp rise in these cases, each situation is unique. "Not every child who cuts off a parent is disordered. Some are wounded. Some are navigating unresolved pain. And in some cases, the estrangement is a necessary boundary from a parent who really did harm." Nonetheless, she believes many modern estrangements stem from the increase in emotional fragility, which in turn stems from the diminishing importance given to the job of parenting. "There's a lack of resilience. A kind of developmental arrest."

According to Spier, part of the cultural solution is to stop downplaying how hard parenting is and how much help it takes. "It's not just two people and a child. It takes extended family, mentors, a community. That's why we live so long—new parents need their parents to help raise the next generation." Downgrading the importance of family has fed the instability of identity. Generational ruptures further cut us off from such connections.

Spier acknowledges that time, maturity, and especially becoming a parent can help many young people grow out of this pattern. But her counsel to parents echoes what many find hardest to hear: You can't force your child to return. "Stop trying to fix it," she says. "Stop chasing. You'll only reinforce the story that you're controlling. Instead, keep the door open."

Advice from Estranged Parents

At the end of every interview I conducted for this book, I asked one final question: What advice would you give to parents, either preventative or for someone walking the same path? What have you learned, and what wisdom might you offer? The answers were diverse, but patterns emerged.

1. Parent for the World Your Children Live In, Not the One You Grew Up In

Awareness of the modern cultural context is crucial. Parenting strategies must account for the vastly different pressures and environments children face today, including the pervasive impact of social media. Greg's wife, Tammy, offers, "I wish I had recognized how toxic online culture was. Our daughter was part of the first generation deeply shaped by social media. I underestimated its influence." Many parents echoed some version of this sentiment: that they had parented for the culture they were raised in, not the culture their kids were being raised in.

"The thing that hangs most heavily on my heart and mind is to not take for granted the danger facing them," Greg adds. "That danger concept is important because it triggers the right parental instincts."

2. Create a Storehouse of Positive Memories

Greg also thinks back on how demanding his work was at the time and how he needed to be present to the other kids and duties and how all of that perhaps let him excuse himself from throwing himself into his relationship with his angsty daughter. "The advice I would give to fathers is to give your daughters as much love as you can—not in order to persuade her, but to give her a whole host of positive memories that are going to quietly rest in her heart."

Greg wrestles with the inevitable self-recrimination. "Would it have made any difference? I don't know. Would it have damaged my relationship with the other two kids? I don't know. You can go crazy with all the what-ifs," he admits. For fathers of sons, he thinks the same principle applies but with a different dynamic. "With daughters, it's more long conversations, more connecting," he says.

3. Resist Magical Thinking

Several parents emphasized the importance of letting go of control. One mother echoed an old adage: "You pray like it depends on God, and you work like it depends on you. . . . In the end, you can't control everything."

Another mother spoke of finding a balance between maintaining hope and ruminating over wishful thinking. "For a long time, I thought, *She will come back*," she admits. "Now I don't know. Acceptance, I guess, is the key. If they're open to talking, I'd do everything to make it happen. But if they're not, you just have to find God."

Acceptance doesn't mean resignation. It allows parents to focus their energy on what they *can* nurture—relationships with other children, marriage, faith, and community. One mother told me quietly, "My deepest wish is that we'll be together in heaven, even if it doesn't happen here." Over time, she has learned to attend to what she has. "I try to focus on my blessings. I have other children and grandchildren nearby, and we're building beautiful relationships."

Another estranged mother spoke of how their fiftieth wedding anniversary was coming up. She hesitated to plan a celebration, knowing that their son and his wife and their children wouldn't be there. But her husband insisted that they have it with the other children and the grandchildren who are still in their life. "'Nope, we're having it,' he said.

And he's right." Then she adds with resolve, "We're going to celebrate what we *do* have."

4. Be Vulnerable with Others

Roger, a father from chapter 6, offers this piece of wisdom: "I would tell any parents that are in a similar situation to be open with their circle of friends and family about the strained relationship with their child. It can be embarrassing, but from a Catholic point of view, that's not a bad lesson in humility. It's also very cathartic to explain where things are rather than put some false pretense about everything being okay."

How much to bring others in was a common question for many parents, as estrangement can feel intensely private. Roger's decision to bring in "the godmothers" proved wise; they gave him language for his pain and clarity to see his blind spots. Other parents spoke about how a trusted therapist became their lifeline, helping them navigate the grief and emotional confusion, untangle responsibility from false guilt, and ultimately surrender what lay beyond their control. Others find that a spiritual director greatly helps them course correct. Many lean on a support network of good friends. Hardly anyone can see things clearly on their own.

5. Find a Way to De-Center Your Pain

One mother who is estranged says of the pain, "It was a different level of suffering. We had normal suffering before. This was something else. We try not to talk about it too much."

Another mother estranged from her son says that there were nights when she went to bed in the fetal position while her husband carried on, watching her slowly disappear. One day, maybe eighteen months after the estrangement, something shifted. "My husband came and sat next to me with tears in his eyes. He said he needed me too. I saw how this was affecting him. And I thought, *Okay, I can't do this to him. I need to keep living.*"

She and her husband have had to accept that reconciliation might not happen in their lifetime. "If I could give advice—and I'm not sure I could've heard it at the time, the pain was so great—it would be, don't make this about your pain." She recalls another moment of clarity. "I wrote a prayer about how God loves my son more than I do. That was the beginning of something new." She felt she could entrust him to a good and loving and all-powerful Father who knew the intricacies of his soul and wanted nothing but his good. She's found healing through her faith, her marriage, and her church community. "We really learned about redemptive suffering. That helped us reframe it. God allows hard things. And through it we can draw closer to him."

In the end, Greg's conclusion is as much spiritual as it is practical: "Probably the best outcome is that you don't really start to trust God until you have nowhere else to go. You think you trust him—but when there's nothing left, then you start. You go through the whole process: *Why do I have to do this? Why is this happening?* But this is the paschal mystery. Those whom he loves, he chastises. Right up to the eighth beatitude: 'Blessed are you when they hate you. . . . Rejoice and be glad on that day.' I never thought that would be happening to me." For Greg, that's the paradox: The deeper the suffering, the deeper the participation in God's own fatherhood.

To move through the pain of estrangement, it helps to place it in a larger context—one that gives suffering a sense of purpose. Simply marinating in pain doesn't help. But when we ask how this pain might be used for good, it becomes less paralyzing. Some parents find healing by mentoring others in similar situations or perhaps in the earlier stages, breaking the isolation that estrangement so often brings. Support groups provide not just empathy but solidarity—a reminder that you aren't alone. Others turn their suffering into intercession, offering their pain as a prayer for their child's healing. Meditating on stories of people throughout history who have suffered well can also become a wellspring of strength.

The parents I encountered who have the most peace have discovered meaning in suffering. Ideology, by contrast, tends to strip life of mystery and meaning, calcifying pain into an identity defined by that pain. Healing, however, demands something deeper: not the erasure of pain, but the integration of it into a larger and deeper context.

This meaning need not be tidy or transactional. It doesn't require some sort of facile understanding such as "Now I understand why my child left, because it led to x, y, or z." Often it's something more mysterious and open ended: "I don't know exactly what God is doing with this loss, but I do know that it is drawing me closer to him and to the Cross. And that is enough. He is good, and he is worthy of my trust." In that sort of posture, meaning can emerge, reorienting the sufferer toward something more transcendent and enduring.

Advice for Civic Unity

In addition to the insights gleaned from families, I want to summarize practical steps we can all take to foster civic and familial unity and reduce polarization. Ideology will always follow certain patterns to divide us in new ways. Here are concrete resolutions that can help shape a healthier society now and in the future by inoculating us against its seductive power.

1. Disavow Identity Politics Utterly, on Every Level and in Every Direction

Identity politics reduces human beings to their politicized categories and encourages us to define others by those categories rather than their character. It's never a principled position, and it only invites others to engage in their own version of it. It incentivizes victimhood and accusation and dehumanizes everyone it affects. Treat each person as a unique individual, not an avatar of a politicized group identity. Only then can real dialogue and understanding take place.

Recognize that the line between good and evil doesn't run along tribal or political divisions but exists in the heart of every person.[12] Victim culture, which encourages perpetual grievance, self-righteousness, and simplistic thinking, fosters constant conflict and undermines the ability to self-examine. A healthy society requires seeing beyond these divisions.

2. Attend to the Good in Others

What we give our attention to can form or deform us. When we focus too much on what we hate, we tend to become a mirror image of it. If we want better personal relationships, we need to scan for what is good in others and consider that more than we consider what we might not like in them. Create a habit of noticing the good wherever you see it—at home, in your community, in your ideological opponents. Such habits of thought more easily turn into habits of action and acts of affection. Feed your affection with words and actions.

Small gestures of recognition can build bridges of trust and shared humanity.

3. Attend Less to the Daily News Cycle

Realize that outrage is pleasurable and feeding it attaches us to a vicious addiction. Resist the pull of constant media churn. We don't need to stay on top of the froth and frenzy of an accelerated news cycle. If you sit down to cable news every evening, remind yourself that news networks are there as your drug supplier—to redirect the work of virtue into the ease of outrage and a tribalistic in-group belonging. If you take to social media to express your indignation over every political development, you look unhinged and unhealthy.

Limit your consumption and seek sources that encourage thoughtful reflection rather than emotional reaction. And perhaps reinvest some of that time and energy in something of far more enduring cultural value like literature or nature or human interaction—things that take us out of the slavery of the now.

4. Commit to the Rules of Logic

As discussed in the previous chapter, we need to learn and love the rules of logic, as they are guardrails that keep discussion charitable. Don't discredit a legitimate position by assuming malicious motives; don't attack the person instead of the argument. Beware of false dichotomies—such either/or thinking is often a form of emotional manipulation meant to bypass careful thought and other possibilities. Strive to defeat the strongest argument on the other side rather than a straw man version of it. Stick to reason, evidence, and fair-minded analysis. Logical fallacies escalate conflict, cement ideological walls, and make dialogue impossible. If we want a healthier public sphere, we must train ourselves to think and argue logically.

Knowing the rules of logic also helps you know when to bow out of a discussion. When an interlocutor repeatedly engages in fallacies, recognize that continued discussion is likely futile and will lead only to escalation. This doesn't mean bow out of the relationship, just that reasoned discussion is unlikely to be a shared dynamic for now.

5. Be Curious

Curiosity slows the impulse to react. Letting our immediate reactions dictate our behavior is precisely what fuels division and conflict. It's the rage spiral that leads to civil war. Cultivating curiosity interrupts that cycle. It also helps us foster relationships across the aisle, seeing those who disagree not as enemies but as potential partners in a shared pursuit. Instead of approaching someone with the goal of proving them wrong, try approaching with the goal of understanding why they see things differently. This posture can disarm the other and invite them to engage more humanly as well.

6. Be Inauthentic

This might be the most provocative line in the book. Authenticity, in its current conception, treats being true to yourself as the highest moral mandate—and it's making us absolutely miserable. Modern authenticity means that what you feel determines what you should do. The self is reduced to a bundle of desires, feelings, and impulses untethered from stable commitments or objective goods. But such an inner self is inherently fluid, and basing action on it makes our behavior unreliable and our relationships unstable.

True freedom, by contrast, lies in self-governance. Familial bonds shape who we are and provide the first contours of identity. Yet as we mature into moral agents, our actions are within our responsibility, and they can and should shape who we become. In other words, identity ultimately follows action. Exercising this distinctively human capacity to discern the good and to repeatedly choose it makes us truly authentic and in accord with our humanity, not by following our hearts, but by leading them.

Forgiveness and Hope

It can be tempting to avoid the pain of the present by focusing relentlessly on the past or the future. Many parents voiced the need to stop ruminating on discouragement over the past—by way of either regret or anger. Several mentioned having imaginary arguments with their child, saying things just right and changing the outcome. Others felt intense anxiety by focusing on the future—wondering if reconciliation will come or what more anguish might await them around the corner. It strikes me that there are healthy and unhealthy ways to integrate both past and future. We can be filled with despair over what has been and fear over what will be, or we can learn from the mistakes or hurts of the past and apply that wisdom to the future for ourselves and others. We can prepare for what will come by improving how we live now.

To say it in a more spiritual context, the past needs forgiveness, the future needs hope, and the present needs our attention. Kate, from chapter 6, states emphatically the importance of forgiveness—even if a relationship seems presently irredeemable: "If you leave forgiveness on the table, you're leaving healing on the table. Forgiveness is a call for our own development. It's not the same as saying it's okay what they did."

For parents who've been cut off, forgiveness is also something they find they need to seek for themselves. Those who felt they had done a sincere examination of their contributions to the demise of their relationships, and asked for forgiveness for those contributions, tended to have a deeper level of peace.

In each conversation, hope seemed to be as tricky to navigate as forgiveness. Many hesitated to harbor hope, afraid that it might set them up for more heartache. One father counseled that you need to keep hope alive: "Pack it in there. Put a lot of nice padding around it and leave it safe to one side because you might need to access it one day."

His wife holds hope carefully: "If she ever came to the door, wanting a hug, I'd give her one. I would be there for her completely. If she came to demand something, I'd be cautious. It would depend entirely on her disposition."

I asked another mom how she felt about hope in the face of what seems like a permanent estrangement. "I have a lot of hope in my life," she told me. Her prayer life has taken on a new depth, as she feels acutely her need to rely first and foremost on God. "I think I hope in other things now."

Who Are We Becoming?

Forgiveness is often characterized as weakness or enabling of evil, especially in a culture steeped in therapeutic jargon and ideological rigidity. But true forgiveness is neither passive nor naïve—it's a refusal to let bitterness define the terms of one's life.

In his book *The Power of Parting*, Eamon Dolan tells a story that presents a case for bitterness as the right and just response. As one *New York Times* writer summarizes in a review, "In the absence of sufficient atonement for such trespasses, Dolan suggests, forgiveness is overrated and in some cases 'see ya wouldn't want to be ya' is exactly what the doctor should order. One adult child, visiting her brain-dead father after 15 years of not talking to him, resumed contact with a bang. 'I punched him in the arm!' she tells Dolan. 'I dug my fingers into his skin at one point.'"[13]

I wouldn't presume to sit in judgment of how a person who has endured abuse seeks relief. Trauma leaves no road map, and survivors must find their own way to peace. But even as I grant that (and note that abuse-related estrangements aren't the subject of this book), I can't help but see something tragic in this moment—not for the brain-dead father so much as for the daughter. And beyond that, for the society that seems hungry not for justice (and certainly not mercy) but for a ferocity of vengeance made clean by the sacralizing of victimhood.

According to this new ethos, forgiveness becomes unintelligible. It's a philosophy that admits nothing of mercy because it can't conceive of transformation. And that, I fear, is not strength or justice but nihilism. When a culture finds its catharsis not in healing but in ritualized denunciation and retribution, it signals a turning point toward something exacting and self-destructive. This apocalyptic spirit of finality now has its own cultural prestige.

The irony is sharp: In our attempt to escape pain, we often deepen it. What begins as self-protection can harden into self-rejection—a refusal to risk healing, whether in relationship or within the self. The very people who cut others off in the name of self-care often find themselves lonelier, more brittle, more consumed by the very wounds they hoped to leave behind.

We should ask ourselves, "What kind of people are we becoming?"

It's good and right to mitigate suffering where we can, through medicine, policy, science, and social reform. But something insidious happens when we come to see the elimination of pain as the highest good. Utopian ideologies promise to reengineer society in such a way that makes suffering no longer necessary. This is the hallmark of totalizing systems: the promise that pain is not necessarily a permanent feature of the human condition to be endured and redeemed but the result of social problems to be controlled. When suffering is seen as an intolerable aberration, we become incapable of bearing it.

A society that loses its sense of transcendence loses its capacity to suffer well. If there is no ultimate horizon, no divine purpose beyond the self, pain ceases to be something that can be meaningfully integrated. It becomes a glitch in the system, an offense to our self-concept, or a trauma to be surgically removed.

This disordered rejection of suffering leads to a disordered celebration of comfort. When lesser goods—like safety, pleasure, and comfort—are elevated to ultimate ones, they eventually betray us. It's the moral of the Midas myth: Material pursuits can be fine and good, but when they are made into the ultimate good, they devour all else. Likewise, comfort and the avoidance of suffering aren't bad in themselves, but when we treat them as the highest goods, we lose our grip on deeper human goods. We become incapable of enduring, of forgiving, even of loving. Real love is the willingness to sacrifice for the beloved—and such sacrifice becomes nonsensical in the logic of no contact. The pursuit of a painless life eventually robs us of a meaningful one.

Suffering, then, either has meaning or does not. If it has no meaning, there is nothing to do but detest it and try to escape. But if it does—even if we can't fully see it—we are given a way to endure it and to be changed by it. As Viktor Frankl, Holocaust survivor and founder of logotherapy, observes, "suffering ceases to be suffering at the moment it finds a meaning, such as the meaning of a sacrifice." Frankl emphasizes that when there is a "why" to live for, the "how" becomes tolerable.[14]

This insight is all the more urgent in a culture that has largely abandoned belief in the transcendent. For a mechanistic materialist age, it's not only suffering that has no meaning but our lives as well.

Meaning, in contrast, invites us into interior freedom and responsibility. It asks each of us to consider not only "What happened to me?" but also "Who am I becoming in response?"

I think of Natalie, who did the painful work of setting aside her certainty that her daughter was in the wrong. Rather than obsessing over her daughter's rejection, she turned inward and asked, with humility, what role she might have played in the pain. After the estrangement, Natalie began to spiral around one persistent question: *What if I'm the one at fault?* She could have drowned in that. But she didn't. She chose honesty, taking responsibility without self-condemnation or self-justification. In doing so, she found a place to put her hope.

I think, too, of Kier Adrian Gray in chapter 9. Her life as a social justice warrior had been one rupture after another. Immersed in a culture of ideological purity so rigorous that it demanded constant distancing and denunciation, she was trained to see accusation as the pinnacle of the moral life. And yet, one day, in a default state of simmering rage and misery, a single question pierced through her thoughts so intently that she wrote it down and stuck it to a wall: "How do I contribute to my own misery?"

Rupture is the heartbeat of ideology because all ideologies grow through division. But it's all of us who lose. As Václav Havel, dissident intellectual under Communism and later president of Czechoslovakia, wrote, "Ideology is a specious way of relating to the world. It offers human beings the illusion of an identity, of dignity, and of morality while making it easier for them to *part* with them."[15] Ideology traffics in promises it can't keep—belonging, virtue, meaning—while separating us from what makes those promises real.

The Immaterial Architecture

In the beginning of this book, I employed the metaphor of a wildfire, a disturbingly common occurrence in my home state of California. In the fires of early 2025, the devastation was catastrophic. Residents of the Pacific Palisades and Altadena areas saw homes ignited, engulfed, flattened. The wildfire consumed not only homes but also entire communities—civilizations unto themselves.

For those who've lost homes, there is a deep and real grief, not unlike the loss of a loved one. A home is very much like a body. Indeed, it is the body of the family—reinforcing the sense that the individuals within are members of a whole. We can even misuse it as we misuse bodies—either treating both like vanity projects or reducing them to mere tools to use and, in so doing, misuse. But the loss of home is mourned, not like the loss of a tool nor the demise of a vanity project, but—much like a body—like the loss of something sacred, a physical reality that meant far more than its material components and permanently affected those who knew its ins and outs.

This metaphor can illuminate the layers of devastation left by family rupture and the ways those layers reverberate beyond any one broken bond. It also reminds us that the causes of ideological estrangement are complex. After every wildfire, people look for the culprit: climate, incompetent or corrupt leadership, negligent land management, delinquents with illegal open flames, arsonists. It's both devastating and complex to clearly identify one cause, though everyone likes to think they know who is to blame.

The truth is blame usually rests a bit on all of us. The trees should have been cut back. Dangerously neglected dry brush dotted the landscape. There were unprecedented hot high winds. Was it one person's negligence or government corruption that left a reservoir bone dry? The city hadn't allocated enough resources, and the firefighters were overwhelmed.[16] Police caught a suspected arsonist who was allegedly at the Palisades fire's origin and another man with a blowtorch in Los Angeles. You wouldn't expect that level of malevolence in humanity, but some people really do want to burn things to the ground.

The estrangement epidemic wasn't born of ideology alone. Countless small and large failures laid the groundwork—failures of generosity, the affliction of hyper-individualism, the spiritual disease of "me," the malformation of therapeutic culture, the elevation of the victim identity, the totalization of the political, the decline of the spiritual. All of this has created a dry landscape of fuel and tinder ripe for a wildfire. But if the conditions have been set in these deeper ways, today's media influencers and craven TikTok therapists light a match. Headlines that celebrate cutting off your parents light a match. Academics who blithely write off the family as a social construct—or, worse, an oppressive institution—light a match. Politicians and pundits urging young people to "educate" their backward families at the Thanksgiving table light a match. Each of us, insofar as we are afflicted with a terminal paucity of love when it's difficult, lights a match.

My sister posted a video after the destruction of the recent California fires. The video captured her friends, a large Catholic family with their hearts broken at the site of the smoldering remains of their longtime family home, singing in resplendent choral spontaneity the Regina Caeli—a hymn of rejoicing in what God has done for us. It rightly went viral. National news carried the story, and celebrities shared it on their feeds. Observers sensed that this unknown family was speaking, or singing, a love and longing heretofore unarticulated publicly in the stew of news stories about the calamity. The family lost not just a tool, nor a material treasure, but something more—the very same something more that made them sing in its wake.

Fire reveals what's underneath. It exposes not only loss but also longing. The politics of estrangement have rendered millions bereft—not of a physical home but of the immaterial architecture that holds a family together. That invisible structure, which once tied each member to a history, a context, a purpose—and, through that purpose, to one another—has been left in ruins.

We can't stamp out all human failure or erase every wound, but we can clear away the cultural underbrush, cut back some overgrowth, and keep the reservoirs flush with water. While we may never prevent every spark, we can work to reset social and personal conditions that will determine whether the landscape is parched and tinder-dry or cared for and maintained.

If this fire is to be stopped, it will be not by ideology but by another sort of fire altogether—one that brings things back to life, draws us in, moves us to remember, and stirs a longing in us to remind those who have forgotten. This reclamation of memory will spread not through mere argumentation or education but through igniting witnesses to go forth and spark in others a deep burning desire for the things that hold us together individually and collectively—and beckon us to return to what we once knew: where we have come from, why we are here, and to whom we belong.

Acknowledgments

Not many people are willing to invite a stranger into their grief. I am deeply indebted to those who did, entrusting me to enter such personal and painful places. This book would not exist without them. They, and all who suffer similarly, remain in my daily prayers.

I am very grateful to my agent, Keely Boeving, a consummate professional with an incisive intellect and a generosity of spirit. My deep thanks also go to my brilliant editor, Matt Burdette, who is insightful and honest to the point of irreverence—one of my favorite qualities in a person. It's hard for me to imagine a better agent and editor experience. Their care and wisdom shaped and strengthened this book every step of the way.

I am fortunate to work among extraordinary colleagues at the Ethics and Public Policy Center. Ryan Anderson and Mitch Muncy especially offered encouragement as well as invaluable counsel throughout this process from book conception to publication. Great thanks also to Hunter Estes for his excellent communications expertise and skill.

I am indebted to Mary Rice Hasson for her generosity to me, especially for her pivotal help reviewing and strengthening a section on parental rights. I'm also grateful to Nina Saadat for her thoughtful early research assistance. Thanks to Clare Morell for facilitating an introduction to Keely, and to Fran Maier for his kindness and help with ideas and proposals along the way. Thank you also to Carrie Gress for her advice and encouragement of this book and our collaboration over the years.

I am very grateful to the wider publishing team at Forum Books whose great work brought this manuscript to completion, including those responsible for the excellent copyediting, proofreading, production, marketing, and publicity. Thanks also to Jeff Miller for the jacket design.

Thank you to all the experts who generously gave me their time and insight through interviews, including Aaron Kheriaty, Sarah Mittermaier, Rachel Haack, Hannah Spier, Marcella Burke, Michael Gasparro, Kim Zember, and Fr. Bochanski. And thanks to those who helped facilitate family interviews by spreading the word through their networks.

I am rich in friendships. To my many dear friends, thank you for the countless conversations around the fire—for your prayers, advice, and emotional investment.

To my extended family members, many thanks with great love and affection: my parents Phil and Irene to whom I dedicate this book, my beloved sister Nicole and brother-in-law Ray, to Dave and Nancy, Jenna and Dexter, Jon and Oli. Thank you for your advice, feedback, and love.

Finally, my deepest thanks go to my family, who remain the daily reminder of why this subject matters so much. To our children—Abby, Jack, Campion, Caroline, Vivienne, and Vera, and now Thomas and Evangeline—you are the greatest delights to dad and me. And to my best friend and love, Adam, whose profound goodness, strength, generosity, and humor I'm honored to be a daily witness to and beneficiary of. You are, in so many ways, a model of St. Joseph to me.

Notes

Introduction

1. "While Most Americans Align with Close Family Members on Controversial Political Issues, One in Five Report Family Estrangement Based on These Topics," American Psychiatric Association, October 3, 2024, www.psychiatry.org/news-room/news-releases/family-members-and-political-controversy.
2. Kate Mulvey, "Why I'm Disinviting My Unvaccinated Friends from My Dinner Parties," *Telegraph*, June 2, 2021, www.telegraph.co.uk/women/life/wont-have-vaccine-no-friend-mine.
3. Kate Mulvey, "I'm a Single Woman of 63, and I Feel Friendless and Lonely," *The i Paper*, April 21, 2025, https://inews.co.uk/inews-lifestyle/single-woman-63-friendless-lonely-3642624?srsltid.
4. "Jimmy Kimmel Makes Controversial Comment on Vaccinated vs. Unvaccinated," CNN, September 9, 2021, www.cnn.com/videos/media/2021/09/09/jimmy-kimmel-coronavirus-vaccine-hospital-newsroom-vpx.cnn.

Chapter 1: The New Shape of Estrangement

1. "Frequently Asked Questions (FAQs)," Cornell Family Estrangement & Reconciliation Project, accessed December 9, 2025, www.familyreconciliation.org/faqs.

2. Joshua Coleman, "Family Estrangement Is on the Rise. A Psychologist Offers Ways to Cope," interview by Adrian Ma, *All Things Considered,* NPR, December 31, 2023, www.npr.org/2023/12/31/1222370607/family-estrangement-is-on-the-rise-a-psychologist-offers-ways-to-cope.
3. "While Most Americans Align with Close Family Members on Controversial Political Issues, One in Five Report Family Estrangement Based on These Topics," American Psychiatric Association, October 3, 2024, www.psychiatry.org/news-room/news-releases/family-members-and-political-controversy.
4. Taylor Orth, Director of Survey Data Journalism, "All on the Family: Ties, Proximity, and Estrangement," YouGov, December 20, 2022, https://today.yougov.com/society/articles/44817-poll-family-ties-proximity-and-estrangement.
5. Anna Russell, "Why So Many People Are Going 'No Contact' with Their Parents," *New Yorker,* August 30, 2024, www.newyorker.com/culture/annals-of-inquiry/why-so-many-people-are-going-no-contact-with-their-parents.
6. Russell, "Why So Many People."
7. Russell, "Why So Many People."
8. Kylie Agllias, "Disconnection and Decision-Making: Adult Children Explain Their Reasons for Estranging from Parents," *Australian Social Work* 69, no. 1 (2016): 92–104, doi.org/10.1080/0312407X.2015.1004355.
9. Patrick Teahan, quoted in Ellen Barry, "Is Cutting Off Your Family Good Therapy?" *New York Times,* updated July 17, 2024, www.nytimes.com/2024/07/14/health/therapy-family-estrangement.html.
10. Secondary identity markers might include one's talents, loves, occupation, and so on. Identity issues will be further discussed in later chapters.
11. "Differentiation of Self," The Bowen Center for the Study of the Family, accessed January 16, 2026, www.thebowencenter.org/differentiation-of-self.
12. Sarakshi Rai, "White House Releases Turkey Day 'Talking Points' for Family Dinner," *The Hill,* November 23, 2022, https://thehill.com/homenews/3747822-white-house-releases-turkey-day-talking-points-for-family-dinner.

13. Barack Obama (@BarackObama), "How do you plan to spend the cold days of December?," Twitter (now X), December 17, 2013, https://x.com/BarackObama/status/41307986192250880.
14. Nick Haslam, "Concept Creep: Psychology's Expanding Concepts of Harm and Pathology," *Psychological Inquiry*, 27(1), 1–17, February 12, 2016, https://doi.org/10.1080/1047840X.2016.1082418.
15. Sade Pullen, "Chico State Offers Post-Election Student Counseling," *Action News Now*, November 7, 2024, www.actionnewsnow.com/news/chico-state-offers-post-election-student-counseling/article_46c14cfe-9d64-11ef-b69e-4ff59b5b0e42.html.
16. Greg Lukianoff and Jonathan Haidt, *The Coddling of the American Mind: How Good Intentions and Bad Ideas Are Setting Up a Generation for Failure* (Penguin, 2018), 5–11.
17. Abigail Shrier, *Bad Therapy: Why the Kids Aren't Growing Up* (Sentinel, 2024), 7–10.
18. Abigail Shrier, *Bad Therapy: Why the Kids Aren't Growing Up* (Sentinel, 2024), audiobook, narrated by the author, Audible, chapter 3, 08:40–19:27.
19. Patrick Teahan (@patrickteahanofficial), "Toxic families only see us as cardboard cut outs and roles," TikTok, October 25, 2022, www.tiktok.com/@patrickteahanofficial/video/7158453014267825454.
20. Patrick Teahan, "My Response to the NYT," July 24, 2024, YouTube, 23 min., 7 sec., www.youtube.com/watch?v=yTbxhaVJi-o+%2820%3A20%29.
21. Patrick Teahan, in Barry, "Is Cutting Off?"
22. Audrey Helen Linden and Elizabeth Sillence, "'I'm Finally Allowed to Be Me': Parent-Child Estrangement and Psychological Wellbeing," *Families, Relationships and Societies* 10, no. 2 (2021): 334, https://doi.org/10.1332/204674319x15647593365505.
23. Kristen Carr et al., "Giving Voice to the Silence of Family Estrangement: Comparing Reasons of Estranged Parents and Adult Children in a Nonmatched Sample," *Journal of Family Communication* 15, no. 2 (2015): 130–40, https://doi.org/10.1080/15267431.2015.1013106.

24. Ana Yudin, "Why Adult Children Go No Contact, According to Science," April 24, 2024, YouTube, 23 min., 23 sec., www.youtube.com/watch?v=SgxW9SfhB5U.
25. Christopher Lasch, *The Culture of Narcissism: American Life in an Age of Diminishing Expectations* (W. W. Norton, 1979).
26. Jean M. Twenge et al., "Egos Inflating over Time: A Cross-Temporal Meta-Analysis of the Narcissistic Personality Inventory," *Journal of Personality* 76, no. 4 (2008): 875–902, https://doi.org/10.1111/j.1467-6494.2008.00507.x.
27. Jean M. Twenge, W. Keith Campbell, and Elise C. Freeman, "Generational Differences in Young Adults' Life Goals, Concern for Others, and Civic Orientation, 1966–2009," *Journal of Personality and Social Psychology* 102, no. 5 (2012): 1045–62, https://psycnet.apa.org/doi/10.1037/a0027408.
28. John Burn-Murdoch, "The Troubling Decline in Conscientiousness," *Financial Times*, August 17, 2025, www.ft.com/content/5cd77ef0-b546-4105-8946-36db3f84dc43.
29. Israa Nasir, quoted in Molly Longman, "When Did We Start Calling Every Ex a Narcissist?," Popsugar, updated June 9, 2025, www.popsugar.com/relationships/narcissist-label-overused-49358385.
30. Agllias, "Disconnection and Decision-Making."
31. Bronnie Ware, "Regrets of the Dying," Bronnie Ware, accessed February 3, 2026, https://bronnieware.com/blog/regrets-of-the-dying.
32. Rose McDermott, James H. Fowler, and Nicholas A. Christakis, "Breaking Up Is Hard to Do, Unless Everyone Else Is Doing It Too: Social Network Effects on Divorce in a Longitudinal Sample," *Social Forces* 92, no. 2 (December 2013): 491–519, https://doi.org/10.1093/sf/sot096.

Chapter 2: The Road to Cultural Amnesia

1. Jeffrey Marsh, "The Vine Account You Need to Follow for Daily Inspiration," Oprah.com, May 2016, www.oprah.com/inspiration/jeffrey-marshs-vines-are-all-about-positivity-and-self-acceptance.
2. Jeffrey Marsh (@thejeffreymarsh), "Go no contact. You can

do it," TikTok, December 15, 2022, www.tiktok.com/@thejeffreymarsh/video/7177548607648697646.

3. Jeffrey Marsh (@thejeffreymarsh), "How to Know If No Contact Is the Answer," TikTok, April 11, 2022, www.tiktok.com/@thejeffreymarsh/video/7085517563291094318.
4. Eugenia, "I am just gonna get real about this whole estrangement thing . . ." Gransnet, January 7, 2025, www.gransnet.com/forums/estrangement/1344209-I-am-just-gonna-get-real-about-this-whole-estrangement-thing.
5. Sheila Fitzpatrick, *Everyday Stalinism: Ordinary Life in Extraordinary Times—Soviet Russia in the 1930s* (Oxford University Press, 1999), 15.
6. Fitzpatrick, *Everyday Stalinism*, 18, emphasis added.
7. Robert Service, "The Death of a Comrade," *Guardian*, May 13, 2005, www.theguardian.com/books/2005/may/14/featuresreviews.guardianreview23.
8. "A Soviet Legend Dies Hard," *Los Angeles Times*, November 12, 2002, www.latimes.com/archives/la-xpm-2002-nov-12-fg-pavlik12-story.html.
9. Serge Schmemann, "Soviet 'Hero' Informer, 13, Leaves a Bitter Legacy," *New York Times*, September 16, 1982, www.nytimes.com/1982/09/16/world/soviet-hero-informer-13-leaves-a-bitter-legacy.html.
10. Holocaust Encyclopedia, "Indoctrinating Youth," United States Holocaust Memorial Museum, accessed January 13, 2026, https://encyclopedia.ushmm.org/content/en/article/indoctrinating-youth.
11. Xi Van Fleet, "An Interview with Xi Van Fleet, Author of Mao's America: A Survivor's Warning," interview by Adam Rozakis, Hachette Book Group, accessed January 13, 2026, www.hachettebookgroup.com/articles/an-interview-with-xi-van-fleet-author-of-maos-america-a-survivors-warning.
12. Ji-li Jiang, "Ji-li Jiang: Red Scarf Girl—A Memoir of the Cultural Revolution—BookTV Presentation (2001)," March 21, 2001, YouTube, 1 hour, 3 min., 17 sec. www.youtube.com/watch?v=9g8FCIbQ9Cg.
13. George Orwell, *1984* (Signet, 1949), 46.
14. Orwell, *1984*, 177–78.

15. Wilhelm Reich, *The Sexual Revolution: Toward a Self-Governing Character Structure,* trans. Theodore P. Wolfe (Orgone Institute Press, 1945).
16. Jeffrey Marsh, "A Bookmark for Unconditional Love: In Conversation with Jeffrey Marsh," interview by Billy Lezra, Rough Cut Press, accessed January 13, 2026, https://roughcutpress.com/jeffrey-marsh.
17. Milan Kundera, *The Book of Laughter and Forgetting,* trans. Aaron Asher (Perennial Classics, 1996), 4.
18. Sarah Mittermaier, "The Story of Estrangement: Why the Parents of Trans Adults Stay Silent," *Fairer Disputations,* January 3, 2025, https://fairerdisputations.org/estrangement.

Chapter 3: The Psychology of Estrangement

1. Jennifer Huizen, "Examples and Signs of Gaslighting and How to Respond," Medical News Today, updated March 22, 2024, www.medicalnewstoday.com/articles/gaslighting.
2. Peter Sokolowski, quoted in Leanne Italie, "'Gaslighting' Is Merriam-Webster's 2022 Word of the Year," PBS News, November 28, 2022, www.pbs.org/newshour/arts/gaslighting-is-merriam-websters-2022-word-of-the-year.
3. Nigel Barber, "Why Narcissism Is Rising," *Psychology Today,* February 1, 2024, www.psychologytoday.com/us/blog/the-human-beast/202402/why-narcissism-is-rising.
4. Erica Komisar, "How a Narcissistic Society Created the Mental Health Crisis (and Vice Versa)," February 20, 2025, YouTube, 19 min., 38 sec., https://youtu.be/wKSo1KgrOmU?si=riZOdKyxvo0LIWfw.
5. Katy Waldman, "The Rise of Therapy-Speak," *New Yorker,* March 26, 2021, www.newyorker.com/culture/cultural-comment/the-rise-of-therapy-speak.
6. "The Share of Young Adults Who Received Mental Health Treatment Jumped 45% from 2019 to 2022, the Largest Increase Among Any Age Group," KFF, August 1, 2024, www.kff.org/affordable-care-act/press-release/the-share-of-young-adults-who-received-mental-health-treatment-jumped-45-from-2019-to-2022-the-largest-increase-among-any-age-group.

7. Emily P. Terlizzi and Jeannine S. Schiller, "Mental Health Treatment Among Adults Aged 18–44: United States, 2019–2021," U.S. Centers for Disease Control and Prevention, September 7, 2022, www.cdc.gov/nchs/products/databriefs/db444.htm.
8. Rose Horowitch, "Accommodation Nation," *The Atlantic*, January/February 2026, www.theatlantic.com/magazine/2026/01/elite-university-student-accommodation/684946/?
9. Jillian Nestor, "Social Contagion," The Decision Lab, accessed January 15, 2026, https://thedecisionlab.com/reference-guide/sociology/social-contagion.
10. Waldman, "The Rise of Therapy-Speak."
11. Rob Henderson, "'Luxury Beliefs' That Only the Privileged Can Afford," *Wall Street Journal*, February 9, 2024, www.wsj.com/us-news/education/luxury-beliefs-that-only-the-privileged-can-afford-7f6b8a16.
12. Katherine Dee, "Tumblr Transformed American Politics," *The American Conservative*, August 11, 2021, www.theamericanconservative.com/tumblr-transformed-american-politics.
13. Dee, "Tumblr."
14. Heather Schwedel, "'It's Not History, It's Blood': A *Glee* Fan Remembers the Tumblr Wars the Show Inspired," *Slate*, October 4, 2017, https://slate.com/culture/2017/10/looking-back-on-the-glee-fandom-of-tumblr-s-volatile-personal-prolific-heyday.html.
15. A detransitioner is someone who underwent some degree of gender transition and now seeks to reverse it.
16. Helena Kerschner, "My Story of Rapid Onset Gender Dysphoria," interview by Preston Sprinkle, THINQ Media, April 25, 2021, YouTube, 2 min., 2 sec., www.youtube.com/watch?v=GjOmko-9hSg.
17. Helena Kerschner, quoted in Gillian Richards, "These 3 Women Tried Transgenderism, and Then Stopped," *Washington Stand*, September 20, 2022, https://washingtonstand.com/news/these-3-women-tried-transgenderism-and-then-stopped.
18. Kerschner, "My Story."
19. Richards, "These 3 Women"; Helena Kerschner, "By Any Other Name," *Prude Posting*, February 19, 2022, https://lacroicsz.substack.com/p/by-any-other-name.

20. Somsamay Vidamaly and Soon Li Lee, "Young Adults' Mental Illness Aesthetics on Social Media," *International Journal of Cyber Behavior, Psychology and Learning* 11, no. 2 (2021): 13–32, https://doi.org/10.4018/ijcbpl.2021040102.
21. Erin Kerns Vazquez, "The Danger of Self-Diagnosis Through Social Media," Medens Health, October 10, 2024, www.medenshealth.com/blog/the-danger-of-self-diagnosis-through-social-media.
22. Mariam Hull, Mered Parnes, and Joseph Jankovic, "Increased Incidence of Functional (Psychogenic) Movement Disorders in Children and Adults amid the COVID-19 Pandemic: A Cross-Sectional Study," *Neurology Clinical Practice,* October 2021, https://doi.org/10.1212/CPJ.0000000000001082.
23. Caroline Olvera and Alana Kirby, "Functional Tic Disorder: A Pandemic in a Pandemic," *Practical Neurology,* March/April 2022, https://practicalneurology.com/articles/2022-mar-apr/functional-tic-disorder-a-pandemic-in-a-pandemic.
24. Azeen Ghorayshi, "TikTok Tics: Why Tic-Like Behaviors Are Surging Among Young People," *New York Times,* February 13, 2023, www.nytimes.com/2023/02/13/health/tiktok-tics-gender-tourettes.html.
25. Fortesa Latifi, "Why So Many Young People Are Cutting Off Their Parents," *Cosmopolitan,* June 22, 2023, www.cosmopolitan.com/lifestyle/a44178122/family-estrangement-cut-off-parents.
26. Latifi, "Why So Many Young People."
27. @savannahghost, "The ones who stay away suddenly don't seem so selfish," TikTok, February 1, 2025, www.tiktok.com/@savannahghost/video/7466625403147373856.
28. @kaneelkoffje, "They make me the villain now, after they made me a victim," TikTok, March 2, 2023, www.tiktok.com/@kaneelkoffje/video/7205861462361853189.
29. Patrick Teahan, "Toxic Family Test," Patrick Teahan Therapy, accessed January 14, 2026, https://patrickteahantherapy.webflow.io/toxic-family-test.
30. Teahan, "Toxic Family Test."
31. Patrick Teahan, "Childhood PTSD Questionnaire," Patrick Teahan Therapy, accessed January 14, 2026, www.patrickteah

antherapy.com/wp-content/uploads/2017/04/CHILDHOOD-PTSD-QUESTIONNAIRE-FULL-.pdf.

32. Teahan, "Childhood PTSD Questionnaire."
33. Carl R. Trueman, *Strange New World: How Thinkers and Activists Redefined Identity and Sparked the Sexual Revolution* (Crossway, 2022), 19–30.
34. Carl R. Trueman, *Strange New World*, 31–50.
35. u/AdamantMischief, "No Contact—Is It Permanent?," Reddit, accessed January 14, 2026, www.reddit.com/r/trans/comments/1b6ekf3/no_contact_is_it_permanent.
36. u/Markedly_Mira, "You can extend an apology," reply to u/AdamantMischief, accessed January 14, 2026, www.reddit.com/r/trans/comments/1b6ekf3/no_contact_is_it_permanent.
37. u/Markedly_Mira, "You can extend an apology."
38. u/AdamantMischief, reply to u/Markedly_Mira, accessed January 14, 2026, www.reddit.com/r/trans/comments/1b6ekf3/no_contact_is_it_permanent.
39. u/Malkavian_Grin, "No, i went no contact with my folks," reply to u/AdamantMischief, accessed January 14, 2026, www.reddit.com/r/trans/comments/1b6ekf3/no_contact_is_it_permanent.

Chapter 4: Chosen Family

1. Jeremy Mullins, quoted in Emanuella Grinberg, "Polyamorous Relationships: When Three Isn't a Crowd," CNN, January 28, 2020, www.cnn.com/2020/01/28/health/polyamorous-relationship-meaning-wellness/index.html.
2. Mullins, quoted in Grinberg, "Polyamorous Relationships."
3. "True Believers: One Big, Happy (Poly) Family," NBC News, June 11, 2024, www.nbcnews.com/video/true-believers-one-big-happy-poly-family-277969475789.
4. Amy C. Moors, Amanda N. Gesselman, and Justin R. Garcia, "Desire, Familiarity, and Engagement in Polyamory: Results from a National Sample of Single Adults in the United States," *Frontiers in Psychology* 12 (2021), https://doi.org/10.3389/fpsyg.2021.619640.
5. Russell Moul, "Polyamory Is on the Rise and Society Should Be More Accommodating, Research Argues," IFLScience,

April 3, 2023, www.iflscience.com/polyamory-is-on-the-rise-and-society-should-be-more-accommodating-research-argues-68281.

6. David M. Schneider, *A Critique of the Study of Kinship* (University of Michigan Press, 1984).
7. Kath Weston, *Families We Choose: Lesbians, Gays, Kinship* (Columbia University Press, 1991).
8. Emily St. James, "The Modern Family," *Vox*, November 25, 2021, www.vox.com/the-highlight/22784054/estrangement-family-friends-friendsgiving.
9. Harper Keenan and Lil Miss Hot Mess, "Drag Pedagogy: The Playful Practice of Queer Imagination in Early Childhood," *Curriculum Inquiry* 50, no. 5 (2020): 455, https://doi.org/10.1080/03626784.2020.1864621.
10. Keenan and Lil Miss Hot Mess, "Drag Pedagogy," 455–56.
11. Judith Butler, *Undoing Gender* (Routledge, 2004), 126.
12. Elizabeth Brake, *Minimizing Marriage: Marriage, Morality, and the Law* (Oxford University Press, 2012), 1, 5.
13. Brake, *Minimizing Marriage*, 20.
14. Elizabeth Brake, foreword to *Why It's OK to Not Be Monogamous*, by Justin L. Clardy (Routledge, 2023).
15. Brake, foreword to *Why It's OK*.
16. Sophie Lewis, *Abolish the Family: A Manifesto for Care and Liberation* (Verso, 2022), 2–3.
17. St. James, "The Modern Family."
18. "Found Family Books," Goodreads, accessed December 23, 2025, www.goodreads.com/shelf/show/found-family.
19. St. James, "The Modern Family."
20. Michael Warner, introduction to *Fear of a Queer Planet: Queer Politics and Social Theory*, ed. Michael Warner (University of Minnesota Press, 1993), xxvi.
21. Raj Chetty et al., "Where Is the Land of Opportunity? The Geography of Intergenerational Mobility in the United States," *Quarterly Journal of Economics* 129, no. 4 (2014): 1553–623, https://doi.org/10.1093/qje/qju022.
22. "Changing Family Structures Play a Major Role in the Fight Against Poverty," Brookings, December 3, 2015, www.brookings.edu/articles/changing-family-structures-play-a-major-role-in-the-fight-against-poverty.

23. Robert Rector, "Marriage: America's Greatest Weapon Against Child Poverty," The Heritage Foundation, September 5, 2012, www.heritage.org/poverty-and-inequality/report/marriage-americas-greatest-weapon-against-child-poverty.
24. Brent Hartinger, "The 'Chosen Family' Isn't All It's Cracked Up to Be," *Brent and Michael Are Going Places*, January 6, 2022, www.brentandmichaelaregoingplaces.com/p/the-chosen-family-isnt-all-its-cracked.
25. Hartinger, "Chosen Family."
26. Hartinger, "Chosen Family."
27. u/c0balt_60, "I'm Sick of the 'Creating Your Chosen Family' Narrative," Reddit, accessed December 23, 2025, www.reddit.com/r/EstrangedAdultChild/comments/u5m2h4/im_sick_of_the_creating_your_chosen_family.
28. u/thistooistemporary, "The Implicit Power Imbalance with 'Chosen Family,'" Reddit, accessed December 23, 2025, www.reddit.com/r/EstrangedAdultChild/comments/w6vhee/the_implicit_power_imbalance_with_chosen_family.
29. u/AmaltheaDreams, "Does 'Chosen Family' Ever Work Out?," Reddit, accessed December 23, 2025, www.reddit.com/r/AskWomenOver40/comments/1g4d4pq/does_chosen_family_ever_work_out.
30. Grinberg, "Polyamorous Relationships."
31. "True Believers," NBC News.

Chapter 5: The Overton Cage

1. Bari Weiss, "Resignation Letter," Bari Weiss, accessed December 22, 2025, www.bariweiss.com/resignation-letter.
2. Jessica Valenti, "'Vote Shaming' Trump Supporters Is Fair. What They Have Done Is Shameful," *Guardian*, November 19, 2016, www.theguardian.com/commentisfree/2016/nov/19/hamilton-mike-pence-trump-voters-safe-space.
3. Gary Pollakusky, quoted in Gabrielle Fonrouge, "My Best Man Unfriended Me Because I Support Trump," *New York Post*, November 16, 2016, https://nypost.com/2016/11/16/my-best-man-unfriended-me-because-i-support-trump.
4. Brittany Wong, "The Advice Therapists Give People Considering Severing Ties with Family over Politics," *HuffPost*,

November 3, 2024, www.huffpost.com/entry/advice-family-estrangement-politics-ano_l_6723db99e4b00acf55d94798.

5. Jessica Valenti (@jessica), "Cutting Trump supporters out of your life is not petty or vengeful," Substack, November 19, 2024, https://substack.com/@jessica/note/c-77920540.
6. "Yale Psychiatrist Urges MSNBC Viewers to Shun Trump-Voting Family Members over the Holidays," *New York Post*, November 9, 2024, YouTube, 40 sec., www.youtube.com/watch?v=D0n6G1rqqpE.
7. "Stress, Politics, and the Holidays: A Postelection Survey," American Psychological Association, December 2024, www.apa.org/pubs/reports/stress-in-america/2024/postelection-survey.
8. Quoted in Kwame Anthony Appiah, "My Mom Voted for Trump. Can We Let It Go?," *New York Times Magazine*, November 22, 2024, www.nytimes.com/2024/11/22/magazine/mom-trump-vote-ethics.html.
9. Quoted in Appiah, "My Mom."
10. Joseph Lehman, "The Overton Window with Joseph Lehman," interview by Eric Kohn, Acton Institute, March 2, 2022, YouTube, 48 min., 35 sec., www.youtube.com/watch?v=-QVB3EwOUC8.
11. Lehman, "The Overton Window."
12. Quoted in Allie Volpe, "Can You Still Be Close to Someone Whose Politics You Despise?," *Vox*, December 23, 2024, www.vox.com/even-better/391249/maintaining-relationships-trump-estrangement-reconciliation.
13. Jonathan Haidt, *The Righteous Mind: Why Good People Are Divided by Politics and Religion* (Vintage, 2013), 150–79.
14. *Assassination Culture: How Burning Teslas and Killing Billionaires Became a Meme Aesthetic for Political Violence* (Network Contagion Research Institute, April 7, 2025), https://networkcontagion.us/reports/4-7-25-ncri-assassination-culture-brief.
15. Libs of TikTok (@libsoftiktok), "This is so sad . . . student at @LexRich5Schools slams her Conservative Christian parents at board meeting," X, January 26, 2024, https://x.com/libsoftiktok/status/1750944232121245700.

16. Libs of TikTok, "This is so sad."
17. Libs of TikTok, "This is so sad."

Chapter 6: Reengaging Relationships

1. "Differentiation of Self," The Bowen Center for the Study of the Family, accessed January 16, 2026, www.thebowencenter.org/differentiation-of-self.
2. Joshua Coleman, *Rules of Estrangement: Why Adult Children Cut Ties and How to Heal the Conflict* (Harmony, 2020), 60–62.
3. Washington Free Beacon (@FreeBeacon), "WATCH: Jimmy Kimmel's wife, who is also his head writer and executive producer, said," X, November 10, 2025, https://x.com/FreeBeacon/status/1987995860139938198?s=20.
4. Andrea Giles, host, *Heal from Infidelity*, podcast, episode 193, "Relational Bypassing: The Hidden Ways We Bypass Real Healing," June 6, 2025, https://andreagiles.com/relational-bypassing-the-hidden-ways-we-bypass-real-healing.
5. Maia Poet, "How Trans Activists Alienated Me from My Parents," *Maia's Substack*, Substack, March 16, 2025, https://maiapoet.substack.com/p/how-trans-activists-alienated-me.
6. Poet, "How Trans Activists."
7. Poet, "How Trans Activists."
8. Maia Poet, "My Kid Came Out as Trans. Now What?," *Maia's Substack*, Substack, July 15, 2025, https://maiapoet.substack.com/p/my-kid-came-out-as-trans-now-what.
9. Poet, "How Trans Activists."
10. Poet, "How Trans Activists."
11. Poet, "How Trans Activists."
12. Adam Lane Smith, "How No Contact Creates a Cortisol-Fueled Enemy Bond," July 22, 2025, YouTube, 42 sec., www.youtube.com/shorts/0r6q7M8IcUQ.
13. Smith, "How No Contact."
14. Robert Barron, "Everything He Has Is Yours," March 26, 2022, YouTube, 14 min., 44 sec., www.youtube.com/watch?v=9sgd91rGpnw.

Chapter 7: Family Is Humanizing

1. Jonathan Sacks, *Covenant and Conversation: Exodus—The Book of Redemption* (Maggid, 2010), 24.1.
2. Isidore Epstein, trans. and ed., *Seder Nashim: Kiddushin*, The Babylonian Talmud (Soncino, 1936), 30b–32a.
3. Dennis Prager, *The Ten Commandments: Still the Best Moral Code* (Regnery, 2015), 36.
4. Dennis Prager, "You Don't Have to Love Your Parents," *National Review,* December 9, 2014, www.nationalreview.com/2014/12/you-dont-have-love-your-parents-dennis-prager.
5. Epstein, *Seder Nashim: Kiddushin,* 30b.
6. Prager, "You Don't Have To."
7. Jonathan Sacks, *Morality: Restoring the Common Good in Divided Times* (Basic, 2020), 72.
8. Forrest Hanson, in Forrest Hanson and Rick Hanson, hosts, *Being Well,* podcast, season 3, episode 185, "Navigating Estrangement Situations," December 20, 2021, www.youtube.com/watch?v=N9YGABOCwH8.
9. Rick Hanson, in Hanson and Hanson, "Navigating Estrangement Situations."
10. Iris Zaki, "M/other," *New York Times,* May 13, 2025, www.nytimes.com/video/opinion/100000009447387/m-other.html.
11. Gideon Lewis-Kraus, "The End of Children," *New Yorker,* February 24, 2025, www.newyorker.com/magazine/2025/03/03/the-population-implosion.
12. Ayaan Hirsi Ali, "We Have Been Subverted," *Free Press,* June 4, 2024, www.thefp.com/p/ayaan-hirsi-ali-we-have-been-subverted.
13. Hirsi Ali, "We Have Been Subverted."
14. Hirsi Ali, "We Have Been Subverted."
15. Rachel Haack, "We've Been Subverted—and It's Showing Up in Our Families," *Thoughts from a Therapist,* March 20, 2025, https://rachelhaack.substack.com/p/weve-been-subvertedand-its-showing.
16. Hirsi Ali, "We Have Been Subverted."
17. Haack, "We've Been Subverted."
18. Hirsi Ali, "We Have Been Subverted."

19. G. K. Chesterton, *The Superstition of Divorce* (Chatto & Windus, 1920), 32.
20. Christopher Lasch, *The Culture of Narcissism: American Life in an Age of Diminishing Expectations* (W. W. Norton, 1979), 100–120.
21. Hannah Arendt, *The Human Condition*, 2nd ed. (University of Chicago Press, 1998), 28–73.
22. Haack, "We've Been Subverted."
23. Dan Quayle, "Address to the Commonwealth Club of California," May 19, 1992, Dan Quayle, accessed January 20, 2026, www.vicepresidentdanquayle.com/speeches_StandingFirm_CCC_3.html.
24. *13 Reasons Why*, created by Brian Yorkey, Netflix, 2017–20.
25. Madeleine Kearns, "How Catholicism Got Cool," *The Free Press*, June 4, 2025, www.thefp.com/p/meet-americas-newest-catholics?hide_intro_popup=true.
26. Byung-Chul Han, *Saving Beauty*, trans. Daniel Steuer (Polity, 2018), 1–3, 72–76.
27. Stephen R. Covey, *The 7 Habits of Highly Effective Families* (Golden, 1997), 195–97.
28. Wendell Berry, "Economy and Pleasure," in *The World-Ending Fire: The Essential Wendell Berry*, ed. Paul Kingsnorth (Counterpoint, 2019), 273.
29. Fyodor Dostoevsky, *The Brothers Karamazov*, trans. Constance Garnett (Macmillan, 1922), 54.
30. Josef Pieper, *Faith, Hope, Love*, trans. Richard Winston, Clara Winston, and Mary Frances McCarthy (Ignatius, 1997), 174.

Chapter 8: Authority Is Stabilizing

1. Thomas Aquinas, *Summa Theologiae*, II-II, q. 138, a. 1, respondeo.
2. Lawrence Patihis and Mario E. Herrera, "Reappraising a Parent Can Occur with Non-Suggestive Questions: Changing Emotions and Memories of Emotion," *Psychological Reports* (2024), https://doi.org/10.1177/00332941241283413.
3. Lawrence Patihis, quoted in "Asking a Person to Talk About Their Parents in Therapy Can Distort Memories of Childhood Emotions," University of Portsmouth, October 11, 2024,

www.port.ac.uk/news-events-and-blogs/news/asking-a-person-to-talk-about-their-parents-in-therapy-can-distort-memories-of-childhood-emotions.
4. "Asking a Person to Talk."
5. Patihis and Herrera, "Reappraising a Parent."
6. Patihis, in "Asking a Person to Talk."
7. Terrence Sanvictores and Magda D. Mendez, "Types of Parenting Styles and Effects on Children," StatPearls, updated September 18, 2022, www.ncbi.nlm.nih.gov/books/NBK568743.
8. Aristotle, *Nicomachean Ethics* 1106b, 1107b.
9. Diana Baumrind, "Effects of Authoritative Parental Control on Child Behavior," *Child Development* 37, no. 4 (1966): 887–907, https://doi.org/10.2307/1126611.
10. A fourth category was later added for neglectful parents who are low in responsiveness and demandingness. They might pay the bills and provide food but are otherwise fairly checked out of their kids' lives.
11. Gwen Dewar, "Parenting styles: An evidence-based, cross-cultural guide." *Parenting Science,* July 15, 2024, https://parentingscience.com/parenting-styles/9.
12. Charles Dickens, *Hard Times,* ed. Kate Flint (Penguin Classics, 2011).
13. Jane Austen, *Pride and Prejudice,* ed. Vivien Jones (Penguin Classics, 2009).
14. Albert Bandura, "Self-Efficacy: Toward a Unifying Theory of Behavioral Change," *Psychological Review* 84, no. 2 (1977): 191–215, https://doi.org/10.1037/0033-295X.84.2.191.
15. Kevin Majeres, in Sharif Younes and Kevin Majeres, hosts, *The OptimalWork Podcast,* episode 248, "Optimal Parenting IV: Teaching Family Ideals with Consistency," OptimalWork, May 19, 2025, www.youtube.com/watch?v=dJe0pQT1GI8.
16. Eli R. Lebowitz and Jennifer M. Majdick, "SPACE, Parent-Based Treatment for Childhood and Adolescent Anxiety: Clinical Case Illustration," *Journal of Cognitive Psychotherapy* 34, no. 2 (2020), https://doi.org/10.1891/jcpsy-d-19-00028.
17. Eli Lebowitz, "Breaking Free of Anxiety: A Journey Through SPACE," SPACE, June 1, 2022, YouTube, 20 min., 22 sec., www.youtube.com/watch?v=BoMyqockXV4.

18. Taffel, "Decline and Fall."
19. Jordan Peterson, in John Bickley, host, *Morning Wire,* podcast, "Parenting as Sacred Duty," The Daily Wire, May 25, 2025, https://podcasts.apple.com/us/podcast/jordan-peterson-interview-parenting-as-sacred-duty/id1576594336?i=1000709770627.
20. Peterson, in "Parenting as Sacred Duty."

Chapter 9: Disagreeing Well Is Civilizing

1. Pamela Paul, "College Students Are Using 'No Contact Orders' to Block Each Other in Real Life," *Wall Street Journal,* June 6, 2025, www.wsj.com/us-news/education/college-students-are-using-no-contact-orders-to-block-each-other-in-real-life-4e3272b1?st=zd4P3Z.
2. Paul, "College Students."
3. David Karp, in Paul, "College Students."
4. Caroline Mehl, in Paul, "College Students."
5. Paul, "College Students."
6. @majoreyeroll, "Explaining to my republican grandfather who I went no contact with, why I cannot have a relationship with him," TikTok, April 29, 2025, www.tiktok.com/@majoreyeroll/video/7498928729721294110.
7. Herbert Marcuse, "Repressive Tolerance," in *A Critique of Pure Tolerance,* by Robert Paul Wolff, Barrington Moore Jr., and Herbert Marcuse (Beacon Press, 1965), www.marcuse.org/herbert/publications/1960s/1965-repressive-tolerance-fulltext.html.
8. Bob Altemeyer, *The Authoritarian Specter* (Harvard University Press, 1996), 216–34.
9. Bob Altemeyer, "The Other 'Authoritarian Personality,'" in *Advances in Experimental Social Psychology,* vol. 30, ed. Mark P. Zanna (Academic, 1998), 71.
10. John T. Jost et al., "Political Conservatism as Motivated Social Cognition," *Psychological Bulletin* 129, no. 3 (2003): 339–75, https://doi.org/10.1037/0033-2909.129.3.339.
11. Thomas H. Costello et al., "Clarifying the Structure and Nature of Left-Wing Authoritarianism," *Journal of Personality and Social Psychology* 122, no. 1 (2022): 135–70, https://doi.org/10.1037/pspp0000341.

12. Costello et al., "Clarifying the Structure and Nature."
13. Luke Conway, "The Left Has an Authoritarian Problem (but Doesn't Know It)," Presser, September 2024, www.pressermag.com/september-2024/the-left-has-an-authoritarian-problem.
14. Herbert Marcuse, "Repressive Tolerance," in *A Critique of Pure Tolerance* (Beacon, 1969), 81–117.
15. Conway, "The Left Has an Authoritarian Problem (but Doesn't Know It)."
16. Ibram X. Kendi, *How to Be an Antiracist* (One World, 2019), 19.
17. Jason Baxter, in Rich Moss, host, *HeightsCast*, podcast, "Dr. Jason Baxter on Why Beauty Matters: The Postmodern Pressure on Our Interior Life," The Heights Forum, November 6, 2025, https://heightsforum.org/podcast/why-beauty-matters-the-postmodern-pressure-on-our-interior-life.
18. Ellie Lisitsa, "The Four Horsemen: Contempt," Gottman, updated October 10, 2025, www.gottman.com/blog/the-four-horsemen-contempt.
19. John M. Gottman and Nan Silver, *The Seven Principles for Making Marriage Work*, rev. ed. (Harmony, 2015), 34.
20. Charles M. Blow, "Whose Country Is It?," *New York Times*, March 26, 2010, www.nytimes.com/2010/03/27/opinion/27blow.html.
21. See, e.g., Donna Haraway, "Situated Knowledges: The Science Question in Feminism and the Privilege of Partial Perspective," *Feminist Studies* 14, no. 3 (1988): 575–99, https://doi.org/10.2307/3178066; Patricia Hill Collins, *Black Feminist Thought: Knowledge, Consciousness, and the Politics of Empowerment* (Unwin Hyman, 1990); Sandra Harding, *Whose Science? Whose Knowledge? Thinking from Women's Lives* (Cornell University Press, 1991).
22. Lisitsa, "The Four Horsemen: Contempt"; Gottman and Silver, *Seven Principles*, 34.
23. Arthur C. Brooks, *Love Your Enemies: How Decent People Can Save America from the Culture of Contempt* (Broadside, 2019), 153–74.
24. Conway, "The Left Has an Authoritarian Problem."
25. Kier Adrian Gray, "Confessions of a Former SJW," *Recovering Anarchist*, May 27, 2022, www.recoveringanarchist.ca/p/007.

26. Gray, "Confessions of a Former SJW."
27. Gray, "Confessions of a Former SJW."
28. Kier Adrian Gray, "The Right Looks for Converts; the Left Looks for Traitors," *Recovering Anarchist*, April 12, 2024, www.recoveringanarchist.ca/p/the-right-looks-for-converts-the.
29. Gray, "Confessions of a Former SJW."
30. Kier Adrian Gray, "Why I Left Social Justice," *Recovering Anarchist*, July 15, 2022, https://kier.substack.com/p/013.
31. Gray, "Confessions of a Former SJW."
32. Gray, "Why I Left Social Justice."
33. Gray, "Confessions of a Former SJW."
34. Gray, "Confessions of a Former SJW"; Gray, "Why I Left Social Justice."
35. Kier Adrian Gray, "Leaving Wokeworld, Finding Hope," *Recovering Anarchist*, August 26, 2022, www.recoveringanarchist.ca/p/018.
36. It's for this reason that I never advise people to use words that are untrue. Even at the risk of the relationship, using pronouns or other such language that perpetuates a lie is a short-term Band-Aid with a long-term time bomb embedded in it.
37. Josef Pieper, *Abuse of Language, Abuse of Power* (Ignatius, 1992).

Chapter 10: Carrying On Without Closure

1. David Litt, "Is It Time to Stop Snubbing Your Right-Wing Family?," *New York Times*, July 13, 2025, www.nytimes.com/2025/07/13/opinion/family-politics-arguments-right-wing.html.
2. Litt, "Is It Time?"
3. Litt, "Is It Time?"
4. Michael J. Stern, "It's Time to Start Shunning the 'Vaccine Hesitant.' They're Blocking COVID Herd Immunity," *USA Today*, May 2, 2021, www.usatoday.com/story/opinion/2021/04/30/require-covid-vaccine-resume-normal-life-herd-immunity-column/4886673001.
5. Michael Hiltzik, "Mocking Anti-Vaxxers' COVID Deaths Is Ghoulish, Yes—but May Be Necessary," *Los Angeles Times*, January 10, 2022, www.latimes.com/business/story/2022-01-10/

why-shouldnt-we-dance-on-the-graves-of-anti-vaxxers, cited in Litt, "Is It Time?"

6. Litt, "Is It Time?"
7. @feelsdesperate, "I want to write something longer about this piece when I get the time," X, July 15, 2025, https://x.com/feelsdesperate/status/1945275141476508161.
8. Lee, July 13, 2025, comment on Litt, "Is It Time?," www.nytimes.com/shared/comment/48r69t.
9. Prince Buster, July 13, 2025, comment on Litt, "Is It Time?," www.nytimes.com/shared/comment/48r6ei?rsrc=cshare&smid=url-share.
10. Robert, July 13, 2025, comment on Litt, "Is It Time?," www.nytimes.com/shared/comment/48r8nk?rsrc=cshare&smid=url-share.
11. Tom, July 13, 2025, comment on Litt, "Is It Time?," www.nytimes.com/shared/comment/48r9ap?rsrc=cshare&smid=url-share.
12. Aleksandr Solzhenitsyn, *The Gulag Archipelago: An Experiment in Literary Investigation,* trans. Thomas P. Whitney, vol. 2 (HarperPerennial, 2007), part 4, chap. 1.
13. Alexandra Jacobs, "When Cutting Ties Is the Best Thing a Child Can Do," *New York Times,* March 30, 2025, www.nytimes.com/2025/03/30/books/review/the-power-of-parting-eamon-dolan.html.
14. Viktor E. Frankl, *Man's Search for Meaning* (Beacon, 2014), 75, 106.
15. Václav Havel, "The Power of the Powerless," in *The Power of the Powerless: Citizens Against the State in Central-Eastern Europe,* ed. John Keane (M. E. Sharpe, 1985), 28.
16. Alene Tchekmedyian, "After Palisades fire failures, L.A. promises to beef up staffing during high-risk fire weather," October 8, 2025, www.latimes.com/california/story/2025-10-08/los-angeles-firefighters-were-hampered-by-a-lack-of-resources-in-initial-fire-attack-report-says?utm.

About the Author

NOELLE MERING is a fellow at the Washington, D.C.–based Ethics and Public Policy Center. She is author of *Awake, Not Woke: A Christian Response to the Cult of Progressive Ideology* and co-author of the popular *Theology of Home* book series. She writes on culture, politics, and religion and has published in *National Review, Newsweek, The Daily Wire, The Federalist, The American Mind, Catholic World Report,* and *National Catholic Register*. Noelle has been featured on Fox News multiple times (including *Primetime*), on EWTN, in various documentaries, and on numerous radio shows and podcasts. She is a highly sought-after public speaker on topics of family, human flourishing, and navigating the complexities of hot-button ideologies with grace. Noelle is a wife and a mother of six children in Southern California.